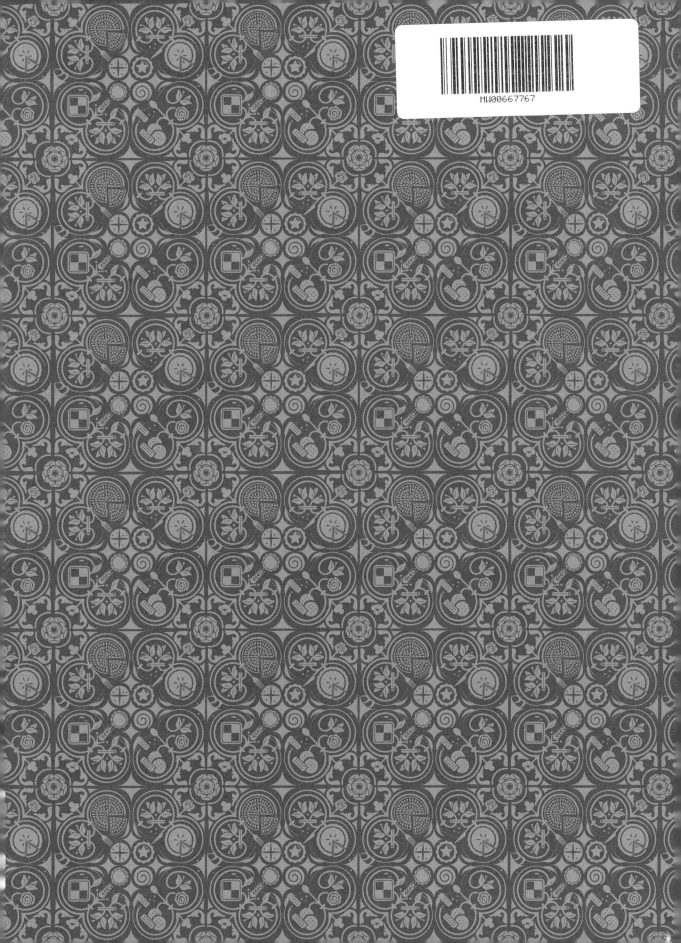

For my husband, Bruno.

I want to acknowledge that most of the cakes, gingerbreads, and
biscuits in this book would not have existed if not for sugar imports that were made possible due to
slavery, which was particularly concentrated in the Caribbean islands of Barbados, St. Kitts, Nevis,
Antigua, and Jamaica, and later Grenada and Trinidad in the 17th, 18th, and 19th centuries, until
the British Slavery Abolition Act took effect on August 1, 1834—which
unfortunately only resulted in partial liberation.

Sugar has a cost, and that cost was paid by those held in bondage.

The British Baking Book

Words and photography

Regula Ysewijn

weldon**owen**

Five Sisters of Kintail (*Cinn Tàile*), Northwest Highlands of Scotland

Simon the Pieman, Rye, East Sussex

FOREWORD

I first met Regula when we were sitting in a London restaurant, filming a documentary on British puddings. She lit up the room with her smile, her style, and her effervescent enthusiasm for British baked goods.

Growing up in the 1980s, my Britain was not like hers. It was far from that of quaint streets and polite customs. I read Austen, Wordsworth, and Dickens at school under duress, and my holidays involved freezing on a rain-swept beach with a gritty picnic. I grew up in a Britain in which the supermarket sticky bun was a Saturday treat, white sliced bread was king, and our village had long since lost its bakery.

But even then, all was not lost, and I recognize that Regula's fascinating Britain co-existed with my own gastronomically challenged version. I envy Regula her travels as a teen, roving around a country I took for granted, eating flavors I would not encounter until, as an adult and a historian, I deliberately sought them out. But while I never roved, I nevertheless ate. I remember curd tarts from my Grandma's local bakery, simultaneously sweet and savory and bitter with nutmeg. She made her own bread, and would smack our fingers for stealing rolls, smothering them in butter while the loaves cooled on racks in her kitchen. I discovered a tiny back-street bakery in the town where I spent my Saturdays, and together with a friend we would buy an apple tart for four and tear it apart, the crust crumbling instantly to let us plunge hungry fingers into its fluffy interior.

By the 1990s the rediscovery of a rich and brilliant British culinary heritage was in full flow, and bakes that were teetering on the edge of extinction – or had already disappeared completely – were being reinvented, brought back for a modern generation. I moved to France, and only then did the unique nature of British baking really strike home. As I gorged on delicate gâteaux and pastry confections, which no one would ever dream of making at home, I realized the fundamental truth that there are some things that do not translate: cake, buns, puddings, and afternoon tea. (I'll be fair, cake in French is *le cake*, pudding is *le poudding* and afternoon tea is *le five o'clock*.) British baking isn't about the ethereal, sweet treats of the pâtisserie, originally destined for the dinner table; it offers you something more solid. Our bakes are sturdy, doughy, packed with fruit, spice, and flavor. They don't dance around your palate; they grab you and hug you, and tell you it's all going to be all right.

Food tells us so much about who we are – as individuals, as communities, and as a nation. The myths we weave about foods are so often invented, crumbling like shortbread when faced with the reality of life in the past. Yet the need to invent backstories, to mythologize our pasties and our simnels is as valuable and as fascinating as the foods themselves. Reading this book, I'm reminded of both how intensely local Britain could (and can) be, and yet how connected every tiny community, baking its own bun, was (and is). Most of these recipes were born in the 18th century, a time of huge cultural and social change. Britain was busy abroad, exploring, trading, colonizing, and it was a time of enormous scientific and artistic discovery, as well as unbelievable exploitation and cruelty. Those who baked or ate baked goods were all playing their part. Sugar came from the West Indies, spice from the East. In the 19th century, strong flour was imported from Eastern Europe and Northern America, eggs from France, and butter from Ireland. Yet locality was also crucial – the South favored wheat, the North clung to its oats. Ovens were rarer in the North than the South, and fuel types and working conditions also played a role in cementing the specialities of each area. But it is the interplay of these practicalities, along with the stories – whether true or invented – which make a whole so much greater than either on their own.

That, then, is the joy of this book. It's a love letter to British baking and all that that implies. It brings together buns and bakes that you'll find in every local shop, and cakes and breads that have long since disappeared. Here you'll find recipes both old and new, resurrected for the future, together with the stories that make them such a window onto both the past and the present. The joy of Regula's writing is that through it all, we realize that it takes an outsider looking in to show us who we truly are. This is a beautiful book. It is a lyrical book. It is a book full of good things, modern and old, with a multitude of real heritage and imagined tradition behind them. Enjoy.

– Dr Annie Gray, food historian

Mermaid Street, Rye, East Sussex

INTRODUCTION

A love story

Ever since I was little, I have been fascinated by Britain. The butterflies in my belly stirred when I heard a lullaby about England at the age of five, painting a picture of an evergreen island, hills crowned with castles, prehistoric monuments, impressive queens, brave knights, and mystical creatures. I wanted nothing more than to go there and live in a limestone cottage by a stream. My mother and I made trips to the only English store in Belgium to pretend we were in London. We bought shortbread, placed it on an English china plate, and ate it while watching historical dramas and documentaries on the BBC.

When I turned nine, my parents finally gave in to my greatest wish and we went to Britain. They had previously thought that the childhood infatuation would fade, but it only grew stronger. We started to spend all our family vacations in Britain, and I looked forward to them all year. When I couldn't be there I spent my time with my nose in books about British history. The kings and queens of England became like the characters of a novel, and a portrait of Elizabeth I hung above my bed as if she were Madonna. A powerful woman, the Virgin Queen of England, my idol.

The anticipation for our trips to Britain started when my mother came home from the library with the travel guides. My parents then spent the evenings hunched over the road map that covered the round dining table in our little flat in Antwerp. They marked our trip with a neon highlighter – the routes to take and the things we had to see. When my parents were done, I took the map to my room, jumped onto my bed, and ran my finger across the marked road, memorizing every town. I dreamed about castles, stone circles, dramatic coastlines, and desolate moorland. I learned English from reading Jane Austen's novels and did not miss a single episode of *EastEnders* on the BBC. Some of my British friends have remarked in recent years that I was training to be British.

On our travels through England, Scotland, and Wales, I was constantly looking for regional bakes and local bakeries. I was quite surprised that British bakeries were so small that they usually had only one window in an ordinary village house. I would press my nose to the window to see which buns and cakes were on offer. I ate soup every afternoon because I knew it would come with the advertised "warm soft white roll." The roll came wrapped in a white napkin and was served with small packaged butters that quickly softened from the warmth of the bread. Did you know that the British have more than seven local names for this generic white roll? I wanted to taste them in all their forms. It was a time when every tearoom, pub, and cafe served homemade bread or rolls from the local baker. It was the glorious '90s, before Britain became obsessed with the "French baguette," which was just a pale prebaked shadow of the good stuff you get in France. A time in which the gastropub flourished and you could eat well and locally in almost every pub that you passed. I experienced the renaissance of British food and saw how proud people were about their local produce. Even then, notes were made on the menus to say the meat or fish was local. It was something I did not see in Belgium, where pride in provenance and heritage was missing in everything.

The British also have a sense of humor when it comes to food. In addition to a rare-breed steak and potatoes from the island of Jersey, or a fragrant chicken curry, the menus also offered pizza served with fries. I know that the latter may sound strange, but even the Italians do it and I enjoyed it immensely as a child, just like fries with a topping of Cheddar cheese, a chip butty (sandwich), or fish finger bap (roll). There must be a place for these types of dishes. It should certainly not be on the menu every week or month, but sometimes you just need these simple dishes. Sometimes all you need is carbs.

I never ate much cake during our travels because we did not eat many sweet foods in our family. I experienced a traditional afternoon tea only in my late teens when I traveled to Glastonbury, looking like a hippy. I still vividly remember my first muffin, though. It was dense and moist, stained with blueberries and almost the size of my head. I bought it on a foggy summer's day in a small bakery near the port of Ullapool in the Highlands of Scotland. It took me two days to eat the thing. After every bite, I put it neatly back in the brown paper bag in which the baker had wrapped it. I enjoyed every bite, picked the berries out and loved the moist blue spots that they left behind. It was the most glorious thing ever. This was the moment that I realized I loved cake, and when I got home, I started baking.

While in French pàtisserie the expertise lies with the pastry chef and pastries are usually bought in a pàtisserie, British people bake at home. The uniqueness of their baked goods has something to do with that. Scones taste best when they have just come out of the oven and are still steaming when you break them open. If you offer simple, modest bakes, you ensure that the taste is 100 percent spot on. You cannot hide behind cheerful colors and delicate frills. I often find with French cakes that they look far better than they actually taste, and wonder about the amount of gelatin and food coloring needed to get the "perfect" look.

British baking is coziness and warmth. The British make time for cakes. If they could, they would drop everything each day at four o'clock for afternoon tea. Recently a police notice showed a picture of some goods they wanted to trace the ownership of and in the background was a plate with a half-eaten Victoria sandwich cake. All the comments on the picture were about the cake, not the police notice! Cakes, biscuits, pies, and other sweet and savory pastries are entwined with the identity of the inhabitants of the green British Isles. It is not surprising that the baking program *The Great British Bake Off* is a British invention, and I often pinch myself when I stand in that iconic white tent, trying to fill Mary Berry's shoes. For the British, a village fair is not complete without a baking competition. Baking and competitions for the best cake, biscuit, jam, or biggest gooseberry are an important community happening and a pinnacle of Britishness.

The day before our wedding in Britain we encountered such a village fair. We were too early for the baking competition, but on the lawn next to the white tent a coquettish lady was sitting behind a table with a large fruit cake, of which you had to guess the weight. My guess was completely wrong, but when the lady heard that we were getting married in her village, she gave me the first prize.

"British baking is coziness and warmth."

Authenticity

I developed the recipes in this book based on those I encountered during my historical research – not as straightforward as you might think, since recipes were not explained as extensively in the past as they are today. Ingredients were often left out on the assumption that the cook would know what was required. For example, one recipe for a tart gave the ingredients and method for the filling, but did not reveal anything about the dough for the base. Guidelines for assessing the doneness of a cake were omitted, as well as the preparation times and oven temperatures. The ingredients were also different. Eggs are much larger nowadays and flour is a lot finer. The recipes needed countless tests to bring them to what they are today.

I deliberately did not make a pimped-up version of the British bakes because it would be arrogant to drastically change anything in a book that is trying to paint a picture of the history of British baking. For example, if I gave a Chelsea bun a twist by adding pistachios or pecans, leaving out the currants, it would no longer be a Chelsea bun. It would be good, but it would no longer be that iconic, slightly square, rolled-up sticky bun, dotted with currants and dusted with fine sugar.

When it comes to more recent classics such as carrot cake, coffee and walnut cake, lemon drizzle, flapjacks, and a few pies, I have given you the recipes that I have been baking for years. Often these are based on memories of what I ate in Britain on my many travels over the last two decades.

My many historical cookbooks and diaries tell a story about the origin and evolution of flavors and thus about the evolution of a recipe due to changes in cooking methods. Delicately rich pastries and confectionery were the privilege of the higher class. From the Victorian era, there were also books for the working class. The new generation of cookbooks "for the people," as the 19th-century chef Alexis Soyer wrote on the cover of his book, were written with the home baker in mind. This was not always realistic, since many people of the lower classes lived in houses without kitchens.

Many manuals for bakers were published around the 20th century. Confectioners who made delicate sweet treats disappeared from the stage as the parties in large houses became less decadent and there were fewer and fewer domestic workers who could spend hours creating a lavish feast. The bakery continued to exist, and took over part of the repertoire from the confectionery, but the focus was mainly on bread, buns, cakes, and biscuits. The handbooks provided bakers with tools to get to know their customers and, depending on who ordered, they chose a rich or economical version of a recipe. In one book there were three recipes for Bath buns, one more expensive to make than the others.

Oats in the North, Wheat from the South

The recipes in this book also paint a picture of the British landscape. The many bakes made with oats in the North tell the story of a rougher and wetter climate in the northern areas, where oats and barley were the most important crops because they could withstand the adverse weather. Here developed a culture for quick breads like soda bread, griddle cakes, oatcakes, and scones, as well as the paper-thin crispbread called clapcake (see page 150) from Northern England and Scotland, which we usually associate with Scandinavia. The cakes of the North were usually heavily spiced, containing unrefined sugars and often rum or sherry. The large trading ports such as Dundee in Scotland and Whitehaven in the north of England traded with the Caribbean and Spain, making imports of sugar, rum, currants, sherry, and other raw materials possible. The uniqueness of the Dundee cake therefore consists of these imported goods and it is not surprising that many gingerbreads, cakes, and parkins also originate from these northern areas.

Wheat is the grain "par excellence" in the Centre, South, and South-west because the climate is drier and the summers are longer. Saffron characterizes the bakes in Cornwall. This southwest peninsula was a trading place for tin that, according to Slow Food UK, was exchanged for saffron and other goods. To meet the need for this mysteriously fragrant spice, saffron was also grown in Cornwall and in Essex around the town of Saffron Walden.

Over the centuries, some bakes disappeared from the scene entirely or changed extensively. Others survived because they were the staple food of workers in certain regions. In Staffordshire's potteries in the Midlands, the most important food was the Staffordshire oatcake, a thick pancake made from soured oat flour dough. In the tin mines of Cornwall that staple was the pasty, a hand-held pie filled with meat and vegetables. In the Highlands of Scotland, the Aberdeen buttery kept the workers fed.

Superstition, religion, and regional customs also influenced British baking traditions. Fairings were biscuits that were sold at the farmers' fair or village fairs. There was a time when girls believed that if they bought a gingerbread man at the fair, they would bag themselves a husband that year. The Twelfth cake, a yeast-leavened cake that has been all but forgotten, was baked for Twelfth Night, the last day of Christmas, and was accompanied by a role-playing game choosing a "king" and "queen."

As a symbol of life, bakes were also central to some festivities. The harvest loaf is a large decorative bread in the form of a bunch of corn, traditionally made from the first grain of the season for the harvest festival of Lammas. According to Florence Marian McNeill in her 1929 book *The Scots Kitchen*, a decorated form of shortbread was the wedding cake of rural Scotland. The shortbread was broken over the bride's head, on the threshold of her new home.

Dedicated to cake

There are few peoples, not even the French, who dedicate a time of day and a whole etiquette to cakes and tea. I am not fond of dessert, because I want sweet treats to be the main affair rather than the afterthought in the dessert course. There is much to say about the afternoon tea ritual and history (page 166) and the importance of toast in British culture (page 178).

This book is not divided into chapters, although the table of contents does provide a guideline for ease of use. We are not going to put the cakes into boxes because buns and biscuits sometimes bear the name cake, and some biscuits are actually gingerbread and a gingerbread can also be a parkin. Pies can be savory or sweet, and sometimes they are both.

Much has changed in Britain in recent years, and although the iconic Britishness may have taken a bit of a beating due to recent political changes, I think there is no better time to gather around the table and get to know each other with a good piece of cake and a cup of strong English tea.

– Regula Ysewijn

By whose tough labours,
and rough hands,
We rip up first, then
reap our lands.

1625–1660, Robert Herrick
The Hock Cart, or Harvest Home

INGREDIENTS

I think that when baking, and when cooking in general, the rule should be that you have to use the best ingredients to get the best results. Budgets for food differ, of course, but I prefer to eat less cake and make it the best cake I can afford. That means that I am always looking for fresh flour from a good source. Flour that's left unused for many months will become dry and that will affect your baking. Preferably buy all organic ingredients. For example, I buy only organic eggs or eggs straight from the farm. Firstly, because I think it is not right that we keep hens in confined barns where they never see the light of day and can never roam freely. Secondly, because an egg from a chicken that has had the space to live and breathe has much more flavor. So you can decide why you choose organic eggs – is it because you say no to animals suffering for your dinner, or because you simply want the best eggs? The two are naturally connected. That, of course, also applies to meat; good provenance ensures good taste.

Flour

I think it's important that you understand why I ask you to use a certain flour, because the protein content of flour has an influence on your results. The higher the protein content of your flour, the more elasticity your dough will get. A flour with a high protein content is therefore good for bread and other pastries that are supposed to be light or would benefit from a little elasticity. Unlike white flour, 100 percent whole-wheat flour is brown because it is made from the entire grain and still contains bran. It therefore also contains fiber and vitamins that are no longer present in white flour. Wheat is the most common cereal used for whole-grain flour, but it can also be made from rye, spelt, oats, and barley, as well as a lot of other rare, ancient, or less-common crops.

Strong white bread flour – around 12.6 g (½ oz) of protein per 100 g (3½ oz) of flour (12–13%)

British recipes for bread and other bakes sometimes require completely or partially strong white bread flour, which can be compared to patent flour. This flour is made from harder wheat, which means that the flour contains more gluten. Gluten is needed for a light and well-raised result. There are several varieties of patent flour and the difference is in the protein content. French flour, which has the designation T65, usually contains 13 g (½ oz) of protein. American flour may be made from either winter or summer wheat. Winter wheat is sown in the fall and harvested in the summer. This wheat produces more protein than wheat that grows in the summer. These types of flour are available only in specialty shops or online, but are very accessible to hobby bakers.

Plain white flour – around 10 g (¼ oz) of protein per 100 g (3½ oz) of flour (10%)

Recipes for more delicate bakes use what the British call "plain white flour." Where I live in Flanders, close to Holland, we have Zeeland flour, made from soft wheat that grows in a maritime climate. Zeeland flour has a low protein content of 10% and will therefore develop little gluten. It's ideal for brittle cookies such as shortbread and short dough for shortcrust cake bases. Your local area may have a flour that is similarly low in protein, or you can choose the regular all-purpose flour you can get everywhere.

Oats

There are many varieties of oatmeal and oat flakes:

Rolled oats, also called old-fashioned, are made by steaming whole oat groats, then running them between rollers to make flat flakes. The steaming partially cooks the oats, which makes them cook faster when you use them in your cooking. Rolled oats are sold in the traditional size and also as jumbo oats.

Steel-cut oats, also called "pinhead oats," are whole oats that have been cut into two or three pinhead-sized pieces. Steel-cut oats are also used for porridge, and are considered the Irish way of making porridge. They have more bite and a nuttier flavor.

Porridge oats, or oatmeal, are made by grinding steel-cut oats or rolled oats about halfway to flour, leaving lots of coarse pieces. They come in a fine, medium, or coarse variety. In the United States, look for porridge oats online, or substitute quick-cooking oats.

Oat flour is a much finer substance than oatmeal. It is ground from whole oat groats, steel-cut oats, or rolled oats. It's completely soft and resembles whole-grain flour. You can create oat flour by grinding rolled oats with the blade attachment of a food processor.

Cornstarch

Cornstarch has the ability to reduce the amount of protein in flour. It's ideal for brittle cookies, but also for light cakes. Cornstarch is the starch that is obtained from the endosperm of the corn grain. The extraction of this starch is done by soaking the corn grain in sulfur dioxide, a substance that has been used since time immemorial to preserve food. The surplus of this process is the proteins from the corn grain, which go directly to the animal fodder industry. Because corn is often genetically modified, I advise you to look for organic cornstarch.

To lower the protein content of your flour (which should contain a minimum of 10 percent protein), use the following rule: replace 2½ Tbsp (20 g) of every 1 cup (125 g) of all-purpose flour with cornstarch.

Self-rising flour

You can buy this flour, but you can easily make it yourself. The advantage of making it yourself is that you only have to buy one type of flour and simply add baking powder when a recipe calls for self-rising flour. An old bag of self-rising flour that you've found in the back of your cupboard may not be active anymore and may therefore yield an unrisen result. There is generally 1½ tsp (4 g) of baking powder in 1 cup (125 g) of self-rising flour. You can play with this ratio if you want the dough to rise a little more or less. I haven't used self-rising flour in this book and have supplied the amount of baking powder needed separately for each recipe.

Baking soda and baking powder

Both powders ensure the raising of a dough or batter, but are definitely not the same. Baking soda is a natural carbonate that works only if you add acid to your dough or batter, such as lemon juice, yogurt, buttermilk, black treacle (or molasses), or vinegar. In baking powder, to which a stabilizer has been added, the acid is already in the carbonate. You need three times as much baking powder to replace baking soda.

Yeast

Yeast ensures the production of carbon gas and ensures that your dough rises. I mainly use dry yeast because you can keep this handy in your larder, and I therefore also use dry yeast in the recipes in this book. If you prefer to use fresh yeast, double the quantity of the dry yeast. Fresh yeast does not have to be immersed in lukewarm liquid before use.

Lard

British recipes often call for lard, which is the belly fat from a pig. You can make it yourself or simply buy it at the store. I make it myself by boiling the belly fat for a few hours, straining it, and then pouring it into containers, which I then freeze – it keeps forever. A pie pastry made with a portion of lard has a nice savory touch that goes well with a sweet filling as well. You can use the surplus of lard to fry eggs or roast potatoes. Delicious.

Suet

Shredded suet is kidney fat that is processed into small grains. It is often called for in British recipes for pie pastry, but also in puddings and in the filling of mince pies. You can buy ready-shredded suet in boxes, but you can also make it yourself, even if it is a rather long process. Because the fat has settled around the kidneys, it is full of fibers that you have to pick out. Then you have to boil and strain this fat, pour it into containers to harden, and then grate it with a coarse grater before use. It is important that you process the suet into fine pieces. You can replace suet with butter or lard, although it does not give exactly the same result. Pastries made with suet have a longer shelf life than pastries made with butter.

Butter

By butter I always mean unsalted butter, preferably organic, and with a fat content of at least 82 percent. Most cheap butter has a lower fat content. That does not mean that this butter is healthier, but that it is not suitable for making delicious cakes and bakes. Do not use margarine for the recipes, even though this was recommended 50 years ago and our parents still swear by it. Your baking skills deserve the best butter. Fat is flavor.

Cream and milk

I do like some fat and therefore also cream. The recipes in this book call for double cream, a British name for cream with a fat content of at least 48 percent. In many countries full cream has a fat content of between 33 and 35 percent. Look carefully on the packaging, choose the fattiest, and stay away from light versions.

The milk used in this book is always whole milk. If you are making cheese, I specify raw milk, which you can buy from the farm and some markets. It has a very short shelf life because it is not pasteurized. You can also make cheese with sour milk or milk to which an acid has been added, but you won't have the exact result needed for these recipes because cheese made with sour or soured milk is more acidic, while cheese made with raw milk is sweet. If you can't find raw milk, it's better to use ricotta in recipes that ask for curd cheese.

Eggs

I use medium-sized organic eggs for my recipes. Eggs ensure that your cakes increase in volume and also add nutritional value, but also make your cakes drier. The egg yolk gives your cakes a nice color. For the recipes, assume that one medium egg weighs around 50 g (1¾ oz).

Apricot kernels

In the past, bitter almonds were used instead of almond flavoring. These almonds contain a toxin that can be harmful if you eat too many of them. Apricot kernels contain the same toxin but to a much lesser extent, making them a good alternative. Bashed apricot kernels to which rosewater is added give the same marzipan-like odor and taste as bitter almonds. Adhere strictly to the quantities in this book and do not eat the kernels without incorporating them into the bake. The kernels may not be eaten in any case like regular nuts. Therefore keep them out of the reach of small children and housemates who are looking for something to nibble.

Golden syrup and black treacle

Golden syrup and black treacle are two typical English sugar syrups that are by-products from the sugar refinery. Golden syrup can be replaced by maple syrup or honey, while black treacle can be replaced by molasses, although the latter tastes much harsher than treacle. You can also use honey for treacle, but then you will miss out on that beautiful dark color.

Candied citrus peel

In England this is simply called candied peel or mixed peel, and it is often a mix of candied lemon and orange peel. For convenience, I have asked for candied citrus peel in the recipes – just use what you can find, unless it is specified in the recipe what kind of peel is needed. A good citrus peel is equal to or thicker than ¼ inch. The skin must be sticky and not as tough and dry as candy. In some recipes I also talk about candied cedro, which is a type of lemon with a very thick skin. This candied skin is usually pale yellowish green and may be purchased from online sources.

Currants and raisins

Currants and raisins are often soaked for a few hours before use, but this isn't preferable for all bakes. When it comes to some cakes, fruit loaves, and buns, it's better to use currants and raisins that haven't been soaked. If you add soaked fruit to a bread or bun dough, it will get damaged during the kneading process, and if you add it before shaping, it might introduce an unnecessary amount of moisture to the dough, often making it annoyingly sticky. I prefer to work with a wetter dough that compensates for the fact that the fruit isn't soaked. I add the fruit before the first rise and it attaches itself perfectly to the structure of the dough. You should, however, always rinse the fruit to remove any dust, and then pat it dry with paper towels.

BEFORE YOU BAKE

Preparing baking tins

Unless the recipe indicates a different method, the following techniques should be used to prepare the different baking tins.
If you prepare the baking tins in the correct way, your cake will come out of the tin more easily after baking.

Square, rectangle, or loaf tin

Apply a thin layer of butter with a folded sheet of paper towel and divide it nicely into the corners of the baking tin. Apply a strip of parchment paper in the tin that covers two sides and protrudes slightly above the top of the tin so that you can remove the cake more easily after baking.

Round tin

With a folded sheet of paper towel, apply a thin layer of butter nicely around the edge of the baking tin. Place a layer of parchment paper on the bottom of the baking tin: trace around the tin onto the parchment paper, then cut out the circle. Stick the parchment paper to the butter so that the paper stays in place.

Baking sheet

A large, shallow baking sheet is simply lined with a sheet of parchment paper.

Oven

If I have learned anything in recent years, it is that you should never blindly trust in your built-in oven thermometer, no matter how strongly the manufacturer claims it is accurate. Get yourself a separate oven thermometer – they cost very little. You can then be assured that your bread will not fail because the temperature in the oven is only $325\,^\circ$F instead of $425\,^\circ$F, even though the oven itself claims to be up to the required temperature.

The temperatures given in these recipes are the temperatures that turned out to be the best when testing, but above all learn to judge your pastry on how it looks and how it smells. The more you bake, the more certain you will become about the cooking times of your cakes and bakes.

In addition, I never bake with the convection function as I find it much too aggressive. If you have a preference, feel free to use this function, but reduce your oven temperature by 25 degrees or according to the manufacturer's instructions.

I also have an Esse stove at home – a stove with heat storage that works with a heavy cast-iron frame that can absorb heat from a relatively low intensity but continuously burning source. Cooking or baking with such an oven is slightly different, because you do not have a glass door in front of the oven and therefore cannot see the cake to judge it during baking. I have tested all recipes on this stove and given an extra tip where needed, but usually the cooking time and temperature are the same as the recipe indicates. As with regular ovens, always use an oven thermometer.

Measuring ingredients

In Britain, dry ingredients are measured by weight rather than by volume, as is customary in America. Weights for dry ingredients are given in these recipes, and a basic kitchen scale will let you measure out your ingredients more accurately, for better results.

Egg washing

Egg washing is used to give cakes a nice golden-brown color during baking. You can also use it to stick toppings, such as pearl sugar nibs or currants, to your cakes. For a tart with a very liquid filling, you can egg wash the blind-baked pie crust and then bake it for another 5 minutes. This ensures that all the holes in the crust close nicely and the crust becomes firmer as you create a kind of barrier against moisture. It is important that you beat your egg yolk well with the milk before use – some people even strain it to ensure an even result. The quantity for a typical egg wash is 1 egg yolk plus 1 tablespoon of milk. Apply it with a brush in a thin layer.

Romney Marsh, Kent and Sussex border

Seven Sisters, South Downs, Sussex

You can't have your cake *and* eat it.

1538, Thomas Duke of Norfolk

"A man cannot have his cake and eat his cake."

Proverb
You cannot eat your cake
and keep it at the same time.

Meaning
You can't have it all.

Cakes

At every important moment in the cycle of life – on birthdays, weddings, and religious and traditional holidays – there are baked goods to share and mark the occasion. This can be bread or biscuits, but mostly and more commonly today it is a cake. Cake is so significant at royal weddings in Britain that pieces of the wedding fruit cake are wrapped carefully and packed into commemorative boxes to be sent to foreign relations, friends, and members of the public. A boxed slice of Queen Victoria's wedding cake, dating from 1840, recently fetched £1500 at auction, while a slice of Kate and William's royal wedding cake was sold for a whopping £6000 in 2014.

We often assume that cake has always existed, but in reality, cake as we know it today is quite recent. The word "cake" comes from Old Norwegian *kaka*. From their inception, cakes were usually small, like biscuits or buns. Cakes were more breadlike than cakelike in the past, and they were sweetened with small amounts of honey because sugar was not available.

Many biscuits, buns, and pastries were and are called cakes. Eccles cakes and tea cakes are certainly not cakes, but they do bear that name. Funnily enough, "cake" is also the word used in Dutch, although the word doesn't occur in old Dutch or Flemish cookbooks.

Cakes and buns were used in pagan religious ceremonies. Round cakes symbolized life, and they were often pressed with a cross depicting the four seasons, later adopted by Christianity as a symbol for the crucifix. An example of this is the hot cross bun.

Recipes of early cakes appear more frequently in English cookbooks from the 17th century when sugar imports increased. Sugar consumption in Britain even doubled between 1690 and 1740. The book *The Compleat Housewife* from 1727 contains 40 cake recipes that could have been already about 30 years old at the time of publication.

The cakes that were baked until the end of the 18th century were either small and not really cake as we know it today, or they were very large. John Mollard's Twelfth cake contained 7 pounds of flour and had to be baked for many hours on end. These cakes were made in cake hoops made from paper, wood, or tin or other metal without an attached bottom. The hoops were often wrapped with moist newspaper to prevent the outside of the cake from baking faster than the inside. These large cakes were intended for special occasions because their ingredients, such as dried fruits and spices, were expensive and depended on imports. To be celebrated with something as precious as a cake was quite an honor.

Before baking powder came on the market in 1843, bakers used eggs – which sometimes had to be beaten for an hour – and yeast to get their cakes to rise. The texture was rather more bready than cakelike. The flour used in the past was also much coarser and denser due to old milling techniques that couldn't create a flour as finely milled as we are used to today. Cakes were often first cooked and then baked, something that can still be seen in the stories about the simnel cake (see page 62).

When the use of baking powder for baking cakes became the norm in the second half of the 19th century and finer flour was imported from places like Austria and Hungary, cake recipes became more refined. But because the British have always respected their old traditions, we can still find the old-style cakes in today's Christmas and fruit cakes. These are much heavier and firmer than, for example, a Victoria sandwich cake. And many people still wrap their Christmas cake in a moist newspaper like their mothers and grandmothers did. It is still relevant because these cakes require a long baking time at a low temperature.

Some cakes get better if you let them mature. Fruit cakes such as Christmas cake, simnel cake, tea loaf, and bara brith only improve if they get some time or are fed with brandy or another liqueur. The same goes for gingerbreads such as the parkin, which is quite dry at first and then becomes wonderfully moist.

In any case, a cake is something that you bake to share, either with your loved ones or colleagues, or with strangers if you bake your cakes to sell.

Savoy cake

Large, airy cakes such as this one were extremely difficult to make in the temperamental ovens of the 19th century. They really tested the chef's skill. In *The Modern Baker, Confectioner and Caterer*, published in 1907, author John Kirkland said that the shape of copper Savoy cake molds was often too complicated to be practical. That's why less intricate copper pudding molds were often used for the Savoy cake instead.

In my *National Trust Book of Puddings*, I give a recipe for a tipsy pudding where this cake is made a few days ahead and left to dry out, then soaked in sweet wine and served with custard.

Use the most beautiful, decorative tin that you have for this cake – the higher, the better – or use a Kugelhopf tin. It's important to follow the instructions using lard to grease the tin. When you're using an intricate tin that doesn't have a non-stick coating, this method will ensure that the cake releases from the tin. Double the recipe for a larger tin.

For 4–6 people

4 egg yolks

4 egg whites

½ cup (100 g) superfine sugar

grated zest of 1 lemon or 1 orange

6 Tbsp (45 g) plain white flour

6 Tbsp (45 g) cornstarch

pinch of sea salt

lard, for greasing

cornstarch, for dusting

confectioners' sugar, for dusting

For a decorative cake tin of at least 4 cups

Preheat your oven to 375°F. Grease the cake tin with lard and dust with cornstarch, then tip out the excess cornstarch and do the same with the confectioners' sugar.

Beat the egg yolks in a small bowl. In a large bowl, beat the egg whites until stiff peaks form. Gradually add the sugar, one teaspoon at a time, until the egg whites are stiff and shiny. Add a teaspoon of the egg white mixture to the egg yolks, add the lemon zest, and mix. Fold the egg yolks through the egg whites.

Sift the flour and cornstarch over the mixture, add a pinch of salt, and fold in, ensuring that the mixture is well mixed but retains its volume.

Spoon the batter into the tin and then place it in the bottom of the oven if you are using a high mold, or in the middle if you are using a normal mold or tin.

Bake for 30–40 minutes until the top of the cake is golden brown. Let it rest for 10 minutes in the tin and then take it out of the tin to cool on a rack. The cake should look very pale.

Caraway seed cake

Caraway seed was a very popular addition to British baking in the past. Nowadays, however, it is a taste we usually associate with Scandinavia. Around 1900, May Byron gave regional recipes for seed cakes from Gloucestershire, Cheshire, Kent, Yorkshire, and Ireland, but we know from other books that seed cake was also very popular in Cornwall. Old recipes also say to add caraway comfits. These are caraway seeds that have been given a white sugar coating, a tedious task that took hours over an open fire, applying the sugar coat seed by tiny seed. Caraway comfits can be compared to Indian *mukhwas*, the difference being that they use fennel seeds and add a colored sugar coating rather than white. The different colors of the *mukhwas* add a nice touch to the cake. I usually use a combination of *mukhwas* and caraway seeds, but you can easily use just seeds and have an equally nice cake. You can also replace the caraway seeds with crushed cardamom seeds.

For 6–8 people

14 Tbsp (200 g) butter, at room temperature

1 cup (200 g) superfine sugar

4 eggs

2 cups (250 g) plain white flour

1 Tbsp caraway seeds and/or 2 Tbsp *mukhwas*

1 Tbsp baking powder

butter, for greasing

flour, for dusting

For a 3½ x 6-inch loaf tin

Preheat your oven to 350°F and prepare the loaf tin (see page 21).

Beat the butter and sugar together until creamy. Beat in the eggs, one at a time, and make sure that each egg is completely incorporated before adding the next one. Add a teaspoon of the flour with the last egg to prevent the mixture from separating.

Stir the caraway seeds and/or *mukhwas* (if using) into the batter, then fold in the remaining flour and the baking powder so that the volume is retained. Spoon the batter into the cake tin and smooth out the top. Place in the middle of the oven and bake for 45–50 minutes. A skewer inserted in the center of the cake should come out clean.

Allow the cake to cool in the tin for 5 minutes, then remove from the tin and let cool on a rack.

Carrot cake

Carrot cake is loved by young and old. It has its origins in the Middle Ages, when sugar and honey were far too expensive to use lavishly. In those days, carrots were considered a sweet food. During the Second World War, many carrot cakes were made in Great Britain because there was a surplus of carrots. Carrots are, of course, very healthy, which is why the Ministry of Food promoted cooking with carrots and a special leaflet with carrot dishes was distributed. Children became fond of carrots and were even given a thick carrot on a stick instead of a lollipop as the latter were not available during the war.

I like to use whole-grain flour for this cake, because it gives the cake more body and it works well with the rest of the ingredients. Although carrot cake is often made with cream cheese icing or buttercream, I love it with this cashew nut topping because the nuts go beautifully with the carrots and spices in the cake. Feel free to use cream cheese icing or buttercream if you prefer.

For 6–8 people

For the topping

1¾ cups (200 g) cashews, soaked overnight in cold water or in hot water for 1–2 hours

2 Tbsp maple syrup or golden syrup

pinch of sea salt

6 Tbsp Greek yogurt, skyr (Icelandic yogurt), or coconut yogurt

unsalted pistachio nuts or marzipan carrots, to garnish

For the cake

1 cup extra-virgin olive oil

1 cup (225 g) demerara (coarse raw sugar)

4 eggs

2½ cups (300 g) whole-wheat flour or whole-grain spelt flour

grated zest of ½ orange

2 tsp ground cinnamon

2 tsp ground nutmeg

1 tsp ground ginger

5 large cloves, ground

pinch of pepper and sea salt

14 oz (400 g) carrots, grated

2 tsp baking powder

1 cup (100 g) pecans or walnuts, broken

butter, for greasing

flour, for dusting

For two 7- to 8-inch round cake tins

Start with the topping. Drain the cashews and pat dry with paper towels. Place in a food processor or blender, add the syrup and blend until smooth. Add the salt and yogurt and blend until smooth and creamy. Spoon into a small bowl and place in the fridge.

Preheat your oven to 350°F and prepare the tins (see page 21).

For the cake, beat the oil and sugar together in an electric mixer for 5 minutes. Add the eggs, one at a time, beating well after each addition. Add a teaspoon of flour with the last egg to prevent the mixture from separating.

Add the orange zest, spices, and salt, followed by the grated carrot. Mix well with a spatula. Mix in the remaining flour and the baking powder until the batter is well combined. Finally, stir in the nuts.

Divide the batter between the two tins. Firmly tap the tins on the bench to distribute the batter and remove any air bubbles.

Bake in the middle of the oven for 35–40 minutes, then test the cakes with a skewer – if it comes out clean, the cakes are ready.

Allow the cakes to cool completely before assembling. If you've made the cakes a day ahead, place them in the fridge 1 hour before decorating.

Spread or pipe one-third of the topping over the bottom cake layer. Add the second cake layer and spread the rest of the topping over the cake. Decorate with whole and chopped pistachio nuts or marzipan carrots. Place the cake in the refrigerator after assembly if you're not serving it immediately.

Battenberg cake

The first Battenberg cake appeared in Frederick Vine's *Saleable Shop Goods for Counter-Tray and Window* from 1898 and had nine panels instead of four. Presumably it became four panels when the big cake manufacturers started baking the cake on an industrial scale in the 20th century. Mrs Marshall, a distinguished cookbook writer, publisher of her own magazine, and owner of a store that sold cooking appliances she invented herself, gave a recipe in 1898 for a cake that looked exactly the same but had a different name. She added flavor to her marzipan by adding maraschino liqueur.

Special Battenberg cake tins are available, and although buying a tin especially for this cake may seem extravagant, it neatly yields four bars of cake that need only minor trimming and therefore will lead to less cake waste (if there ever is such a thing!). I can also guarantee you will be enjoying this tin for many Battenberg combinations to come. Why not try chocolate and vanilla?

For 6–8 people

For the homemade marzipan
(or use 14 oz/400 g ready-made marzipan)
¾ cup (100 g) confectioners' sugar
½ cup (100 g) superfine sugar
2 cups (180 g) almond meal
3 Tbsp (20 g) apricot kernels (see page 19)
1 tsp rosewater or maraschino liqueur
1 egg, beaten

For the cake
¾ cup (175 g) butter, at room temperature
¾ cup (175 g) superfine sugar
3 eggs
1 cup + 2 Tbsp (135 g) plain white flour
6 Tbsp (35 g) almond meal
1 tsp baking powder
natural pink food coloring
3–4 Tbsp apricot jam
butter, for greasing
flour, for dusting

If you can't find apricot kernels, use an extra ¼ cup (20 g) of almond meal and add a few drops of natural almond extract or maraschino liqueur to your homemade marzipan.

For a Battenberg tin

It is best to make the marzipan a day in advance. Sift the confectioners' sugar, superfine sugar, and almond meal into a large bowl and mix well. Soak the apricot kernels in boiling water for 5 minutes, then remove the skins. Using a mortar and pestle, finely crush the apricot kernels and add the rosewater or maraschino liqueur.

Make a well in the dry ingredients and add the egg and the apricot kernel mixture. Use a spatula or wooden spoon to mix everything well, then use your hands to knead the marzipan. If necessary, add a teaspoon of water at a time until it comes together but doesn't become sticky. Wrap the marzipan in plastic wrap and let it rest at room temperature.

Preheat your oven to 350° F and prepare the tin (see page 21).

For the cake, put the butter and sugar in a bowl and beat until creamy. Add the eggs, one at a time, beating well after each addition. Add a teaspoon of the flour with the last egg to prevent the mixture from separating.

Add the remaining flour, the almond meal, and the baking powder and mix well. Divide the batter in half and add coloring to one half. Pour the batter into the cake tin, keeping the colors separate. Bake in the middle of the oven for 25–30 minutes.

When the cake has cooled completely, cut out 1¼ x 1¼–inch bars from each color, making sure they are nicely square and uniform. You can skip this step if you have a Battenberg tin, and just trim where necessary.

Gently heat the apricot jam. Spread a little of the warm jam on the sides of the cake bars where they will be stuck together to create the iconic stained-glass window effect.

Roll out your marzipan to about ¼ inch thick. Brush the marzipan with the jam and place the assembled cake on top. Trim the marzipan and wrap it around the cake. Trim the ends of the cake for a neat finish.

Coffee and walnut cake

Coffee and walnut cake can be found in every tearoom. Even though it's old fashioned, it hasn't fallen out of favor. You can make one cake and decorate it with buttercream, or you can make several layers with buttercream in between.

You can make buttercream in several different ways. Italian buttercream is made with Italian meringue, which is made by whipping egg whites together with hot sugar syrup. The meringue is then beaten until it has cooled, after which the butter is added. This buttercream has a very white appearance. For Swiss buttercream, a mixture of egg white and sugar is heated in a bain-marie to 160°F, then the egg whites are whipped and butter is added. The French method isn't that different: they first make a *pâte à bombe* by boiling water with sugar at 250°F. In the meantime, they whip the egg whites, then add the sugar syrup and beat until cold. Subsequently, cubes of butter are added to create a creamy, smooth buttercream. The Germans do it completely differently and make a mousseline cream that consists of one part butter and two parts pastry cream. There are many more versions, but here I've used the simplest, which is the English or American version. This buttercream is not really smooth, but its advantage is the simplicity – anyone can make it.

For 6–8 people

For the cake

1 cup (225 g) butter, at room
  temperature
1 cup (200 g) demerara (coarse raw
  sugar)
4 eggs
1¾ cups (225 g) plain white flour
3 tsp instant coffee dissolved in
  1 Tbsp hot water, cooled
pinch of cocoa powder
pinch of ground cinnamon
pinch of sea salt
2 tsp baking powder
¾ cup (75 g) walnuts, roughly chopped
butter, for greasing
flour, for dusting
walnut halves, to garnish

For the buttercream

1 cup (240 g) butter, at room
  temperature
3½ cups (400 g) confectioners' sugar
heaping 2 tsp instant coffee dissolved in
  1 Tbsp hot water, cooled

For two 7- to 8-inch round cake tins

Preheat your oven to 350°F and prepare the tins (see page 21).

Put the butter and sugar in a bowl and beat until creamy. Add the eggs, one at a time, and make sure that each egg is completely incorporated before adding the next one. Add a teaspoon of the flour with the last egg to prevent the mixture from separating. Stir in the instant coffee, cocoa, cinnamon, and salt.

Carefully fold the remaining flour and the baking powder into the batter so that the volume is retained. Mix in the walnuts, divide the batter between the cake tins, and smooth the tops. Firmly tap the tins on the bench to distribute the batter and remove any air bubbles. Bake in the middle of the oven for 20–25 minutes.

Let the cakes rest for 5 minutes before taking them out of the tins, then let them cool further on a wire rack.

For the buttercream, beat the butter in an electric mixer until it turns white; this is an important step. Add the confectioners' sugar, one spoonful at a time, until it is completely absorbed. Finally, add the instant coffee and mix well until the buttercream is fluffy.

To assemble the cake, choose the cake with the smoothest top and set it aside. Spread the other cake with buttercream or use a piping bag fitted with a star nozzle to pipe a pattern over the cake. Place the second cake on top and lightly press down. Decorate the top of the cake with buttercream and walnut halves.

Swiss roll

Swiss roll, or jelly roll, originated in the 19th century. Its origins are not entirely certain because many cultures have a similar cake. The British are extra enthusiastic because it reminds them of that other classic, jam roly-poly. You can experiment with the flavors of fillings and toppings, but my favorite will always be the classic combination of strawberry and cream.

For 8–12 people

For the cake

4 egg whites

½ cup (100 g) superfine sugar

4 egg yolks

grated zest of ½ lemon

⅓ cup (45 g) plain white flour

⅓ cup (45 g) rice flour or 7 Tbsp (45 g) cornstarch

butter, for greasing

superfine sugar, for dusting

For the filling

¾ cup cream with at least 40% fat

1 Tbsp granulated white sugar

4-6 Tbsp strawberry jam

chopped pistachio nuts, to garnish

fresh strawberries and raspberries, to garnish

For a 10 x 15–inch jelly roll tin

Preheat your oven to 400°F. Grease the jelly roll tin with butter, line with parchment paper, and sprinkle with superfine sugar.

In a bowl, beat the egg whites to stiff peaks and then add the superfine sugar, one spoonful at a time. Keep beating until the mixture forms a meringue. Beat the egg yolks in another bowl.

Add a teaspoon of meringue to the egg yolks, then mix in the grated lemon zest. Transfer the egg yolk mixture to the meringue and mix well. Carefully fold in the flour and rice flour or cornstarch so that the volume is retained. Spoon the batter into the tin and smooth the top.

Bake for 6–8 minutes until the cake has a golden blush. Remove the cake from the tin and place it on a sheet of parchment paper with a tea towel underneath, then roll it up from the short side and let it rest until you are ready to assemble. This will make rolling up the filled cake much easier.

For the filling, whip the cream with the granulated sugar. Unroll the cake and spread it with the jam, followed by the whipped cream. Re-roll the cake and decorate it with chopped pistachios and fresh berries.

If you aren't going to serve the cake immediately, it's best to stabilize the cream with gelatin. Soak 2 gelatin sheets in a bowl of cold water. Beat the cream until it has the consistency of yogurt, then drain the gelatin and heat it in the microwave for 10–15 seconds. Let it cool slightly, then beat the cream further, pour in the liquid gelatin, and beat until the cream is stiff.

You can also replace the cream with vanilla ice cream. Re-roll the cake with the paper around it and freeze before serving.

Cornish heavy cake

It's not certain when this cake came into existence, but Cornwall locals claim it's an age-old cake. This recipe comes from a booklet from around 1920 that contained Cornish recipes. It's a flat, rough cake with currants that actually looks more like a rock cake.

For 6–8 people

3½ Tbsp (50 g) butter, at room temperature

3½ Tbsp (50 g) lard

2¾ cups (340 g) plain white flour

¼ cup (50 g) granulated white sugar

½ tsp sea salt

½ cup milk or water

1¼ cups (180 g) currants

⅓ cup (50 g) candied citrus peel

1 egg yolk + 1 Tbsp milk, for egg wash

granulated white sugar, for dusting

For a 9 x 13-inch baking sheet

Preheat your oven to 375 °F and line the baking sheet with parchment paper.

Roughly mix the butter and lard with the flour, sugar, and salt.

Add the milk or water and knead until combined. Add the currants and candied peel and knead to distribute them throughout the dough. Cover the dough and set aside for 1–2 hours.

Turn the dough out onto the baking sheet and gently push it into a large rectangle. Use a knife to lightly score the portions into diamonds. Brush the egg wash over the dough and sprinkle with sugar.

Bake in the center of the oven for 40–50 minutes.

Victoria sandwich cake

The first version of this cake was made in small, individual, elongated cakes similar to the sandwiches that were served for an afternoon tea. In *The Modern Baker, Confectioner and Caterer* from 1907, John Kirkland gives different versions for cakes such as coffee and walnut, but the Victoria sandwich with raspberry or strawberry jam and/or cream is the most popular. Traditionally, for this cake, the eggs are first weighed in their shells and then the same weight of butter, sugar, and flour is used.

For 6–8 people

4 eggs

1 cup (250 g) butter, approximately, at room temperature

2 cups (250 g) plain white flour, approximately

1¼ cups (250 g) granulated white sugar, approximately

1 Tbsp milk

2 tsp baking powder

2–3 Tbsp raspberry or strawberry jam

butter, for greasing

flour, for dusting

confectioners' sugar, for dusting

For two round 7- to 8-inch loose-based cake tins

Preheat your oven to 350° F and prepare the cake tins (see page 21).

Weigh the eggs in their shell, then measure out the same weight of butter, flour, and sugar.

Put the eggs in a large mixing bowl. Add the butter, sugar, milk, flour, and baking powder. Mix the batter until it is smooth.

Divide the batter between the two cake tins and smooth the tops. Tap the tins on the bench to remove any air bubbles. Bake in the middle of the oven for 20–25 minutes. Leave in the tins for 5 minutes, then remove from the tins and let cool on a wire rack.

When the cakes have cooled, cover one cake with the jam and place the second cake on top. Sprinkle with confectioners' sugar.

For a richer version, cover the bottom cake with whipped cream (with at least 40% fat) in addition to the jam. In summer, it's also very nice to add slices of fresh strawberries to the filling and on top.

A collaboration
between the hen,
the cow, and the cook.

Custard

Madeira cake

This cake is named after Madeira wine, a fortified wine from Madeira in Portugal that became popular in England in the mid-19th century. The wine was served to be enjoyed with the cake, just as vin santo is served with biscotti in Tuscany. One of the earliest recipes was that of Eliza Acton in her 1845 book *Modern Cookery for Private Families*. Madeira cake still often appears on the table, although today it is served with a steaming cup of tea rather than a glass of Madeira wine.

For 6–8 people

¾ cup (175 g) butter, at room temperature

¾ cup (175 g) superfine sugar

3 eggs

2 cups (250 g) plain white flour

grated zest of 1 lemon

1 tsp baking powder

1–2 thin slices of candied lemon or lemon zest

butter, for greasing

flour, for dusting

candied fruits, to garnish

For a 7- to 8-inch round cake tin

Preheat your oven to 350°F and prepare the cake tin (see page 21).

Put the butter and sugar in a bowl and beat until creamy. Add the eggs, one at a time, and make sure that each egg is completely incorporated before adding the next one. Add a teaspoon of the flour with the last egg to prevent the mixture from separating. Stir in the lemon zest.

Carefully fold the remaining flour and the baking powder into the batter so that the volume is retained. Stir in the candied lemon. Spoon the batter into the cake tin and smooth the top. Bake in the middle of the oven for 30–40 minutes.

Allow the cake to cool in the tin for 5 minutes, then remove from the tin and let cool on a wire rack. You can decorate the cake with candied fruits to give it a wonderful retro appearance.

Serve with a cup of Earl Grey tea or a glass of Madeira, sherry, or port.

Variation: In the past, fine pieces of cedro (see page 19) were used in this recipe. For a tasty twist, add ⅓ cup (50 g) of candied cedro to the batter.

Lemon drizzle cake

This cake is at home in rustic tearooms as well as hip coffee bars. The secret that makes this simple cake so beautiful is the sharp lemon syrup that soaks into the velvety soft cake. The best way to bake it is as a tray bake (sheet cake) – it loses its effect as a round cake. This is my husband Bruno's favorite cake.

For 8–12 people

For the cake

1 cup (225 g) butter, at room temperature

1 cup + 2 Tbsp (225 g) superfine sugar

4 eggs

2 cups (250 g) plain white flour

¼ cup buttermilk (or regular milk mixed with a little lemon juice)

grated zest of 2 lemons

2 Tbsp baking powder

butter, for greasing

flour, for dusting

For the lemon drizzle topping

juice of 2 lemons

¾ cup (175 g) granulated white sugar

For a 6 x 3½–inch loaf tin

Preheat your oven to 350°F and prepare the tin (see page 21).

Put the butter and superfine sugar in a bowl and beat until creamy. Add the eggs, one at a time, and make sure that each egg is completely incorporated before adding the next one. Add a teaspoon of the flour with the last egg to prevent the mixture from separating. Add the buttermilk and lemon zest and mix well.

Add the baking powder to the flour and combine well. Now carefully but swiftly fold it into the batter, spoon the batter into the tin, and place in the middle of the oven.

Bake the cake for 45–50 minutes. A skewer inserted in the center should come out clean.

For the topping, mix the lemon juice with the granulated sugar.

Use a toothpick to pierce some small holes in the warm cake. Allow the cake to cool for 5 minutes and then transfer to a rimmed plate.

Spoon the topping over the cake and continue to spoon over the topping that drips over the side. Allow the cake to cool further.

Mix 1 teaspoon poppy seeds into the batter to turn the lemon drizzle cake into a lemon and poppyseed cake, another British classic.

Lardy cake

Lardy cakes are known in a few regions in England. I came across them in the Cotswolds, where they are smaller and spiral-shaped, and in Oxford, where the dough is folded into a brick as in this recipe.

For 8–12 people

For the cake

4¾ tsp (15 g) dried yeast

1¼ cups lukewarm water

4¼ cups (500 g) strong white bread flour (see page 16)

¼ cup (60 g) demerara (coarse raw sugar)

½ tsp ground cinnamon

1½ Tbsp (20 g) lard or butter, cubed, at room temperature

1 tsp sea salt

1 egg yolk + 1 Tbsp milk, for egg wash

For the filling

4 Tbsp (60 g) lard

4 Tbsp (60 g) butter, at room temperature

¼ cup (50 g) soft brown sugar

¾ cup (120 g) raisins

⅓ cup (50 g) currants

⅓ cup (50 g) candied citrus peel

For the syrup

⅓ cup (60 g) granulated white sugar

5 tsp water

For a 9 x 13–inch baking sheet

Add the yeast to the lukewarm water to activate it. Put the flour, raw sugar, and cinnamon in the bowl of an electric mixer fitted with a dough hook and put the lard or butter on top. Pour half of the yeast mixture over the lard or butter, wait 1 minute, and then knead for a few seconds. Add the rest of the yeast mixture. The dough will now be very wet, but don't add flour – this is how it should be. Knead for 5 minutes, then scrape all of the dough back together. You can also mix and knead the dough by hand.

Let the dough rest for a few minutes and then add the salt and knead for another 10 minutes. Remove the dough from the dough hook and now use your hands to knead the dough in the bowl for 1 minute until it is a smooth ball – do not use extra flour. Cover the bowl and leave the dough to rise in a warm place for 1 hour until doubled in quantity.

For the filling, start by beating the lard and butter with the sugar.

Roll out the dough to a rectangle about 8½ x 20 inches. Dot the dough with the lard mixture, spread it out with your fingers, and then sprinkle the dried and candied fruit over the top. Start rolling up the dough by folding a 4-inch strip from left to right and then keep rolling it up. Push the tips of your fingers halfway into the dough so that the filling and the dough will mix together slightly.

Line the baking sheet with parchment paper. Place the dough on top and let it rest for 30 minutes while you preheat the oven to 400°F. After rising, flatten the dough by patting it with your hands so that it covers the baking sheet. Brush the dough with the egg wash. Bake for 30–35 minutes until the top is golden brown.

While the cake is baking, prepare the syrup by heating the granulated sugar and water in a small saucepan. Simmer until all the sugar has dissolved. Brush the syrup over the warm lardy cake.

Some people flip the lardy cake over in the fat that is left behind in the tin so it can soak up all that goodness instead of adding a sugar syrup.

Sticky toffee cake

This sticky toffee cake is based on the sticky toffee pudding that you can find in my book *Pride and Pudding*. At one point people started baking the pudding batter as a cake, and so this cake was born. My secret ingredient is *appelstroop*, a reduced apple syrup. It is available online, but if you can't buy it you can replace it with date syrup.

For 6–8 people

For the cake

1 lb (450 g) dates or prunes, pitted

¾ cup (170 g) butter, at room temperature

scant 1 cup (200 g) soft brown sugar

3 eggs

2½ cups (300 g) plain white flour

⅓ cup (100 g) appelstroop or date syrup

3 Tbsp + 1 tsp (50 g) baking powder

pinch of sea salt

butter, for greasing

flour, for dusting

For the toffee sauce

4 Tbsp (50 g) butter

¾ cup (175 g) soft brown sugar

¾ cup cream with at least 40% fat

1 Tbsp appelstroop or date syrup

pinch of sea salt

For two round 8-inch loose-based cake tins

Put the dates or prunes in a saucepan of boiling water. Simmer for 15 minutes, then drain and purée.

Preheat your oven to 350°F and prepare the cake tins (see page 21).

Put the butter and brown sugar in a bowl and beat until creamy. Add the eggs, one at a time, and make sure that each egg is completely incorporated before adding the next one. Add a teaspoon of the flour with the last egg to prevent the mixture from separating. Add the fruit purée and the appelstroop or date syrup, then add the remaining flour, the baking powder, and the salt. Mix well.

Divide the batter between the two cake tins and smooth the tops. Tap the tins on the bench a few times to remove any air bubbles. Bake in the middle of the oven for 45–50 minutes. A skewer inserted in the center of the cake should come out clean. Leave in the tins for 5 minutes, then cool on a wire rack.

While the cakes are baking, make the toffee sauce by melting the butter in a saucepan with the brown sugar, cream, appelstroop or date syrup and salt. Let it bubble until the sauce gets heavier on your spoon. Set aside to cool slightly.

When the cakes have cooled, cover one cake with half of the toffee sauce and place the second cake on top. Poke holes in the top cake with a skewer. Pour the rest of the sauce over the cake.

Serve slices of cake with clotted cream or custard (see recipe opposite).

You can also cook this as one large cake using a round 8½-inch loose-based cake tin. You'll only need half the toffee sauce, so halve the recipe. For a sticky toffee apple cake, add 1¾ cups (220 g) apple cubes to the batter.

Dorset apple cake

The landscape of southwestern England has been marked by its many apple orchards for centuries. It is therefore not surprising that Dorset is proud of its apple cake, which is eaten hot. Of course, you'll find apple cakes all over Great Britain, but there are regional differences. For example, there are no spices in the apple cakes from the South, but the further north you go, the more spices and dried fruits make their way into the cake. Because we already have a rich selection of cakes with lots of spices, I decided to make the Dorset apple cake here because simplicity can sometimes be a relief between all the complex flavors.

This cake is usually baked in a tray and is less than 2 inches thick and very compact in structure. Cox apples are ideal because of their fresh, sour taste, but you can use any red cooking apples.

For 6–8 people

For the cake

8 oz (225 g) Cox, Braeburn, or other red
    apples, chopped

¾ cup (180 g) butter, at room
    temperature

scant 1 cup (180 g) granulated
    white sugar

2 eggs

¼ cup buttermilk or regular milk

1¾ cups (220 g) plain white flour

1 Tbsp (15 g) baking powder

butter, for greasing

flour, for dusting

For the custard

1 cup milk

1 cup cream with at least 40% fat

2 Tbsp (25 g) demerara (coarse raw
    sugar)

1 blade of mace

1 fresh bay leaf

5 egg yolks

For an 8-inch square cake tin

Preheat your oven to 325°F and prepare the cake tin (see page 21).

Toss the apple pieces in some flour (this will prevent sinking during baking).

Beat the butter and granulated sugar together until light and creamy. Add the eggs and make sure they are completely incorporated before adding the buttermilk or milk.

Sift in the flour and mix well, then sift in the baking powder and mix well. Fold the apple pieces through the batter and then spoon into the cake tin. Bake for 30 minutes.

Meanwhile, for the custard, heat the milk and cream in a saucepan with the raw sugar, mace, and bay leaf. Beat the egg yolks in a large bowl. Discard the mace and bay leaf, then pour a little of the warm milk onto the egg yolks and beat well; this prepares the egg yolks for the warm mixture. Pour the rest of the milk onto the egg yolks, whisking constantly.

Pour the custard back into the saucepan and cook over low heat, stirring with a spatula, until it starts to thicken. Make sure the mixture doesn't get too hot, or you will end up with scrambled eggs. Pour the thickened custard into a jug. Cover the jug with foil to prevent a skin from forming on the custard.

Serve the apple cake warm, cut into squares, and drizzle it with the hot or cold custard.

Tottenham cake

In 1901, pieces of Tottenham cake were given away to children from the London neighborhood of Tottenham to celebrate the victory of the Tottenham Hotspurs in the FA Cup. The pink icing is traditionally colored with mulberry juice, and sometimes the cake is finished with "hundreds and thousands" sprinkles or desiccated coconut.

John Kirkland writes in *The Modern Baker, Confectioner and Caterer* that this is an easy and quick cake for children's parties and other occasions for which many pieces must be baked in a short time. His recipe is for a giant cake that is made with more than eleven pounds of flour, but it is not tasty at all because it contains no egg and almost no sugar and butter. It clearly had to be cheap to make! The version that I give here is the version that is still sold today – a simple cake, but also delicious.

"For one penny piece, soft sponge could be bought,
mis-shapen, a ha'penny, a feast that was sought.
Pink icing with colour from mulberry so red,
So sticky, delicious, the people were fed ..."
"Tottenham Cake," by Henry Jacobs

For 12 portions

For the cake

1 cup + 5 Tbsp (300 g) butter, at room temperature
1½ cups (300 g) granulated white sugar
6 eggs
4 cups (500 g) plain white flour
3 Tbsp + 1 tsp (50 g) baking powder
⅓ cup milk
butter, for greasing
flour, for dusting

For the icing

3 cups (350 g) confectioners' sugar
2 Tbsp red currant juice or water
natural pink coloring (if you don't use red currant juice)
desiccated coconut and/or "hundreds and thousands" sprinkles, to garnish (optional)

For a 9½ x 11–inch cake tin

Preheat your oven to 325°F and prepare the cake tin (see page 21).

Put the butter and granulated sugar in a bowl and beat until creamy. Add the eggs, one at a time, and make sure that each egg is completely incorporated before adding the next one. Add a teaspoon of the flour with the last egg to prevent the mixture from separating.

Carefully fold the remaining flour and the baking powder into the batter so that the volume is retained. Stir in the milk, a little at a time. Spoon the batter into the tin and smooth the top. Bake in the middle of the oven for 30–40 minutes. Allow the cake to cool completely.

For the icing, mix the confectioners' sugar with the red currant juice or the water and the pink coloring.

Put the coconut and/or sprinkles in a shallow bowl. Trim the cake edges. You can freeze the trimmings for filling Banbury cakes (see page 134). Spread the cake with the icing and cut it into 12 pieces, wiping the knife after each cut. Dip the cake pieces into the coconut or sprinkles or just leave them plain.

It is best to eat this cake on the day it's made or the following day.

Flapjacks

Many of my English friends really love flapjacks. You can buy them at almost any bakery, but they are so simple to make yourself that you will never buy them again. A flapjack – not to be confused with an American pancake – is actually a muesli bar made with oats, sugar, syrup, and butter. A flapjack is a blank canvas – often nuts, currants, other dried fruits, and chocolate are added, but you can get creative and add whatever you like. I've given some variations below.

"Come, thou shalt go home, and we'll have flesh for holidays, fish for fasting-days, and moreo'er puddings and flap-jacks; and thou shalt be welcome."
From *Pericles, Prince of Tyre*, by William Shakespeare

For 8–10 bars

2½ cups (220 g) rolled oats or
  spelt flakes
14 Tbsp (200 g) butter
⅓ cup (100 g) golden syrup, maple
  syrup, or honey
¼ cup (50 g) soft brown sugar
pinch of sea salt
butter, for greasing
flour, for dusting
chocolate chips, for topping (optional)

For an 8-inch square cake tin

Preheat your oven to 325°F and prepare the cake tin (see page 21).

Put the oats in a blender and blitz for 3 seconds (skip this step if you are using fine rolled oats).

Melt the butter in a saucepan over low heat (make sure it does not bubble). Add the golden syrup, brown sugar, and salt and stir until the sugar has dissolved. Remove from the heat and add the oats or spelt flakes, plus any other optional ingredients except chocolate chips for topping (see variations, below), and stir well.

Firmly press the mixture into the tin so the top is even. Bake in the middle of the oven for 20–30 minutes.

For a chocolate topping, add the chocolate chips as soon as the flapjack comes out of the oven. Once they have melted, use a spatula to spread the chocolate.

Leave the flapjack to cool in the tin for 15 minutes. Using the parchment paper, carefully lift the flapjack out of the tin and cut it into bars or squares.

Variations: add a handful of chocolate chips, chopped pecans, cranberries, dried blueberries, dried apricots, or currants, or replace the oats or spelt flakes with your favorite muesli.

Fruit cake for weddings and Christmas

Bruno and I were married in our favorite village in southern England. It was a traditional affair in the old Town Hall. The town crier announced our marriage in front of the Town Hall with his voice like a clock and his hand bell ringing for the villagers and all who had gathered. After the wedding ceremony he guided us to the pub for our wedding toast, via a path that was hidden between the cobblestone streets.

After the toast we left for our honeymoon in Cornwall, and on the way back home we picked up our wedding cake in the seaside town of Brighton. The cake was, according to British wedding tradition, a rich fruit cake, the very best I had ever tasted. Baker Becky Colletti made the cake three months in advance and fed it cognac every few weeks. The ripened fruit cake was then covered with a layer of marzipan and finished with white fondant icing. When we crossed the border, we were picked out by border control because of the large box in the back seat. The man asked us, after the explosives check, whether there was perhaps a fruit cake in the box, to which I replied that we were transporting our wedding cake. If this had been the French border control, we might have had to leave our wedding cake behind. Fortunately, the British know their cake!

When I wrote this book, I wanted to share a fruit cake recipe that was special, so I asked my friends for their family recipes. They were all tasty, but none were like my wedding cake. Maybe it was the special moment that made the cake taste extra sweet, but probably it was because it is the very best recipe that exists. I would never be able to match it.

I decided to ask Becky for her recipe. She had followed my adventures over all the years since my wedding and agreed with pleasure. She told me that the cake was a family recipe and that her father was a master baker who swore by mixing the batter by hand to keep the fruit intact. She also gave me expert instructions on how to protect the cake from the heat during the long baking process. I think this is one of the reasons why I love this cake – it is dense and juicy, not dry and hard as a brick like many other Christmas cakes.

The Christmas cake is a fruit cake that is usually just a little more richly filled. The Dundee cake (see page 60) is closely related to this cake and is often eaten as a lighter version of a Christmas cake. Early Christmas cakes or fruit cakes were called plum cakes, just as the Christmas pudding was first called plum pudding. "Plum" refers to the raisins and currants, and not to plums or prunes. The tradition of eating this cake at Christmas stems from the Twelfth cake (see page 58) that was eaten on Twelfth Night, the twelfth night of Christmas (or, Epiphany eve). This custom has moved to Christmas because the British haven't celebrated twelve days of Christmas for many years.

So hereby I pass on the recipe for my wedding cake – which we now enjoy every year for Christmas – to you. Hopefully it will also be your Christmas cake, or maybe even your typical British wedding cake someday.

This cake, when stored properly, will keep for months. It won't even go moldy for over a century, as we know from a commemorative boxed piece of Queen Victoria's wedding cake that was recently sold at auction. It would be a nice choice for wedding favors even if you aren't a member of the royal family. I kept a piece of my wedding cake for many years until it finally got lost when we moved house last year.

For 8–10 people

For the soaked fruit

5⅓ cups (790 g) sultanas (golden
  raisins)

2 cups (285 g) raisins

1½ cups (225 g) currants

heaping ½ cup (115 g) glacé cherries,
  cut into quarters

⅔ cup (115 g) candied citrus peel

grated zest of 1 lemon

grated zest of 1 orange

¾ cup cognac

For the cake

1½ cups (340 g) butter, at room
  temperature

1½ cups (340 g) light brown sugar

½ tsp natural almond extract

seeds of 1 vanilla bean or
  1½ tsp natural vanilla extract

6 eggs

3⅓ cups (400 g) plain white flour

1 cup (85 g) almond meal

1½ tsp mixed spice (or pumpkin
  pie spice)

½ tsp ground cinnamon

½ tsp ground nutmeg

3 Tbsp orange marmalade

butter, for greasing

cognac, to feed the cake

For a round 8½- to 9-inch springform tin

When it comes to fruit cake, it is very important to wrap the tin so that the sides of the cake don't burn or dry out during baking. Grease the tin with butter and cover the base and sides with a double layer of parchment paper. Fold a piece of brown paper in half, then wrap it around the outside of the tin and secure with kitchen string. Fold a square of brown paper to sit the cake on in the oven, and fold another square to put on top of the tin during baking. Remove this sheet of paper about 20 minutes before the end of the cooking time. Preparing the tin in this way will ensure that your cake cooks evenly. Some people also use newspaper to tie around the tin.

The day before you begin baking, soak all of the fruit and the citrus zest in the cognac. It needs to soak for at least 12 hours.

Preheat your oven to 250°F.

Put the butter and brown sugar in a bowl and beat until light and creamy, then mix in the almond extract and vanilla seeds or extract. Add the eggs, one at a time, and make sure that each egg is completely incorporated before adding the next one. Add a teaspoon of the flour with the last egg to prevent the mixture from separating. Stir in the remaining flour, the almond meal, and the spices, mixing well.

Add the marmalade to the soaked fruit and cognac, then gradually add the fruit mixture to the cake batter while gently stirring it with your hand or a spatula.

Spoon the batter into the tin and bake for about 3½–4 hours. Allow the cake to cool in the tin. When the cake has cooled down, pierce it all over with a thin skewer and feed it by spooning over 4 tablespoons of cognac. Wrap the cake in parchment paper and then in plastic wrap and foil, and store in an airtight container.

You can feed the cake with cognac every few weeks. Becky likes to make the cake three months in advance, but you can also make it just a month ahead. You can, of course, immediately enjoy the cake as it is.

Mermaid Street, Rye, East Sussex

Twelfth cake

From the mid-18th century to the end of the 19th century, Twelfth cakes were very popular, but they had been mentioned in poems and other literature more than a century earlier. The cake was traditionally baked on the 5th of January for Twelfth Night, or the eve of the feast of Epiphany, which – as the name suggests – falls on the twelfth night of Christmas.

The cake was decadently decorated with elaborate scenes of feasting, with little people and filigree made of a white glaze, which was shaped in intricately carved wooden molds. Crowns seem to have been the most popular decoration and are rarely missing from illustrations of the cake. In the British Museum, you can find pictures of gigantic Twelfth cakes that had to be carried by several footmen. In the *Illustrated London News* of January 1849, an engraving of Queen Victoria's Twelfth cake appeared. It was an immense cake with an entire company on it, with a violin player and sugar trees.

In Victorian London, people gathered around the Twelfth cake for games. Special playing cards were developed with different characters, and everyone had to behave like the character on his or her playing card for the rest of the evening. In his 1648 work, the poet Robert Herrick explained that a bean and a pea were hidden in the Twelfth cake, and those who found them in their piece of cake were crowned to play king or queen.

Towards the end of the 19th century, Twelfth cakes finally merged with the Christmas cake. Nowadays, Twelfth cake is not commercially made, and few people remember it.

This recipe is based on the first published recipe for Twelfth cake from John Mollard in 1802. The authentic recipe traditionally makes a very large cake with more than 3 kg (about 7 lb) of flour and 2 kg (about 4½ lb) of currants.

For 8–12 people

4¾ tsp (15 g) dried yeast

¾ cup lukewarm milk

3¾ cups (450 g) plain white flour

⅓ cup (80 g) demerara (coarse raw sugar)

1 tsp ground cloves

1 tsp ground cinnamon

¼ tsp ground mace

¼ tsp grated nutmeg

4½ Tbsp (65 g) butter, cubed, at room temperature

1 egg

2 cups (300 g) currants

apricot jam, for brushing

rolled marzipan, for decorating

white fondant, for decorating

butter, for greasing

flour, for dusting

For a round 9½-inch springform tin

Add the yeast to the lukewarm milk to activate it. Put the flour, sugar and spices in the bowl of an electric mixer fitted with the dough hook. Mix to combine, then put the butter on top. Pour half of the yeast mixture over the butter and start mixing. When the mixture is completely combined, add the remaining yeast mixture, along with the egg, and knead for 10 minutes until the mixture has come together in a smooth dough that isn't too dry. Occasionally scrape the dough off the dough hook and the sides of the bowl.

Cover the dough and leave it to rise for 1 hour until it has doubled in size. Prepare the baking tin (see page 21).

Add the currants to the dough and briefly knead. Place the dough in the tin and let it rise again, covered, for 1 hour. Preheat your oven to 325°F.

Bake the cake in the middle of the oven for 2½ hours. If the top browns too quickly, make a tent of foil and place it lightly on the cake to finish cooking. When a skewer inserted in the center of the cake it comes out clean, take it out of the tin and let it cool for a few hours before decorating.

Brush the entire cake with apricot jam and apply a layer of marzipan, smoothing the surface and covering any holes. Roll out the fondant. Cover the marzipan with another layer of jam, then carefully place the fondant over the cake and use your hands or a fondant scraper to smooth it out. Decorate the cake as you wish.

Dundee cake

According to legend, 16th-century Mary, Queen of Scots, did not like to eat glacé cherries, and a lighter version of fruit cake, the Dundee cake, was developed especially for her. The real story is that the cake was invented by Janet Keiller at the end of the 18th century. She sold the cake in her shop in Dundee, where she also sold her marmalade.

Janet Keiller is the inventor of marmalade as we know it today; previously, it was cut-able rather than spreadable. Her business passed on from generation to generation and thus became the iconic brand Keiller's of Dundee in the 19th century. Keiller's continued to bake the Dundee cake, with its typical decoration of almonds, on a commercial scale to use their surplus of orange peel. The cake was a by-product of marmalade making and something for the company to produce outside the orange season. The almonds, sherry, and raisins arrived from Spain in the port of Dundee by boat, just like the Seville oranges, so the extra purchases helped maintain the company's relationships with the Spanish sellers. The cake shows the landscape and richness of the import port of Dundee.

Soon after Keiller's commercialized the cake, other cake makers followed suit throughout Great Britain, and also offered the cake in a cookie tin and delivered it worldwide. Today, real Dundee cake can be made only in Dundee and under strict rules regarding the ingredients and method. There are no spices in Dundee cake, but you can always add them.

For 6–8 people

For the cake

10 Tbsp (150 g) butter, at room temperature

¾ cup (150 g) light brown sugar

3 eggs

1⅔ cups (200 g) plain white flour

1 Tbsp sherry

heaping ½ cup (100 g) candied orange peel, finely chopped

grated zest of ½ orange

⅓ cup (25 g) almond meal

1 tsp baking powder

pinch of sea salt

1¼ cups (175 g) raisins

butter, for greasing

flour, for dusting

about 45 blanched almonds, to garnish

For the sugar syrup

1 Tbsp granulated white sugar

1 Tbsp water

For a round 8-inch springform tin

Preheat your oven to 350°F and prepare the cake tin (see page 21).

Put the butter and brown sugar in a bowl and beat until creamy. Add the eggs, one at a time, and make sure that each egg is completely incorporated before adding the next one. Add a teaspoon of the flour with the last egg to prevent the mixture from separating. Stir in the sherry, candied peel, and grated zest.

Carefully fold the remaining flour, the almond meal, baking powder, and salt into the batter so that the volume is retained. Stir in the raisins, then spoon the batter into the tin and smooth the top.

Arrange the whole blanched almonds in concentric circles on top of the cake. Don't push the almonds into the batter – lightly place them on top, or they will sink into the batter during baking.

Reduce the oven to 300°F and bake the cake in the lower part of the oven for 50–60 minutes.

Meanwhile, make the sugar syrup by mixing the granulated sugar and water in a small saucepan and heating over low heat until the sugar has dissolved.

Cover the hot cake with the sugar syrup. Allow the cake to cool completely in the tin. It tastes best after a few days, stored in an airtight container.

61

Simnel cake

The simnel cake has a rather mysterious origin. The name could derive from *simile conspersa*, which means "fine flour" in Latin. But England wouldn't be England if she didn't try to make it a more romantic tale. In 1838, a story appeared in an English newspaper entitled "The Sim-Nell" or "The Wiltshire Cake." Simon and Nelly were an old couple arguing at Easter about what to do with a surplus of dough. Simon thought that the dough should be baked in a mold, while Nelly thought it should not be baked, but cooked on the stove top. To prevent further quarrelling, the old couple came to a compromise, cooking the cake first on the stovetop, and then baking it!

Another story became legend when the recipe for simnel cake appeared in a poem. In addition to the recipe, the poem says that the cake should be brought to your mother in mid spring. This inspired the legend that simnel cake was cooked by maids who were allowed to go home on Mother's Day. The cake was apparently made from the rich ingredients found in the household of the maid's employer. Today, in England, simnel cakes are still baked around Easter and especially on Mother's Day.

It's true that 17th-century references show that the cake was indeed first cooked and then baked, which was later forgotten because ovens became more reliable. The rich ingredients have remained, such as the candied skin of fruits, currants, and sometimes saffron. The marzipan is also an important ingredient, and the 11 marzipan balls symbolize the 12 apostles, minus Judas.

This simnel cake is based on a recipe from May Byron's iconic 1914 book, *Pot-luck; or, The British Home Cookery Book*. Byron points out that this is a simnel cake from the Gloucestershire region, because variations of simnels were also baked in Bury, Devizes, and Shrewsbury. These simnels, however, were not finished with the balls of marzipan as has become the custom today.

For 6–8 people

For the homemade marzipan

1¾ cups (200 g) confectioners' sugar

1 cup (200 g) superfine sugar

4¼ cups (360 g) almond meal

6 Tbsp (40 g) apricot kernels
  (see page 19)

1 tsp rosewater or maraschino liqueur

2 eggs, beaten

For the cake

½ cup (115 g) butter, at room
  temperature

heaping ½ cup (115 g) superfine sugar

3 eggs

scant 1 cup (110 g) plain white flour

⅔ cup (55 g) almond meal

1 tsp baking powder

2⅓ cups (340 g) currants

⅓ cup (55 g) candied citrus peel,
  chopped

½ Tbsp apricot jam, to garnish

butter, for greasing

flour, for dusting

1 egg yolk + 1 Tbsp milk, for egg wash

If you can't find apricot kernels, use an extra ¼ cup (20 g) of almond meal and add a few drops of natural almond flavor or maraschino liqueur. If using store-bought marzipan, get two 14-oz (400-g) packs to be safe—you'll need extra for the marzipan balls.

For a round 7- to 8-inch springform tin

It is best to make the marzipan a day in advance. Sift the confectioners' sugar, superfine sugar, and almond meal into a large bowl and mix well. Soak the apricot kernels in boiling water for 5 minutes, then remove the skins. Using a mortar and pestle, finely crush the apricot kernels and add the rosewater or maraschino liqueur.

Make a well in the dry ingredients and add the eggs and the apricot kernel mixture. Use a spatula or wooden spoon to mix everything well, then use your hands to knead the marzipan. If necessary, add a teaspoon of water at a time until it comes together but doesn't become sticky. Wrap the marzipan in plastic wrap and let it rest at room temperature.

Preheat your oven to 325°F. Grease the tin with butter and cover the base and sides with a double layer of parchment paper. Fold a piece of brown paper in half, then wrap it around the outside of the tin and secure with kitchen string.

Divide the marzipan in half and roll each piece out to about ¼ inch thickness. Use the cake tin to cut out two 8-inch circles. Roll 11 marzipan balls from the leftover marzipan.

Put the butter and superfine sugar in a bowl and beat until creamy. Add the eggs, one at a time, and make sure that each egg is completely incorporated before adding the next one. Add a teaspoon of the flour with the last egg to prevent the mixture from separating. Fold in the remaining flour, the almond meal, and the baking powder, followed by the currants and the candied citrus peel.

Spoon half of the batter into the tin, then place one of the marzipan circles neatly on top of the batter. Spoon the other half of the batter on top.

Reduce the oven to 250°F and bake the cake in the lower part of the oven for 2 hours. If a skewer inserted in the center of the cake does not come out clean, bake for another 15 minutes.

Remove the cake from the oven and switch the oven function to broil. Allow the cake to cool in the tin for 15 minutes, then remove it from the tin. Brush the top of the cake with a thin layer of apricot jam and place the remaining marzipan circle on top. Arrange the marzipan balls on the marzipan circle, using a little apricot jam to secure them.

Lightly brush the marzipan balls with the egg wash. Briefly put the cake back in the oven to give the balls a light golden color.

Genoa cake

Although this cake resembles the Italian Christmas cake *Pandolce genovese*, it's still a top British cake, just like the Belgian bun and Battenberg cake. When I was little, my mother sometimes bought a cake in the supermarket with glacé cherries and currants in it; I always called it English cake. Genoa cake is a lovely alternative to a richer Christmas cake. It's nice to decorate the cake with candied fruit that catches the light like little gems.

You can find recipes for Genoa cake in many 19th-century cookbooks. They usually begin with a pound cake recipe. This version is based on Robert Wells' recipe from *The Bread and Biscuit Baker's and Sugar-Boiler's Assistant* from 1890. He gives instructions to make a square cake, but I find a loaf-shaped cake more convenient.

For 6–10 people

14 Tbsp (200 g) butter, at room temperature

1 cup (200 g) granulated white sugar

4 eggs

1⅔ cups (200 g) plain white flour

2 tsp baking powder

¾ cup (150 g) glacé cherries

1 cup (150 g) currants

¾ cup (150 g) candied orange peel

butter, for greasing

flour, for dusting

blanched almonds, to garnish

For a 6 x 3½-inch loaf tin

Preheat your oven to 325°F and prepare the loaf tin (see page 21).

Put the butter and sugar in a bowl and beat until creamy. Add the eggs, one at a time, and make sure that each egg is completely incorporated before adding the next one. Add a teaspoon of the flour with the last egg to prevent the mixture from separating.

Carefully fold the remaining flour and the baking powder into the batter so that the volume is retained. Fold in the fruit, then spoon the batter into the tin and smooth the top.

Bake the cake in the middle of the oven for 2 hours, checking if it is cooked after 1¾ hours and again after 2 hours. A skewer inserted in the center of the cake should come out clean. Garnish with blanched almonds.

Add candied fruits and/or apricot jelly as a garnish, to give the cake an even more decadent appearance.

Bara brith

Bara brith is a currant loaf from Wales, and the name is Welsh for "speckled bread." Just like with an Irish Barmbrack or tea loaf (the modern version of bara brith), the raisins are soaked in tea overnight before being used.

The bara brith is so important to the Welsh people that they took it to the Chubut Valley of Patagonia in Argentina, where Welsh pioneers arrived with their ships more than 150 years ago. Today there are still many tearooms in the area that serve bara brith, and although the main language is Spanish, the Welsh language still lives on there.

This recipe is based on one from a book from the 1940s, *Traditional Fare of England and Wales*. It makes a very compact bread that looks more like a cake. For a lighter version you can make Tea Loaf (page 68) or Fruit Loaf (page 70).

For 6–10 people

¾ cup (110 g) currants

¾ cup (110 g) raisins

1 cup hot black tea or Earl Grey tea

2¾ cups (330 g) plain white flour

6–7 Tbsp (85 g) granulated white sugar
  or golden syrup

½ tsp mixed spice (or pumpkin pie
  spice)

¼ tsp sea salt

6 Tbsp (85 g) lard or butter, at room
  temperature

½ egg (25 g) egg

3½ tsp (11 g) dried yeast

2–3 Tbsp (25 g) candied citrus peel

butter, for greasing

flour, for dusting

For a 9 x 5–inch loaf tin

Soak the currants and raisins in the hot tea overnight.

Combine the flour, sugar, mixed spice, and salt, then rub in the lard or butter. Add the egg and the currants, raisins, and tea, followed by the yeast and candied peel. Knead for 5 minutes.

Cover the dough and set aside for 1 hour until doubled in size.

Prepare the loaf tin (see page 21). Place the risen dough in the tin and set aside to rise again for 1 hour. Preheat your oven to 375°F towards the end of the rising time.

Reduce the oven to 300°F. Bake the loaf in the lower part of the oven for 1½ hours until golden brown.

Serve the loaf with butter.

Black bun

The black bun, or Scotch bun, was once eaten in Scotland on Epiphany, as with the Twelfth cake. In the last century, however, it has been linked to the Hogmanay party on the last day of the year. On this evening it is common to do First Footing. Just before the clock strikes midnight, you have to leave the house and ring the doorbell with a gift of coal, which symbolizes warmth for the new year, and the black bun, which means the family won't go hungry (or without whisky, of course!) that year.

In the past, a bread dough was first made and part of it was kept for the outer crust, then all the ingredients for the black bun were added to the rest of the dough. The modern version of the black bun is a fruit cake with a layer of shortcrust dough on top of and underneath the cake, and sometimes wrapped all the way around it.

For this recipe I used one of the oldest black bun recipes, from Mrs Frazer's 1791 *The Practice of Cookery, Pastry, and Confectionary*. She calls it a "Rich half-peck Bun" and is the first to encase the fruit bread in a pastry layer.

For 6–10 people

For the filling

1 cup (150 g) large black raisins

1 cup (150 g) currants

⅓ cup (50 g) candied citrus peel

2 Tbsp rum

¼ cup (50 g) soft brown sugar

½ tsp ground cinnamon

¼ tsp ground cloves

¼ tsp ground ginger

½ cup (50 g) blanched almond halves

For the pastry

1½ tsp (5 g) dried yeast

1¼ cups lukewarm water

4¼ cups (500 g) strong white bread flour (see page 16)

1 Tbsp fine raw sugar such as turbinado, or superfine sugar

2 Tbsp (30 g) butter, cubed, at room temperature

pinch of salt

butter, for greasing

flour, for dusting

1 egg yolk + 1 Tbsp milk, for egg wash

For a 9 x 5–inch loaf tin

Put the raisins, currants, and candied citrus peel in a bowl with the rum and enough water to cover them. Leave to soak overnight, then drain and mix with the brown sugar and spices.

For the pastry, add the yeast to the lukewarm water to activate it. Put the flour and raw sugar in a large bowl or the bowl of an electric mixer fitted with a dough hook. Mix together, then put the butter on top. Pour half of the yeast mixture over the butter and start mixing. When the liquid and butter have been completely incorporated, add the remaining yeast mixture.

Knead for 5 minutes, then let stand for a few minutes. Add the salt and knead for 10 minutes until all the dough has come together in a smooth dough that is not too dry. Scrape all of the dough back together.

Preheat your oven to 350°F and prepare the loaf tin (see page 21).

Take a third of the dough and knead it with the fruit mixture and the almonds. Roughly shape the mixture into a rectangular log. Press the rest of the dough out into a rectangle large enough to cover the filling. Place the filling on top and fold the dough around it. Press the dough together to seal it, cut away the excess and place the bun in the loaf tin. Brush with the egg wash, then bake in the lower part of the oven for 1 hour until golden brown.

Serve the loaf with butter.

Tea loaf

This tea loaf is a bara brith without yeast – a more modern version of the Welsh cake. The result is a wonderfully moist cake that stays good for days and only gets better with time. It is heavenly when spread with some good butter. This cake is a favorite with my family and friends.

For 6–10 people

1¼ cups (175 g) currants

½ cup (80 g) raisins

1 cup hot strong English tea

2 cups (260 g) plain white flour

½ cup (110 g) demerara (coarse raw sugar)

½ cup (120 g) soft brown sugar

½ tsp mixed spice (or pumpkin pie spice)

⅓ cup (50 g) candied citrus peel

1 Tbsp (15 g) baking powder

1 egg

butter, for greasing

flour, for dusting

For a 9 x 5–inch loaf tin

Put the currants and raisins in a large bowl. Pour in the hot tea and leave to soak overnight.

Preheat your oven to 300°F and prepare the loaf tin (see page 21).

Add the flour, raw and brown sugars, mixed spice, candied peel, baking powder, and egg to the bowl of soaked currants and raisins and mix well. Spoon into the tin.

Bake the loaf in the lower part of the oven for 1½ hours. Check the loaf after 1 hour by gently pressing your finger down in the middle of the cake; it should be lightly springy to the touch. If the batter sticks to your finger, continue baking for another 15 minutes or more, covering with foil if it threatens to get too dark.

Serve the loaf with butter.

Fruit loaf

This is the kind of fruit loaf I grew up with – more loaf than cake. I remember buying a loaf in one of the oldest bakeries in our town and arriving home with just half a loaf left. My mum and I always ate the other half while we walked, as it tastes its sweetest when freshly sliced and eaten straight from the paper bag. What was left was eaten toasted the next day, spread with cold butter as an afternoon treat.

I did the same with my best friend in school, and today I cannot walk past that bakery without buying a loaf and sticking my hand in the bag to grab a slice, then another, and then some more. I have come to associate the street with the scent and flavor of freshly baked fruit loaf.

For 6–10 people

1¼ cups (175 g) currants

½ cup (60 g) raisins

2 Tbsp rum

4¾ tsp (15 g) dried yeast

¾ cup lukewarm milk

4¼ cups (500 g) strong white bread
  flour (see page 16)

¼ cup (50 g) demerara (coarse raw
  sugar)

7 Tbsp (100 g) butter, cubed,
  at room temperature

2 eggs

1 tsp sea salt

¼ cup (35 g) candied citrus peel

butter, for greasing

flour, for dusting

1 egg yolk + 1 Tbsp milk, for egg wash

For a 9 x 5–inch loaf tin

Soak the currants and raisins in the rum for 1 hour, then drain.

Add the yeast to the lukewarm milk to activate it. Put the flour and raw sugar in a large bowl or the bowl of an electric mixer fitted with a dough hook. Mix together, then put the butter on top. Pour half of the yeast mixture over the butter and start mixing. When the liquid and butter have been completely incorporated, add the remaining yeast mixture, together with the eggs. Knead for 5 minutes.

Let the dough rest for a few minutes and then add the salt and knead for another 10 minutes until all the dough has come together in a smooth dough that is not too dry. Scrape all of the dough back together.

Cover the dough and set aside for 1 hour until it has doubled in size. Meanwhile, prepare the loaf tin (see page 21).

Knead the dough for 5 minutes while adding the currants and raisins and the candied peel. Shape the dough into a rectangle and place it in the loaf tin. Cover and set aside to rise again for 1 hour.

Preheat your oven to 350°F. Brush the top of the loaf with the egg wash and bake for 30–35 minutes until it is cooked and sounds hollow when you tap on the bottom.

Cornish saffron cake

Saffron cake was once also baked in other parts of England, but it remained popular in Cornwall, where it is still available today. The yeast makes it more like a fruit bread than a cake. In the West Country, it's eaten with a good layer of butter on it.

For 6–10 people

1⅓ cups lukewarm milk

4¾ tsp (15 g) dried yeast

½ tsp saffron threads

4¼ cups (500 g) strong white bread
  flour (see page 16)

¼ cup (60 g) demerara (coarse raw
  sugar)

2 Tbsp (30 g) lard or butter, cubed,
  at room temperature

1 tsp sea salt

½ Tbsp caraway seeds

½–¾ cup (60–100 g) currants

⅓ cup (50 g) candied citrus peel,
  finely chopped

butter, for greasing

flour, for dusting

1 egg yolk + 1 Tbsp milk, for egg wash

For a 9 x 5-inch loaf tin

Divide the lukewarm milk in half. Add the yeast to one half to activate it. Using a mortar and pestle, crush the saffron threads and add them to the remaining milk.

Put the flour and raw sugar in a large bowl or the bowl of an electric mixer fitted with a dough hook. Put the lard or butter on top. Pour in half the yeast mixture and start mixing. When the liquid and lard or butter have been completely incorporated, add the remaining yeast mixture and knead for 5 minutes.

Let the dough rest for a few minutes and then add the salt and caraway seeds and knead for another 10 minutes until all the dough has come together in a smooth dough that is not too dry. Scrape all of the dough back together. Knead the currants and the candied peel through the dough.

Cover the dough and set aside for 1 hour until it has doubled in size. Meanwhile, prepare the loaf tin (see page 21).

Briefly knead the risen dough, shape it into a rectangle, and put it in the tin. Cover and set aside to rise for 1 hour until the dough has doubled again.

Preheat your oven to 350°F. Brush the top of the cake with the egg wash and bake for 30–35 minutes until it is cooked and sounds hollow when you tap the bottom.

Grasmere, Cumbria, Lake District

Gingerbreads

In Belgium and the Netherlands, gingerbread is known as *speculaas* and *speculoos*, but also *honingkoek* and *peperkoek*. In Dinant in Belgian Wallonia, they have a rock-hard decorative version with beautiful imprinted rural scenes. Germany has its variants, for example *Lebkuchen*, Switzerland has *tirggel*, among others, and the Scandinavian countries have their types of *pepparkakor, brunekager,* and *piparkakut*. In Latvia it is called *piparkukas*, and *piparkoogid* in Estonia. You'll find *mézeskálacs* in Hungary, *pernicky* in the Czech Republic, and *pierniczki* in Poland. Russia has *prianiki,* and France has its *pain d'épice*. If there's one bake that connects us all in the world, it's gingerbread.

We know that gingerbread was very popular in England because even Shakespeare mentioned it in one of his plays:

"An I had but one penny in the world, thou shouldst have it to buy gingerbread ..."

Act V, Scene I, Shakespeare's *Love's Labour's Lost*, 1598

Gingerbread is, of course, not bread, but medieval recipes up to the early 18th century were certainly made with bread. Breadcrumbs were heated together with honey, spices, and sometimes milk or alcohol, and kneaded into a dough. Often the gingerbread was colored with powdered sandalwood, which gave it a red color. There was also white gingerbread, made from almonds instead of breadcrumbs, which looked a bit like a spiced baked marzipan. Both types of gingerbread and their many varieties with different spices were often made in wooden boards carved out in the shape of animals or human figures. The early gingerbreads weren't baked in the oven, but rather dried out from the radiant heat of an open fire and then gilded with gold leaf. In the Middle Ages, gingerbread was eaten at the end of the meal to help digestion, but it soon became a festive treat that was baked and sold on various local and religious holidays.

From the second half of the 18th century we see treacle syrup – a by-product of the sugar refinery – appearing as a sweetener, and sugar is also added. Wheat flour is also used more frequently than breadcrumbs. Eliza Smith's 18th-century book, *The Compleat Housewife*, contains six recipes for gingerbread, including one for Dutch gingerbread and one for white gingerbread. We often see the use of caraway seeds in the spice mix.

In the late 19th century we sometimes even find ten different types of gingerbread in one book, with different ingredients – sometimes black treacle, sometimes golden syrup and sugar. The term "gingerbread" is therefore very broad. Gingerbread varied from region to region, sometimes with negligible differences and sometimes with a completely different result.

Grasmere Gingerbread® from Cumbria is the best known. It is a thin but chewy biscuit. In the same village of Grasmere, rushbearers gingerbread was once available as a soft version that was rather more like a cake. The Yorkshire parkin from the north of England is also a gingerbread, made with oats. In the same region we find in the 19th century Whitley's Original Wakefield gingerbread, which is a ginger cake with candied peel, and Sledmere gingerbread, both of which have disappeared today. Fortunately, Market Drayton gingerbread still exists in Shropshire – Billington's has been baking it since 1817, but according to them the origins date back to 1793. For this gingerbread, the dough is piped into fingers.

Cornish Fairings and Widecombe fair gingerbread are crisp biscuits made with a ball of dough that then forms cracks as it spreads out while baking. Sunderland gingerbread nuts – for which we find a recipe in the 19th-century cookbook of Mrs Beeton – look like the gingerbread nut we still know today. May Byron gives a recipe for the disappeared Hertford hard gingerbread in 1914. Whitby gingerbread, also from Yorkshire, is a rectangular block of soft cakelike gingerbread and is still baked by Botham, a bakery started by Elizabeth Botham in 1865 that remains in the same family today. And then there are the numerous gingerbread recipes in the many cookbooks that are not linked to a region. The recipes in this chapter are but a small selection of Britain's great gingerbread heritage.

Grasmere Gingerbread®

Grasmere is a small picturesque village in the hilly landscape of the Lake District in the north of England. Its surroundings are poetic, so it is not surprising that the poet William Wordsworth took up residence here to write. His sister, Dorothy, wrote in her diary in 1803 that she was going to buy gingerbread for her brother in Grasmere.

Fifty years later, in 1854, Sarah Nelson started baking her version of Grasmere Gingerbread®, which she sold from her little gingerbread house–like stone cottage just a few yards from the final resting place of William Wordsworth. Now, more than 150 years later, you can still buy gingerbread in the same little house. The name Grasmere Gingerbread® has since been given a trademark and no other gingerbread can carry the Grasmere name. This led to a gingerbread war about ten years ago, because Sarah Nelson was not the only one selling her biscuits in the area and gingerbread had clearly been made in Grasmere before she began selling it. In the village, there is talk of the Dixon family, who sold gingerbread in the 18th century, and in a book from 1912 I discovered that in the church a few yards from Sarah's shop, gingerbread was given to the children as early as 1819. They called it rushbearers gingerbread. ("Rushbearing" is an old English church ceremony in which bundles of grass are collected to cover the rough earth floor of the local church. The bundles had to be replaced every year; this usually happened on the name day of the church and was called "Wakes Day." In Britain, there are many bakes connected to these "Wakes Days.")

The same 1912 book says that the Walker family baked gingerbread in their small shop, and that in 1912 a Mrs Gibson ran a gingerbread store after a Mrs Mary Dixon had been the gingerbread maker there for years. Strangely enough, Sarah Nelson is not mentioned in this book. What is special is that it seems that baking gingerbread was a women's task, while at that time bakers were mainly male.

For 4 large pieces and 8 halves

1¾ cups (225 g) plain white flour

½ cup (115 g) soft brown sugar

1 tsp ground ginger

¼ tsp ground nutmeg

¼ tsp baking soda

pinch of sea salt

½ cup (115 g) butter, at room temperature

butter, for greasing

flour, for dusting

For an 8-inch square cake tin

Preheat your oven to 350° F and prepare the cake tin (see page 21).

Put all the dry ingredients in a bowl and rub the butter into the mixture until it is the consistency of breadcrumbs. This is best done in a food processor or blender. The dough won't come together as with other cookie doughs – it will remain as crumbs.

Weigh 2½ oz (70 g) of the crumb mixture and set it aside. Press the remaining crumb mixture into the cake tin, using a mini rolling pin or a sheet of baking paper to push the crumbs down firmly. Spoon the reserved crumbs over the top and press very lightly to distribute the crumbs over the surface of the dough.

Lightly score the top of the gingerbread, first dividing it into four squares and then dividing each square in half.

Bake the gingerbread for 25 minutes, then immediately remove it from the oven. Cut the gingerbread into portions along the marked lines while it is still hot.

75

Yorkshire parkin

Parkin is a type of gingerbread that is mainly associated with the counties of Yorkshire and Lancashire. While a lot of gingerbread is rather biscuit-like, parkin is a cake. Traditionally this ginger cake is made for the festivities around Guy Fawkes Night, also known as Bonfire Night, when the thwarting of the Gunpowder Plot – a failed attack on King James I in 1605 – is commemorated in England. On this evening, large fires are lit throughout England and parades are held through the streets, with fireworks and a bonfire as the climax. It is a very politically charged tradition and although it is customary to carry an effigy of Guy Fawkes (the man caught red-handed with gunpowder to blow up the parliament), effigies of politicians are carried in some parades today, although burning them is avoided.

Bonfire Night is a very exciting and fun evening for children, who are blissfully unaware of political and religious disputes. To them it is an occasion when they are given a lot of goodies and they can stay up late to watch the parade and fireworks. And toffees and parkin are certainly part of the fun.

There are a few theories as to how parkin was linked to Guy Fawkes Night on the 5th of November. In the past it coincided with the harvest of the oats in the first week of November, and oats are an essential part of this cake and the principal crop of the area. For the pagan feast of Samhain on 31 October, on which large bonfires were lit, there surely were cakes made with the local grain, and the primary sweetener was first honey and then treacle, when sugar imports made it cheap. Martinmas on 11 November is also close and marked the end of the agrarian year and the end of the harvest. Both festivals contributed to the way that Guy Fawkes "Bonfire" Night became so important. It carefully replaced a pagan and Christian celebration with a political one.

Modern recipes for parkin often don't contain oats, only wheat flour, resulting in cakes with a finer texture that are more like Aunty Betty's Gingerbread (page 79). The recipe I give you here is made with oats, and is an acquired taste to the modern palate. The cake is best made in advance and left to rest for a few days to a couple of weeks.

For 9 squares

1 cup (100 g) rolled oats (see page 16)

⅔ cup (200 g) golden syrup or maple syrup

2 Tbsp (45 g) black treacle or molasses

14 Tbsp (200 g) butter

2¼ cups (200 g) oat flour

2 tsp baking soda

2 tsp ground ginger

½ tsp ground nutmeg

1 egg

2 Tbsp whisky or milk

pinch of sea salt

butter, for greasing

flour, for dusting

For an 8-inch square cake tin

Preheat your oven to 325°F and prepare the cake tin (see page 21).

Briefly pulse the oats in a food processor fitted with the blade attachment.

Heat the golden syrup, black treacle, and butter in a saucepan until melted and combined. Set aside to cool for a few minutes, then add the chopped oats and the remaining ingredients. Combine well with a wooden spoon or spatula. Spread the mixture into the cake tin.

Bake for 50–60 minutes until a skewer inserted in the center of the cake comes out clean. Let cool in the tin. When the cake is cold, cut it into squares and pack it in an airtight container to rest for at least a day before serving.

The cake gets stickier and more moist every day and can last for 2 weeks if you can hide it for that long.

Aunty Betty's gingerbread

This family recipe ended up in my hands in a special way. I was on the train to London when Joanne came up to me to say that she loved my first book, *Pride and Pudding*, and that she wanted to send me her family recipe for gingerbread.

Joanne told me that she came from Cumbria in the north of England, where Grasmere Gingerbread® also originates, and where, historically, a lot of gingerbread is made. In our later conversations she told me that in the 1980s the recipe was mainly made with margarine because butter was too expensive. Butter was used only for cakes for special occasions, such as Christmas cake and shortbread. When Joanne was a little girl, her mother won prizes with this gingerbread in baking competitions at their local village fair. The family recipe is from Joanne's great aunt, Betty, and it's a privilege to be able to share it with you.

For 16 squares

2¾ cups (340 g) plain white flour

2 tsp baking soda

2 tsp ground ginger

1 tsp ground cinnamon

pinch of sea salt

1 cup (225 g) butter

1 cup + 2 Tbsp (225 g) granulated white sugar

⅔ cup (225 g) black treacle or molasses

1 Tbsp golden syrup, maple syrup, or honey

¾ cup milk

2 eggs

butter, for greasing

flour, for dusting

For an 8-inch square cake tin

Preheat your oven to 325°F and prepare the cake tin (see page 21).

Put the flour, baking soda, spices, and salt in a large bowl and mix well.

Melt the butter, sugar, treacle, and golden syrup together in a saucepan over low heat. Remove from the heat and let the mixture cool a little while you mix the milk and eggs with the dry ingredients.

Add the butter mixture to the batter and mix until well combined. Spoon the batter into the cake tin.

Bake the gingerbread in the center of the oven for 45–55 minutes. Leave it in the tin to cool for 5 minutes, then remove the gingerbread from the tin using the parchment paper and cut it into squares.

You can eat the gingerbread immediately, but it actually gets better and stickier after a day, and even better after a week. Pack it in an airtight container and hide it away until a week has passed.

Eliza's 18th-century gingerbread

This 18th-century recipe comes from Eliza Smith's 1727 book, *The Compleat Housewife, or, Accomplish'd Gentlewoman's Companion*. I have a delicate copy from 1737, and it is one of my most precious possessions.

This gingerbread is one of my favorites from the book, and it takes the form of small cushions. It remains soft on the inside, and is fragrant with coriander and caraway seeds.

If you can't get hold of Lyle's black treacle, you can use another brand or even molasses, but I'm not particularly fond of the stronger taste. It's worth the effort in hunting down Lyle's. A pinch of salt is not called for in Eliza's recipe, but I do find it improves the flavor.

For 20 gingerbreads

6 Tbsp (130 g) golden syrup or maple syrup

1½ Tbsp (35 g) black treacle or molasses

½ cup (115 g) butter

½ egg

¼ cup (55 g) soft brown sugar

3½ tsp (6 g) ground ginger

½ tsp ground cloves

½ tsp ground mace

½ tsp ground coriander seeds

½ tsp ground caraway seeds

1⅔ cups (200 g) plain white flour

scant 1 cup (100 g) whole-wheat flour or 1 cup (100 g) oat flour

For the best result, make the dough one day in advance.

Melt the golden syrup, black treacle, and butter together in a saucepan over low heat. Add the rest of the ingredients and mix well, then set aside to cool.

Preheat your oven to 350°F. Line a large baking sheet with parchment paper.

Knead the dough, then roll it into balls, using about 1 oz (33 g) of dough per biscuit, and place on the sheet. Lightly press the balls down.

Bake for 15–20 minutes, then transfer the gingerbreads to a wire rack to cool.

Cornish Fairings

Fairings are sweet treats, usually gingerbread, that were sold at English fairs for centuries. During the Reformation, fairs and festivals, which were mostly held on holy days, were outlawed – even Christmas and its festivities were abolished by an Act of Parliament in 1647. For nearly two decades, the preparation of food for festivities was a punishable offense. After Charles II was restored to the throne in 1660, people could return to their festivities. Gingerbread experienced a revival because the spices needed to make it became cheaper and, by then, sugar imports from Barbados brought large amounts of sugar to the London sugar refineries.

Fairings were known throughout the country, but became connected to Cornwall when Cornish baker Furniss of Truro started selling Cornish Fairings in 1886. In *The Cornishman* of 3 December 1908, an advertisement for Ginger fairings appeared with the headline "A Genuine Cornish Delicacy for one & all of the Cornish Riviera." Today, Furniss Foods still sells Cornish Fairings and holds the trademark for the name.

In the early 19th century, newspapers describe how at village fairs stacks of gingerbread "husbands" were sold to girls looking for a sweetheart. But gingerbread people are much older. The *Oxford Companion to Sugar and Sweets* tells us the legend that Tudor Queen Elizabeth I enjoyed having gingerbread men made in the image of her potential husbands and other guests, and serving the biscuits at the table. This way everyone could "eat" themselves, and the Virgin Queen could decapitate the men who wanted to tame her with her teeth (which eventually turned black from excessive sugar consumption). She never married and reigned alone, to the great annoyance of the powerful men surrounding her.

For 14 fairings

¾ cup (100 g) plain white flour

¼ cup (50 g) soft brown sugar

pinch of mixed spice (or pumpkin pie spice)

1½ tsp ground ginger

3½ Tbsp (50 g) butter, at room temperature

3 Tbsp (55 g) golden syrup or maple syrup

1 tsp baking soda

1 tsp baking powder

pinch of sea salt

Preheat your oven to 350°F. Line a large baking sheet with parchment paper.

Mix together the flour, sugar, and spices and rub in the butter by hand.

Heat the golden syrup in a saucepan, then add the remaining ingredients and stir until well combined. Set aside to cool.

Knead the dough, then roll it into balls, using about ½ oz (18 g) of dough per biscuit, and place on the sheet. Lightly press the balls down.

Bake for 8–10 minutes, then transfer to a wire rack to cool. The biscuits will flatten as they bake and form nice cracks on the surface. They are best eaten on the day they're baked because they don't stay crisp.

From top: Shrewsbury cakes, Goosnargh cakes, Flakemeal biscuits

Shrewsbury cakes

Although the name could fool you into thinking that these are cakes, a Shrewsbury cake is a brittle, spiced biscuit that looks a bit like a gingerbread biscuit. It is thanks to playwright William Congreve that we know that they are brittle, short biscuits. In his play *The Way of the World* from 1700, he wrote, "You may be as short as a Shrewsbury cake." Shrewsbury cakes appeared as early as the 16th century and, from 1760, Mr Pailin sold them from his store in the town of Shrewsbury in Shropshire.

During the British Raj, Shrewsbury cakes became popular in India, and you can still buy them there to this day at Kayani Bakery in Pune, where the freshly baked round Shrewsburies have been highly sought after since 1955.

Throughout history, Shrewsbury cakes have been made with either nutmeg, cloves, ginger, cinnamon, or mace. Rosewater is the only constant, but it was replaced by lemon in the early 20th century. A handwritten 1907 cookbook in my possession contains a recipe for Shrewsbury cakes without spices but with lemon zest.

For 12 biscuits

1¾ cups (225 g) plain white flour
1 cup (110 g) confectioners' sugar
¼ tsp ground cinnamon
¼ tsp ground mace
¼ tsp ground nutmeg
pinch of sea salt
½ cup (110 g) chilled butter, diced
1 egg yolk
1 tsp water
1 tsp rosewater or additional water

Preheat your oven to 350°F. Line a baking sheet with parchment paper.

Mix the flour, sugar, spices, and salt in a large bowl. Rub in the butter until the mixture is the consistency of breadcrumbs. Add the egg yolk and the water and rosewater and knead until the mixture comes together into a smooth, stiff dough. Make sure you do not overknead the dough. If the dough turns out to be too dry, add extra water, 1 teaspoon at a time, making sure it doesn't become too sticky.

Roll out the dough between two sheets of parchment paper until ¼ inch thick. Use a 3¼-inch cutter to cut out 12 biscuits – traditionally, Shrewsbury cakes are 4½ inches, but I thought that was quite large. You can knead the remaining dough and then cut out more biscuits.

Decorate each biscuit by applying a checkerboard pattern with small holes. Place one more dot in the middle of each square. (I have found that the tip of a clean, old ballpoint pen gives the best result.)

Place each biscuit on the baking sheet and bake for 10 minutes until baked to a pale color. The biscuits are also great when they are baked for longer, although that isn't traditional – simply bake them the way you like them.

Let the Shrewsbury cakes cool on the sheet.

Goosnargh cakes

On 18 June 1859 *The Preston Chronicle* reported that many thousands of the famous Goosnargh cakes were sold in Goosnargh on Whitsun that year. The nearby village of Stalmine had its own version of this biscuit, and called them Tosset cakes. Bakeries in Wirksworth and Winster in Derbyshire also baked them as Wirksworth and Winster Wakes cakes, with currants instead of caraway seeds. "At Winster Wakes there's ale and cakes" goes an old song, and, indeed, these biscuits were mainly eaten with a nice glass of beer instead of tea.

These biscuits are almost extinct today. Slow Food UK thinks this is due to the rationing of butter and sugar, and therefore also Goosnargh cakes, during the Second World War.

The shortbread-like butter biscuits have a distinct taste from the caraway seeds (and sometimes coriander seeds), but cardamom would also be a nice variation.

For 24 biscuits

1¾ cups (225 g) plain white flour

⅓ cup (50 g) rice flour or 7 Tbsp (50 g) cornstarch

½ cup (100 g) superfine sugar, plus extra for sprinkling

pinch of sea salt

1 cup (225 g) chilled butter, diced

2 Tbsp caraway seeds

flour, for dusting

Mix the flour, rice flour or cornstarch, sugar, and salt in a large bowl.

Rub in the butter with your fingers. Add the caraway seeds, then knead the mixture until it comes together into a smooth dough. Do not overknead it, or the biscuits will be less brittle.

Wrap the dough in plastic wrap and refrigerate for 15 minutes. In the meantime, preheat your oven to 325°F. Line a large baking sheet with parchment paper.

Dust your work surface with flour and roll out the dough until it is about ¼ inch thick. Use a 3¼-inch cutter to cut out the cookies. Press the leftover dough back together and cut out more biscuits.

Prick the biscuits all over with a fork, place them on the baking sheet and bake in the middle of the oven for 20 minutes. The biscuits should not be baked for long – a golden blush around the edges is enough. Remove the biscuits from the oven, sprinkle with the extra sugar, and leave them to cool on the sheet.

Flakemeal biscuits

Flakemeal biscuits are sweet oat biscuits that are popular in Northern Ireland. The coconut is not always added, but it really adds value. These biscuits are brought to you with thanks to two Northern Irish ladies with whom I had a conversation about the bakes of Northern Ireland.

For 14 biscuits

6 Tbsp (75 g) superfine sugar

10 Tbsp (150 g) butter, at room temperature

1½ cups (150 g) traditional rolled oats

½ cup (35 g) coconut flakes

pinch of sea salt

⅔ cup (75 g) plain white flour

Preheat your oven to 350°F and line a baking sheet with parchment paper.

Put the sugar in a bowl. Use a fork to rub in the butter, then add the oats, coconut, and salt and push the dough together with a wooden spoon. Knead in the flour.

Roll out the dough between two sheets of parchment paper until ½ inch thick. Use a 2½- to 2¾-inch cutter to cut out 14 biscuits.

Place the biscuits on the baking sheet, making sure there is enough space between the biscuits to expand by ½ inch during baking.

Bake in the middle of the oven for 20–25 minutes until the biscuits are lightly colored. If you want golden-brown biscuits with a deep taste, bake them just a little longer. Leave the biscuits to cool on the baking sheet.

Shortbread biscuits

According to Florence Marian McNeill in a 1929 book, *The Scots Kitchen*, a decorated form of shortbread, known as "infare-cake," was the wedding cake of rural Scotland. On the first day of the marriage, or "Infare day," the infare-cake was broken over the bride's head on the threshold of her new home. This very old custom finds its origin in paganism.

The textbook shortbread is one part sugar for two parts butter and three parts flour. My version contains slightly less sugar and a little more butter. Some of the flour is also replaced by rice flour, cornstarch, or semolina to make the biscuits even more brittle and short. I was looking for the taste and texture of my favorite shortbread fingers, and this recipe is very close.

I've given the method for regular round biscuits, shortbread fingers, and petticoat tails, where the biscuit is baked in a large round and cut into portions like a pie. In the 1990s, it was popular in tearooms to push glacé cherries into the shortbread dough to make cherry shortbread. Today it's popular to add edible lavender, but when it comes to shortbread, I think simplicity wins.

1⅔ cups (200 g) plain white flour

7 Tbsp (50 g) cornstarch, ⅓ cup (50 g) semolina, or ⅓ cup (50 g) rice flour, or a combination

6 Tbsp (75 g) superfine sugar, plus extra for sprinkling

pinch of sea salt

¾ cup (175 g) butter, at room temperature but not soft

butter, for greasing (if needed)

flour, for dusting

Put the dry ingredients in a large bowl and combine well. Rub in the butter until the mixture is the consistency of breadcrumbs. Knead the mixture until it comes together into a smooth dough. Do not overknead, or the biscuits will be less short and brittle.

Wrap the dough in plastic wrap and chill in the refrigerator while you preheat your oven to 325°F.

For 10 round shortbreads

Cover a baking sheet with parchment paper.

Flour your work surface and pat the dough flat with your hands until it is about ¼ inch thick. Do not roll the dough, or the shortbreads will be chewy. You can put a sheet of parchment paper on top of the dough and brush it with the palm of your hand so that your shortbreads have a smooth top.

Cut out biscuits with a 2¾-inch cutter. Pat the leftover dough back together and keep cutting out biscuits until there is no dough left.

Neatly prick the shortbreads all over with a fork, place on the baking sheet, and bake in the middle of the oven for 30 minutes.

The shortbread should not gain too much color – a golden blush around the edges is enough. Remove the shortbread from the oven and immediately sprinkle with superfine sugar. Let the shortbreads cool on the sheet for 5 minutes, then use a spatula to move them to a wire rack to cool completely.

Keep the shortbreads in an airtight container and eat them as quickly as possible.

For 16 shortbread fingers

Prepare an 8-inch square cake tin (see page 21).

Pat the dough flat, place it in the lined tin, and then push it out to cover the base of the tin. Place a second sheet of parchment paper over a baking sheet and flip the tin over to turn the dough out onto the sheet, with the smooth side on top. Slide the dough back into the lined tin, with the smooth side up. Use a knife to gently score lines to cut the shortbread into 16 fingers.

Bake the shortbread in the middle of the oven for 35–40 minutes. The shortbread should not gain too much color – a golden blush around the edges is enough.

Remove the shortbread from the oven, cut it into fingers, and sprinkle it with superfine sugar. Allow to cool for 10 minutes and then use a spatula to carefully transfer the shortbread to a wire rack to cool completely.

For 8 petticoat tails

Pat the dough roughly in the shape of a circle, ½ inch thick. Use a rolling pin or place a sheet of parchment paper on top of the dough to smooth it out. Turn the dough so that the smoothest side is facing upwards. Using an 8½-inch plate as a guide, trim the dough into a neat circle.

Use a knife to gently score the shortbread into portions as you would divide a cake. Prick the shortbread all over with a fork in a decorative pattern. Bake in the middle of the oven for 35–40 minutes. The shortbread should not gain too much color – a golden blush around the edges is enough.

Remove the shortbread from the oven, cut it into petticoat tails, and sprinkle with superfine sugar. Allow to cool for 10 minutes and then use a spatula to carefully transfer the shortbread to a wire rack to cool completely.

Digestives

Digestives were developed by two Scottish doctors in the 1830s with the aim of creating a biscuit that could improve digestion, hence the name "digestive." The most popular digestives are those made by McVitie's, which the company began to bake on a large scale in 1892.

Digestives were often called malt cookies, and the original patent received was entitled "Making Malted Bread." Cassell's *Universal Cookery Book* from 1894 provides a recipe for malt biscuits. The author suggests that the use of ground caraway seeds is a suitable aromatic for people suffering from flatulence, but he also states that any other spices are a possibility.

Today, digestives are one of the most-loved British biscuits, along with shortbread and rich tea biscuits. They are also sometimes made with a layer of chocolate, which is great when you dip the cookie in your coffee and the chocolate melts. I rather like the ground roasted pecans in this biscuit, but if you are a purist, feel free to substitute them with more oat flour.

For at least 40 biscuits

½ cup (40 g) pecans

10 Tbsp (150 g) butter, at room temperature

½ cup (100 g) demerara (coarse raw sugar)

2 eggs

1 tsp baking powder

1 tsp sea salt

1⅔ cups (150 g) oat flour

2¼ cups (260 g) white whole-wheat flour or whole-grain spelt flour

flour, for dusting

Preheat your oven to 400°F and line two baking sheets with parchment paper.

Spread the pecans on one of the sheets and roast for 10 minutes. Allow to cool, then pulse the nuts in a blender until they resemble coarse flour.

Mix the butter and sugar together until creamy (use an electric mixer if you have one), then add the eggs, one by one. Add the baking powder, then add the pecans, salt, and flours, a teaspoon at a time. It will take a while for the mixture to come together. It will appear very dry at first, but don't be tempted to add milk or water.

Use the dough immediately or leave it in the fridge for 15 minutes.

Pat the dough flat on a floured work surface or a sheet of parchment paper. Dust the dough with flour to prevent the rolling pin from sticking, then roll out the dough until ¼ inch thick. Use a round cutter to cut out the biscuits. Push the leftover dough back together, roll it out, and cut out more biscuits until you have used all the dough.

Place the biscuits on the baking sheets and prick all over with a fork. Bake in the middle of the oven for 10–13 minutes. After 13 minutes you will have the darker version that I like best.

Rich tea biscuits

Rich tea biscuits have an uncomplicated flavor, making them ideal for dipping in your hot coffee or tea. Scientists have also proven that rich tea biscuits are the superior dunker or dipper. Research showed that the digestive crumbles after five seconds, while the rich tea holds up for no less than 20 seconds. It's because the rich tea remains crisp that people find it such a superior dunker. Only in Great Britain do they research these kinds of small things!

Prince William requested a rich tea cake for his groom's cake for the royal wedding. A total of 1700 biscuits and 40 pounds of chocolate were used to create this no-bake cake, which is also rumored to be the Queen's favorite cake.

If the royals and almost half of the British population approve of rich tea biscuits, they should certainly be included in this book. Homemade, they are certainly a lot more rustic than the tidy, perfectly smooth rich teas of the iconic British biscuit brands, but they do dip just as well.

For 28 biscuits

2⅓ cups (280 g) plain white flour

1 Tbsp baking powder

pinch of sea salt

⅓ cup (65 g) demerara (coarse raw sugar)

4½ Tbsp (65 g) chilled butter, diced

½ cup + 2 Tbsp chilled milk

flour, for dusting

Preheat your oven to 400°F and line one or two baking sheets with parchment paper.

Mix the flour, baking powder, salt, and sugar in a large bowl. Rub in the butter until the mixture resembles coarse breadcrumbs. Pour in the milk and use your fingers to bring the ingredients together into a dough. Briefly press and knead the dough.

Place the dough on a floured work surface and divide it in half to make it easier to work with. Roll out half the dough as thinly as possible – 1/16 inch would be ideal (keep in mind that the cookies rise to twice their height). Cut out the cookies with a 2¾-inch cutter, then repeat with the other half of the dough.

Prick the biscuits all over with a fork and place them on the lined baking sheets. Bake the cookies for 10 minutes until they are a pale golden color. Leave them to cool on the sheets.

And now brew yourself a cup of tea and start dipping!

Garibaldi biscuits

The Garibaldi was first baked by Jonathan Carr for the English biscuit company Peek, Frean and Co in 1861. John Carr was a celebrity in the biscuit world: he was the first to succeed in producing biscuits on a large industrial scale. He made a name for the Carr family that still produces Carr's Table Water Crackers in Carlisle, England.

The biscuit was named after Italian General Giuseppe Garibaldi, who fought to unite Italy in the 19th century.

For 14 biscuits

¾ cup (100 g) currants

1¼ cups (150 g) plain white flour

⅓ cup (50 g) rice flour or 7 Tbsp (50 g) cornstarch

½ tsp baking powder

¼ cup (50 g) demerara (coarse raw sugar), plus extra for sprinkling

pinch of sea salt

3½ Tbsp (50 g) chilled butter

2 egg yolks

¼ cup milk

flour, for dusting

1 egg yolk + 1 Tbsp milk, for egg wash

Preheat your oven to 350°F and line a baking sheet with parchment paper.

Put the currants in a bowl and lightly bruise them with a pestle or the base of a glass bottle.

Put the flours, baking powder, sugar, and salt in a bowl and rub in the butter with your fingers until the mixture resembles breadcrumbs.

Add the egg yolks and milk. (You can use the egg whites instead of the egg yolk for the egg wash.) Use a blunt knife to mix the wet and dry ingredients together, and then use your hands to briefly knead the mixture into a smooth dough. Put the dough in the fridge for 30 minutes.

Divide the dough in half and roll each half out on a floured sheet of parchment paper into a rectangle about 8 x 12 inches. Brush one of the rectangles with the egg wash (or the reserved egg whites) and spread the currants over it in an even layer. Brush the second dough rectangle with the egg wash, then lay it over the currants on the other sheet of dough.

Lightly roll over the sandwiched dough until the two halves stick together. Don't worry if the currants are visible here and there – it adds to the biscuits' charm.

Cut the sandwiched dough into 14 rectangular biscuits. Lightly push the edges into place and place on the baking sheet. Brush with more egg wash and sprinkle with extra sugar.

Bake the biscuits in the middle of the oven for 10–15 minutes until lightly colored. Leave on the baking sheet to cool.

You can also use whole-wheat flour instead of plain white flour.

Custard creams

Custard creams are sandwich biscuits decorated with a baroque pattern and a custardlike filling, a very popular treat in the UK. In 1837, Birmingham pharmacist Alfred Bird developed the recipe for Bird's egg-free custard powder for his wife because she was allergic to eggs.

The baroque pattern is achieved by pushing a piece of lace or something similar into the dough.

For 12–14 biscuits

For the biscuits

1¾ cups (220 g) plain white flour

⅓ cup (50 g) rice flour or 7 Tbsp (50 g) cornstarch

½ tsp baking powder

3 Tbsp (35 g) superfine sugar

2 Tbsp custard powder

½ tsp sea salt

7 Tbsp (100 g) chilled butter

1 egg yolk

¼ cup milk

For the filling

¾ cup (100 g) confectioners' sugar

1 Tbsp custard powder

3½ Tbsp (50 g) butter

1 tsp warm milk or water

pinch of sea salt

Combine the dry ingredients in the bowl of a food processor fitted with the blade attachment. Add the butter and pulse until the mixture has the consistency of fine breadcrumbs. Add the egg yolk and milk and mix until the dough sticks together in a ball. Briefly knead the dough by hand until smooth.

Wrap the dough in plastic wrap and put it in the fridge for 15–20 minutes while you make the filling. Meanwhile, preheat the oven to 350°F. Line a baking sheet with parchment paper.

Make the filling by mixing the confectioners' sugar, custard powder, butter, milk and salt in the food processor until creamy. If it is too dry, add some more milk, ¼ teaspoon at a time. Cover and set aside.

Roll out the dough on a floured work surface until ⅛ inch thick. Press a lace doily or similar into the dough. Use a 2-inch rectangular cutter to cut out the biscuits.

Place the biscuits on the sheet and bake for 10–15 minutes. Transfer to a wire rack to cool.

Spread a teaspoon of filling on half of the biscuits, then sandwich them with the remaining biscuits, gently twisting to secure.

Serve with strong tea with milk.

Buns

Buns were a Victorian favorite, but they still form an important part of the British baking repertoire today. Sugar became very cheap in the 19th century and therefore found its way into the "fancy goods" and buns that were demanded by the emerging middle class. These small buns were made from yeast dough enriched with either butter, eggs, or cream, with or without a topping or filling, and, most importantly, they were sweetened. Buns are usually eaten as they are, but some are also spread with butter and served with something extra like jam and cream or even treacle. The Yorkshire tea cake is generally only eaten toasted.

The most common buns in British cuisine are the Chelsea bun, hot cross bun, Belgian bun, Yorkshire tea cake, and the iced finger. There are, however, many regional buns that often don't travel beyond the county borders. In Cornwall you will find saffron buns, in Northern Ireland and on the west coast of Scotland there are Paris buns, and in Bath you will find not only the Bath bun but also the Sally Lunn. There are "dough nuts" from the Isle of Wight and rock cakes from Brighton. Some buns are called cakes, while some cakes are called buns – the English language keeps us on our toes!

Chelsea bun, the 18th-century "it" bun

In the early 18th century, there was a bakery in London's borough of Chelsea called The Chelsea Bun House. One of the owners was known as "Captain Bun," and King George II, Queen Caroline, King George III, and Queen Charlotte and their children were among their custom. The newspapers reported that the shop looked more like a ballroom than a bakery, with its luxury furniture, statues, curiosities, and large paintings on the walls. The long shopfront was decorated with a colonnade that stood out on the sidewalk. The interior and exterior were captured by artists, just as we would take a photo for Instagram today. People reportedly walked great distances to buy their buns at the bun house. It was even claimed in a local newspaper that 50,000 people went to The Chelsea Bun House one Good Friday to get hold of a hot cross bun that the bakery baked exclusively on that day. The then-owner noted that from then on there would be only Chelsea buns at the shop because the whole neighborhood had complained about "the immense unruly and riotous London mob" that had gathered there to buy hot cross buns.

Although the store had been a thriving business since at least 1711, the closure in 1804 of the nearby Ranelagh Pleasure Gardens, where the gentry would hang out, impacted the business and it was demolished in 1839 when the last heir of the family died without succession and ownership went to the Crown. It was a pity, because *The Mirror* of 4 May 1839 reported that The Chelsea Bun House still sold more than 24,000 buns on Good Friday of that year. The same newspaper also wrote that the shop would be rebuilt after the regeneration of the street, but unfortunately the Chelsea "New" Bun House was never erected.

According to Elizabeth David, The Chelsea Bun House was indeed resurrected in 1951, albeit briefly, as part of the celebration of the Festival of Britain. She describes the Chelsea bun as an English institution. Today, Chelsea buns no longer have a store dedicated to them, but they are still sold everywhere. One particular bakery that is especially noted for its Chelsea buns is Fitzbillies in Cambridge, which has been baking its celebrated Chelsea buns since 1920.

The buns of Bath

In the majestic city of Bath, nestled in a green valley with its Roman baths and elegant wide Georgian streets and circuses, you will find two famous buns: the Sally Lunn and the Bath bun. Both buns even have their own tearoom dedicated to them.

The Sally Lunn is a soft, white brioche-like bun with a shiny golden-brown head, and has been known in cookbooks since 1776. In these cookbooks it is usually stated that a tea cake without currants is a Sally Lunn bun. But there is also a difference in baking, as the tea cake is baked freely, while in *The Cook's Oracle* from William Kitchiner in 1830, the Sally Lunn is baked in a shallow tin or ring so that the bun has a pale band at the bottom.

The Bath bun was usually called a Bath cake in the 18th century. Bath resident and cookbook author Martha Bradley gave a recipe for Bath seed cake in her 1756 book, *The British Housewife*. According to Elizabeth Raffald's 1769 book, *The Experienced English Housekeeper*, the Bath cake is the size of a French roll and had to be served hot for breakfast. Jane Austen, who lived in Bath for a while, was a fan of Bath buns and wrote in 1801 that she would eat herself sick if her sister, Cassandra, did not accompany her during a visit. This shows that in Austen's time, the Bath cakes were already known as Bath buns.

Both buns were exclusively a treat for the rich. In the 18th century, ordinary people did not eat sweet pastries for breakfast. Sweet yeasted breads and buns were only slightly more widely distributed among the various classes in Victorian times, when bakeries became more industrialized and the price of sugar decreased.

The Bath buns from Martha Bradley's and Elizabeth Raffald's books and those known to Jane Austen would have been very similar. They were flavored and decorated with caraway seeds or caraway comfits, made by covering the seeds with layers of sugar. Making caraway comfits was, and still is, a time-consuming task, with the seeds being dried between each layer, resulting in something that looks like "hundreds and thousands" sprinkles, but is more similar to Indian *mukhwas*, which still contain the seeds. Caraway comfits were, along with other comfits, often served at the end of a meal to aid digestion, just as they still do in India with *mukhwas*.

Towards the end of the 19th century, candied peel, lemon peel and/or dried fruit and mixed spices became popular additions. The Bath buns of today are no longer made or decorated with caraway seeds or comfits. They are now baked with a lump of sugar in them and decorated with a few pearl sugar nibs and currants. I've given the recipe for the pre-19th century and the modern version, so you can decide for yourself which version you like best.

During the Great Exhibition of 1851 in London, organized by Prince Albert, 934,691 Bath buns were sold to visitors. According to the stories, people noticed that the Bath bun sold in London was much less lavish, hence it was renamed the "London bun." In John Kirkland's book, *The Modern Baker, Confectioner and Caterer,* you will find a recipe for cheap Bath buns or London buns, which confirms this story.

Chelsea buns

Chelsea buns were sold in The Chelsea Bun House in London as far back as 1711. They may be considered the first sweet confection that people ever queued for in masses, just to get their hands on a bun or two. It might not be as modern as a cronut or a freakshake, but the Chelsea bun managed to live through the ages without being forgotten along the way. Today it is still the bun you see most frequently sold in British bakeries, although it's getting some competition from the Scandinavian cinnamon bun.

Chelsea buns are made from a rich yeast dough and must have a square shape, with a circular spiral dotted with currants. The pleasure of unrolling them while you eat them and tearing the dough is addictive. The size of the baking tins is important to ensure that the buns touch one another and push each other into a square shape. The trick to making the best Chelsea bun is to roll out the pastry as thinly as you can manage.

For 24 buns

For the buns

3 Tbsp + 1 tsp (30 g) dried yeast

2½ cups lukewarm milk

8⅓ cups (1 kg) strong white bread flour (see page 16)

½ cup (120 g) demerara (coarse raw sugar), or granulated white sugar

10 Tbsp (140 g) butter, cubed, at room temperature

2 eggs, beaten

1¾ tsp fine sea salt

flour, for dusting

For the filling

1 lb (450 g) butter, at room temperature

1⅓ cups (285 g) demerara (coarse raw sugar), or granulated white sugar

3 tsp ground cinnamon

pinch of fine sea salt

2½ cups (350 g) currants

For the sugar syrup

¼ cup (60 g) demerara (coarse raw sugar), or granulated white sugar

5 Tbsp water

superfine sugar, for sprinkling

For two 15 x 10-inch jelly roll tins

Add the yeast to the lukewarm milk and stir briefly and gently to activate it. The yeast will start to foam up in clusters, which means it is ready for use. Combine the flour and sugar in a large bowl or the bowl of an electric mixer fitted with a dough hook and put the butter on top. Pour half of the yeast mixture over the butter and start kneading. When the milk and butter are completely absorbed, add the rest of the yeast mixture, along with the eggs. Knead the dough for 5 minutes, then let it stand for a few minutes (at this point the dough will be very wet). Add the salt and knead for 10 minutes, scraping the dough off the dough hook and sides of the bowl if needed, until the dough has come together in a smooth and elastic dough that is not too dry but also not terribly wet.

Cover the dough and set aside for 1 hour until it has doubled in quantity.

Meanwhile, make the filling by whipping the butter with the sugar, cinnamon, and salt until creamy.

Preheat your oven to 400°F and line the baking tins with parchment paper.

Roll out the dough on a floured surface to a rectangle that's about 24 x 38 inches and 1/16 inch thick (or as thin as possible). Place the dough in front of you horizontally. Cover the top half with a third of the filling, then fold the bottom half over the filling. Roll over the dough with a rolling pin to flatten it out.

Spread the whole surface of the dough with the remaining filling, dot with the currants, and roll up lengthwise to make a long roll. Cut the roll into 2-inch slices and place in the baking tins with the spiral facing upwards and a little space in between each bun. Bake for 20–25 minutes until the buns are golden brown.

Prepare the syrup while the buns are baking by heating the sugar and water in a small saucepan until the sugar has dissolved. Brush the buns with the sugar syrup as soon as they come out of the oven and sprinkle with superfine sugar. The buns are best eaten on the day they're made, but they can be revived in a hot oven for a few minutes the next day, or you can freeze the baked buns, thaw, and then pop them in a hot oven for a few minutes.

Yorkshire tea cakes

Tea cakes are soft, white brioche-like buns with a shiny golden-brown top. Currants are added all over Britain, but not in West Yorkshire, where a tea cake is a plain bread roll. Cookbooks from the 19th century are divided about adding currants, with some stipulating currants in their recipes and others simply leaving the bun plain. It is sometimes also said in books from that period that the bun is the same bun as the Sally Lunn, but with added currants. To make it even more confusing, a tea cake in Scotland is a biscuit with a mallow cloud on top, dressed in a chocolate jacket.

On tearoom menus it always says "toasted tea cake" – they are hardly ever served untoasted. The toasted tea cake is crisp on the outside, with caramelized bits of currant, and soft and doughy on the inside. Tea cakes are best when they are freshly baked or toasted; when a day old, they become heavy. Just heat the oven as hot as you can and stick the buns in for a few minutes to revive them. Then toast them, of course.

For 10 tea cakes

4¾ tsp (15 g) dried yeast

1¼ cups lukewarm whole milk

4¼ cups (500 g) strong white
  bread flour (see page 16)

¼ cup (60 g) demerara (coarse raw
  sugar), or granulated white sugar

2 Tbsp (30 g) butter, at room
  temperature

1 egg

1 tsp fine sea salt

½–¾ cup (60–100 g) currants
  (optional), rinsed and patted dry

1 egg yolk + 1 Tbsp milk, for egg wash

Add the yeast to the lukewarm milk and stir briefly and gently to activate it. The yeast will start to foam up in clusters, which means it is ready for use. Combine the flour and sugar in a large bowl or the bowl of an electric mixer fitted with a dough hook and put the butter on top. Pour half of the yeast mixture over the butter and start kneading. When the milk and butter are completely absorbed, add the rest of the yeast mixture, along with the egg. Knead the dough for 5 minutes, then let it stand for a few minutes (at this point the dough will be very wet). Add the salt and the currants (if using) and knead for 10 minutes, scraping the dough off the dough hook and sides of the bowl if needed, until the dough has come together in a smooth and elastic dough that is not too dry but also not terribly wet.

Cover the dough and set aside for 1 hour until it has doubled in quantity. Meanwhile, line a baking sheet with parchment paper.

Briefly knead the dough and divide it into eight equal pieces. Take a piece of dough and lightly flatten it on your work surface, then pull the outer parts in like a purse and gently squeeze together like a dumpling so that the dough can no longer split open while rising. Turn the dough over so the squeezed ends are on the bottom. It should be nice and smooth on top – if not, flatten it and start again. Place the bun on the baking sheet and continue shaping the other buns.

Cover the sheet of buns with a light cotton cloth and wrap it in a large plastic bag (I keep one especially for this purpose). Rest the dough for 1 hour until the buns have doubled in size. Towards the end of the resting time, preheat the oven to 400°F.

Brush the buns with the egg wash and bake in the middle of the oven for about 15 minutes until golden brown. You can freeze the baked buns, thaw, and then pop them in a hot oven for a few minutes.

For the best toasted tea cake, cut the tea cakes in half. Heat a cast-iron pan over medium heat. When the pan is hot, turn off the heat and place the rolls in the pan, cut side down. Place a lid or plate on top to exert pressure and toast until the rolls are golden brown. Another method that gives a more rustic result is to turn on the toaster and make it very hot. Place the buns on top of the toaster, cut side down. Spread with butter.

Sally Lunns

Where does the name Sally Lunn come from? All the popular legends are variations on the story of Solange Luyon, a Huguenot girl who fled to Bath in the 18th century. She worked in a bakery and sold her buns on the street from a basket on her arm. When the baker discovered that Solange had a gift for baking light, luxurious brioche, he had her bake these buns and named them Sally Lunns. The first known recipe for these also comes from this century and appeared as a poem in 1796 in *The Monthly Magazine*.

In *The Cook's Oracle* of 1830, William Kitchiner tells us that the buns must be baked in tins. As a result, they have a pale band at the bottom and a golden-brown top, just as they still look today in the Sally Lunn's Eating House in Bath.

In the US, recipes with the name Sally Lunn appeared in the 19th century, but these were rich butter cakes, a corruption of a French pastry that Marie-Antoine Carême gives in his book, *The Royal Parisian Pastrycook and Confectioner*, called "Gateau au Beurre" or "Solilemne." In the US, "Solilemne" has grown to become "Sally Lunn," probably because people had heard of this cake in Bath and assumed it would be the same.

In 1937, a woman bought the house in Bath where today Sally Lunn's Eating House is located. During a renovation, she found not only an old baking oven, but also a recipe for Sally Lunn buns hidden in a cabinet behind a panel in the wall.

For 10 buns

4¾ tsp (15 g) dried yeast

½ cup + 2 Tbsp lukewarm whole milk

4¼ cups (500 g) strong white bread flour (see page 16)

¼ cup (60 g) demerara (coarse raw sugar), or granulated white sugar

¼ tsp ground nutmeg

3½ Tbsp (50 g) butter, at room temperature

½ cup + 2 Tbsp cream with at least 40% fat

2 eggs

1 tsp fine sea salt

1 egg yolk + 1 Tbsp milk, for egg wash

butter, for greasing

flour, for dusting

At Sally Lunn's Eating House, the buns are served halved and toasted, with savory toppings on the bottom pale halves and sweet toppings on the top golden halves.

Grease ten 3¼- to 4-inch crumpet rings with butter and dust with flour.

Add the yeast to the lukewarm milk and stir briefly and gently to activate it. The yeast will start to foam up in clusters, which means it is ready for use. Combine the flour, sugar, and nutmeg in a large bowl or the bowl of an electric mixer fitted with a dough hook and put the butter on top. Pour half of the yeast mixture over the butter and start kneading. When the milk and butter are completely absorbed, add the rest of the yeast mixture, followed by the cream and eggs. Knead the dough for 5 minutes, then let it stand for a few minutes (at this point the dough will be very wet). Add the salt and knead for 10 minutes, scraping the dough off the dough hook and sides of the bowl if needed, until it has come together in a smooth and elastic dough that is not too dry but also not terribly wet. Cover the dough and set aside for 1 hour until it has doubled in quantity.

Line a baking sheet with parchment paper and place the crumpet rings on top. Briefly knead the dough and divide it into 10 equal pieces. Take a piece of dough and lightly flatten it on your work surface, then pull the outer parts in like a purse and gently squeeze together like a dumpling so that the dough can no longer split open while rising. Turn the dough over so the squeezed ends are on the bottom. It should be nice and smooth on top – if not, flatten it and start again. Place each bun in a crumpet ring on the baking sheet.

Cover the sheet of buns with a light cotton cloth and wrap it in a large plastic bag (I keep one especially for this purpose). Rest the dough for 1 hour until the buns have doubled in size. Towards the end of the resting time, preheat the oven to 400°F.

Brush the buns with the egg wash and bake in the middle of the oven for about 15 minutes until golden brown. The buns are best eaten on the day they're made.

Bath buns, 18th century

The earliest recipe for Bath buns dates from Elizabeth Cleland's *A New and Easy Method of Cookery* from 1755. The book was published in Scotland, over 400 miles from Bath, which means the bun must have been well established by then. This recipe, as well as that from Bath resident Martha Bradley from 1756 and Elizabeth Raffald from 1769, calls for one part butter to two parts flour. This is the 18th- and 19th-century version of the Bath bun, with much more butter than the modern version, and complete with caraway comfits as decoration.

I discovered that Indian *mukhwas*, which are eaten after meals, are very similar to caraway comfits. Most *mukhwas* are made with fennel seeds, but they look exactly as the caraway comfits would have looked in the past. Pick out the white *mukhwas* from the box of multi-colored *mukhwas*. Use the colored ones for the Caraway Seed Cake on page 29.

For 8 buns

4¾ tsp (15 g) dried yeast

1 cup lukewarm whole milk, plus extra for brushing

3¾ cups (450 g) strong white bread flour (see page 16)

2 Tbsp (30 g) demerara (coarse raw sugar), or granulated white sugar

1 cup (225 g) butter, cubed, at room temperature

1 egg, beaten

1 tsp fine sea salt

1 Tbsp caraway seeds or *mukhwas*, plus extra caraway seeds or *mukhwas*, for decoration

Add the yeast to the lukewarm milk and stir briefly and gently to activate it. The yeast will start to foam up in clusters, which means it is ready for use. Combine the flour and sugar in a large bowl or the bowl of an electric mixer fitted with a dough hook and put the butter on top. Pour half of the yeast mixture over the butter and start kneading. When the milk and butter are completely absorbed, add the rest of the yeast mixture, along with the egg, and knead for 5 minutes. Let the dough stand for a few minutes (at this point it will be very wet). Add the salt and caraway seeds (if using – *mukhwas* are added later because of the sugar coating). Knead for 10 minutes, scraping the dough off the dough hook and side of the bowl if needed, until the dough has come together in a smooth and elastic dough that is not too dry but also not terribly wet.

Cover the dough and set aside for 1 hour until it has doubled in quantity. Meanwhile, line a baking sheet with parchment paper.

Briefly knead the dough, adding the *mukhwas* (if using), and divide it into eight equal pieces. Take a piece of dough and lightly flatten it on your work surface, then pull the outer parts in like a purse and gently squeeze together like a dumpling so that the dough can no longer split open while rising. Turn the dough over so the squeezed ends are on the bottom. It should be nice and smooth on top – if not, flatten it and start again. Place the bun on the baking sheet and continue shaping the other buns.

Cover the sheet of buns with a light cotton cloth and wrap it in a large plastic bag (I keep one especially for this purpose). Rest the dough for 1 hour until the buns have doubled in size. Towards the end of the resting time, preheat the oven to 400°F.

Brush the buns with milk, sprinkle with a few caraway seeds or *mukhwas,* and bake for about 15 minutes until lightly golden brown. The buns are best eaten on the day they're made. The next day they can be revived in a hot oven for a few minutes. You can also freeze the baked buns, thaw, and then pop them in a hot oven for a few minutes.

Bath buns, 20th century

This version of Bath buns became popular in the early 1900s. Professional baking books of that time give several recipes, one richer than the other and therefore also more expensive, so that all classes of people had a version of the bun that they could afford. You can still find this modern version of the Bath bun today in Bath. It uses much less butter than the older recipe.

For 8 buns

4¾ tsp (15 g) dried yeast

1 cup + 2 Tbsp lukewarm whole milk

4¼ cups (500 g) strong white bread flour (see page 16)

¼ cup (60 g) demerara (coarse raw sugar), or granulated white sugar

5 Tbsp (70 g) butter, cubed, at room temperature

1 egg

1 tsp fine sea salt

1 egg yolk + 1 Tbsp milk, for egg wash

¼ cup (35 g) currants, to garnish

4–5 Tbsp (55 g) pearl sugar nibs, to garnish

Add the yeast to the lukewarm milk and stir briefly and gently to activate it. The yeast will start to foam up in clusters, which means it is ready for use. Combine the flour and sugar in a large bowl or the bowl of an electric mixer fitted with a dough hook and put the butter on top. Pour half of the yeast mixture over the butter and start kneading. When the milk and butter are completely absorbed, add the rest of the yeast mixture, along with the egg. Knead the dough for 5 minutes, then let it stand for a few minutes (at this point it will be very wet). Add the salt and then knead for 10 minutes, scraping the dough off the dough hook and sides of the bowl if needed, until the dough has come together in a smooth and elastic dough that is not too dry but also not terribly wet.

Cover the dough and set aside for 1 hour until it has doubled in quantity. Meanwhile, line a baking sheet with parchment paper.

Briefly knead the dough and divide it into eight equal pieces. Take a piece of dough and lightly flatten it on your work surface, then pull the outer parts in like a purse and gently squeeze together like a dumpling so that the dough can no longer split open while rising. Turn the dough over so the squeezed ends are on the bottom. It should be nice and smooth on top – if not, flatten it and start again. Place the bun on the baking sheet and continue shaping the other buns.

Cover the sheet of buns with a light cotton cloth and wrap it in a large plastic bag (I keep one especially for this purpose). Rest the dough for 1 hour until the buns have doubled in size. Towards the end of the resting time, preheat the oven to 400°F.

Brush the buns with the egg wash and sprinkle with the currants and pearl sugar. Bake in the middle of the oven for about 15 minutes until golden brown. The buns are best eaten on the day they're made. The next day they can be revived in a hot oven for a few minutes. You can also freeze the baked buns, thaw, and then pop them in a hot oven for a few minutes.

Many Bath buns contain a lump of sugar inside. You can, if you want to, add a couple of pearls of sugar and shape the dough around them.

Belgian buns, 20th century

The name of these buns is very amusing for a Belgian like me, because you don't see them in Belgium at all. The first time I saw these buns at a bakery in Oxford I had to ask the shop assistant what a Belgian bun was and why they think they are Belgian. Of course, there was no answer, because these buns have been sold for more than a century and nobody remembers where they come from. The 19th-century version of this bun is more like a rock cake and you'll find the recipe on page 114.

We do have a similar pastry in Belgium, but it is made with laminated dough and, although it has a modest amount of icing, the glacé cherry is missing. I think Belgian buns look cheerful, and when I see them lying in rows of two in the bakery window, I always have to smile.

As there is no strict recipe, every bakery makes these buns from their basic bun dough, and so do I.

For 6 buns

For the buns
2¼ tsp (7 g) dried yeast

½ cup lukewarm whole milk

2⅓ cups (275 g) strong white bread flour (see page 16)

2 Tbsp (30 g) demerara (coarse raw sugar), or granulated white sugar

4 Tbsp (60 g) butter, cubed, at room temperature

1 egg

pinch of fine sea salt

flour, for dusting

For the filling
3 Tbsp lemon curd

¾–1 cup (120–150 g) currants, soaked for 1 hour in water or brandy, drained

For the glaze
1¾ cups (200 g) confectioners' sugar

3 Tbsp water

For decoration
3 glacé cherries, halved

Add the yeast to the lukewarm milk and stir briefly and gently to activate it. The yeast will start to foam up in clusters, which means it is ready for use. Combine the flour and sugar in a large bowl or the bowl of an electric mixer fitted with a dough hook and put the butter on top. Pour half of the yeast mixture over the butter and start kneading. When the milk and butter are completely absorbed, add the rest of the yeast mixture, along with the egg. Knead the dough for 5 minutes, then let it stand for a few minutes (at this point the dough will be very wet). Add the salt and knead for 10 minutes, scraping the dough off the dough hook and sides of the bowl if needed, until the dough has come together in a smooth and elastic dough that is not too dry but also not terribly wet.

Cover the dough and set aside for 1 hour until it has doubled in quantity. Meanwhile, line a baking sheet with parchment paper.

Shape the dough into a rectangle on a floured work surface and roll it out until it measures about 10 x 14 inches. Spread the lemon curd over the dough and sprinkle it with the currants. Roll up the dough from the short side like a jelly roll.

Cut the dough into six equal parts with a serrated knife and place on the baking sheet with the spirals facing upwards.

Cover the sheet of buns with a light cotton cloth and wrap it in a large plastic bag (I keep one especially for this purpose). Rest the dough for 1 hour until the buns have doubled in size. Towards the end of the resting time, preheat the oven to 400°F.

Bake the buns in the middle of the oven for 15 minutes until light golden brown. Let them cool completely while you make the glaze by mixing the confectioners' sugar with the water.

Apply a layer of glaze to the cooled buns and finish with half a glacé cherry.

You can freeze these buns before you ice them, thaw, and then pop them into a hot oven to revive them before adding the glaze.

Belgian buns, 19th century

These are George Read's Belgian buns from his 1854 book, *The Complete Biscuit and Gingerbread Baker's Assistant*. Unlike modern Belgian buns, these buns are rather like rock cakes.

For 12 buns

½ cup (80 g) blanched almonds

1¾ cups (225 g) plain white flour

1 tsp baking powder

1 cup (125 g) confectioners' sugar

¼ tsp ground cloves

¼ tsp ground ginger

½ tsp ground nutmeg

6 Tbsp (85 g) butter

1 egg

½ cup (75 g) currants

¼ cup (40 g) candied citrus peel

grated zest of ½ lemon

1 egg yolk + 1 Tbsp milk, for egg wash

Preheat your oven to 325°F and line a baking sheet with parchment paper.

Cut the almonds in half with a sharp knife and then in half again. Reserve some of the almonds to decorate the top of the buns.

Mix together the flour, baking powder, sugar, and spices, then rub in the butter with your fingers until the mixture resembles breadcrumbs. Add the egg and knead until the dough comes together. Fold in the almonds, currants, citrus peel, and lemon zest.

Divide the dough into 12 equal parts and roll each into a ball. Place on the sheet and push down a little. Brush the buns with the egg wash and place a few pieces of almond in the middle of each one.

Bake for 40 minutes until the buns are golden.

Cornish saffron buns

Saffron cakes and buns appeared throughout Britain, but survived only in Cornwall. The tin that was collected from the many mines in Cornwall was sometimes partially exchanged for saffron with foreign merchants, but although saffron was imported and traded for centuries, saffron crocuses have been and still are grown in Cornwall and some other areas in the country. The clue is in the name of the Suffolk town of Saffron Walden, where saffron was grown as far back as the 1600s. For the last decade, there have been several small farms producing saffron in Britain.

These Saffron buns were eaten by Methodists on Good Friday, smeared with clotted cream. Hot cross buns were the preferred bun eaten on Good Friday in other parts of the country, so the Methodists' preference ensured that saffron buns continued to exist on this beautiful peninsula.

For 8 buns

½ tsp saffron threads

1⅓ cups lukewarm whole milk

4¾ tsp (15 g) dried yeast

4¼ cups (500 g) strong white bread flour (see page 16)

¼ cup (60 g) demerara (coarse raw sugar), or granulated white sugar

1½ Tbsp (20 g) butter, at room temperature

2 Tbsp (30 g) lard or additional butter

1 tsp fine sea salt

½ Tbsp caraway seeds

⅓ cup (50 g) candied citrus peel, finely chopped

½–¾ cup (60–100 g) currants

1 egg yolk + 1 Tbsp milk, for egg wash

Use a mortar and pestle to crush the saffron threads. Combine the saffron with half of the lukewarm milk.

Add the yeast to the remaining lukewarm milk and stir briefly and gently to activate it. The yeast will start to foam up in clusters, which means it is ready for use. Combine the flour and sugar in a large bowl or the bowl of an electric mixer fitted with a dough hook and put the butter and lard on top. Pour half of the yeast mixture over the butter and start kneading. When the milk and butter have been completely absorbed, add the rest of the yeast mixture, along with the saffron-infused milk. Knead the dough for 5 minutes, then let it stand for a few minutes (at this point the dough will be very wet).

Add the salt to the dough, then add the caraway seeds, candied peel, and currants. Knead for 10 minutes, scraping the dough off the dough hook and sides of the bowl if needed, until the dough has come together in a smooth and elastic dough that is not too dry but also not terribly wet. (Adding the currants at this point will ensure that they adhere to the dough, whereas they won't adhere properly if you add them after the first rising.)

Cover the dough and set aside for 1 hour until it has doubled in quantity. Meanwhile, line a baking sheet with parchment paper.

Briefly knead the dough and divide it into eight equal pieces. Take a piece of dough and lightly flatten it on your work surface, then pull the outer parts in like a purse and gently squeeze together like a dumpling so that the dough can no longer split open while rising. Turn the dough over so the squeezed ends are on the bottom. It should be nice and smooth on top – if not, flatten it and start again. Place the bun on the baking sheet and continue shaping the other buns.

Cover the sheet of buns with a light cotton cloth and wrap it in a large plastic bag (I keep one especially for this purpose). Rest the dough for 1 hour until the buns have doubled in size. Towards the end of the resting time, preheat the oven to 400°F.

Brush the buns with the egg wash and bake for about 15 minutes until they are golden brown. The buns are best eaten on the day they're made. The next day they can be revived in a hot oven for a few minutes. You can also freeze the baked buns, thaw, and then pop them in a hot oven for a few minutes.

Iced fingers

An iced finger or iced bun is made from sweet yeast dough enriched with eggs, milk, and butter or lard. It can be square, round, or finger-shaped, depending on the bakery, and the icing is either snow white or baby pink. The buns are usually sold unfilled, but sometimes they are filled with jam and whipped cream, or just whipped cream. The bun must be very light and fluffy and baked to a pale golden color. If you see iced fingers in rural bakeries, they are often very large and the first thing you spot as you walk through the door. Around 1900, they often had the glamorous name of "Queen's rolls." Today they are considered a rather plain and uncomplicated bun, which is actually their strength.

When the buns are baking, they should touch as they expand so that you can tear them apart and enjoy that wonderful soft part where they were spooning together. These buns need to be eaten within just a couple of hours of baking, or they lose their lightness and become as heavy as a regular bun. If you aren't eating them all fresh, freeze them before you ice them.

For 14 fingers

For the buns

4¾ tsp (15 g) dried yeast

1 cup lukewarm whole milk

4 cups (500 g) plain white flour

½ tsp baking powder

¼ cup (60 g) demerara (coarse raw sugar), or granulated white sugar

7 Tbsp (100 g) butter, cubed, at room temperature

2 eggs

1 tsp fine sea salt

For the glaze

1¾ cups (200 g) confectioners' sugar

2 tsp lemon juice

5 tsp water

For the filling (optional)

1⅔ cups cream with at least 40% fat

1 Tbsp granulated white sugar

natural vanilla extract (optional)

strawberry or raspberry jam

Add the yeast to the lukewarm milk and stir briefly and gently to activate it. The yeast will start to foam up in clusters, which means it is ready for use. Combine the flour, baking powder, and sugar in a large bowl or the bowl of an electric mixer fitted with a dough hook and put the butter on top. Pour half of the yeast mixture over the butter and start kneading. When the milk and butter are completely absorbed, add the rest of the yeast mixture, along with the eggs. Knead the dough for 5 minutes, then let it stand for a few minutes (at this point the dough will be very wet). Add the salt and then knead for 10 minutes, scraping the dough off the dough hook and sides of the bowl if needed, until the dough has come together in a smooth and elastic dough that is not too dry but also not terribly wet.

Cover the dough and set aside for 1 hour until it has doubled in quantity. Meanwhile, line a baking sheet with parchment paper.

Divide the dough into 14 equal pieces. Take a piece of dough and lightly flatten it into an oval on your work surface, then pull the outer parts in like a purse and gently squeeze together like a dumpling so that the dough can no longer split open while rising. Turn the dough over so the squeezed ends are on the bottom. It should be nice and smooth on top – if not, flatten it and start again. Continue shaping the other buns, then place them on the baking sheet in two neat rows.

Cover the sheet of buns with a light cotton cloth and wrap it in a large plastic bag (I keep one especially for this purpose). Rest the dough for 1 hour until the buns have doubled in size. Towards the end of the resting time, preheat the oven to 400°F.

Bake the buns for 8–10 minutes until pale golden brown. Allow them to cool completely, then make the glaze by mixing the confectioners' sugar with the lemon juice and water. Put the glaze in a piping bag and pipe a line on the top of each finger, then use a palette knife or the back of a spoon to smooth it out. Allow the glaze to set before you fill the fingers, if desired.

To fill the fingers, whip the cream with the sugar and, if desired, vanilla. Spoon into a piping bag. Cut into the buns diagonally from next to the icing, but don't cut all the way through. Pipe the cream into the buns, drizzle with jam, and serve immediately.

Whitby lemon buns

E. Botham & Sons from Whitby have been making Whitby buns and Whitby gingerbread since the 1860s. The company was started by Elizabeth Botham, who began selling her bakes at local markets to make ends meet. She became so famous for her bakes that she opened a shop and later also a tearoom. The company is still owned by the same family today, and you can still enjoy an afternoon tea in the tearoom that Elizabeth founded.

Whitby lemon buns are made from the same dough as the iced finger, but with added raisins or currants, lemon zest, and a lemon glaze. The British store Marks & Spencer adds lemon curd as a filling, which is rather nice.

The buns are usually square from being baked in a baking tin that's small enough that the buns touch when they expand in the oven, but sometimes you find them finger-shaped. Botham's serves them with a generous amount of soft lemon icing. The icing in this recipe will become hard. For a softer version like Botham's, add an extra teaspoon of water.

For 12 buns

For the buns

4¾ tsp (15 g) dried yeast

1 cup lukewarm whole milk

4 cups (500 g) plain white flour

½ tsp baking powder

¼ cup (60 g) demerara (coarse raw sugar), or granulated white sugar

7 Tbsp (100 g) butter, cubed, at room temperature

2 eggs

1 tsp fine sea salt

grated zest of ½ lemon

1 cup (150 g) raisins or currants

For the glaze

1¾ cups (200 g) confectioners' sugar

2 Tbsp lemon juice

For a 15 x 10– inch jelly roll tin

Add the yeast to the lukewarm milk and stir briefly and gently to activate it. The yeast will start to foam up in clusters, which means it is ready for use. Combine the flour, baking powder, and sugar in a large bowl or the bowl of an electric mixer fitted with a dough hook and put the butter on top. Pour half of the yeast mixture over the butter and start kneading. When the milk and butter are completely absorbed, add the rest of the yeast mixture, along with the eggs. Knead the dough for 5 minutes, then let it stand for a few minutes (at this point the dough will be very wet). Add the salt, lemon zest, and raisins or currants. Knead for 10 minutes, scraping the dough off the dough hook and sides of the bowl if needed, until the dough has come together in a smooth and elastic dough that is not too dry but also not terribly wet.

Cover the dough and set aside for 1 hour until it has doubled in quantity. Meanwhile, line the baking tin with parchment paper.

Divide the dough into 12 equal pieces. Take a piece of dough and lightly flatten it on your work surface, then pull the outer parts in like a purse and gently squeeze together like a dumpling so that the dough can no longer split open while rising. Turn the dough over so the squeezed ends are on the bottom. It should be nice and smooth on top – if not, flatten it and start again. Place in the baking tin and continue shaping the other buns, adding them to the tin to form neat rows.

Cover the sheet of buns with a light cotton cloth and wrap it in a large plastic bag (I keep one especially for this purpose). Let rest for 1 hour until the buns have doubled in size. Towards the end of the resting time, preheat the oven to 400°F.

Bake the buns for 8–10 minutes until pale golden brown. Allow them to cool completely, then make the glaze by mixing the confectioners' sugar with the lemon juice. Put the glaze in a piping bag and pipe a line on the top of each finger, then use a palette knife or the back of a spoon to smooth it out. You can freeze these buns before you glaze them, thaw, and then pop them into a hot oven to revive them before adding the glaze.

In the image, I've decorated the buns with dried marigold petals.

Hot cross buns

The tradition of baking bread with a cross placed on top or pressed into the dough is linked to both paganism and Christianity. At the beginning of spring, the pagan Saxons baked bread in honor of the goddess Eostre – which is the origin of the name Easter, according to Bede the Venerable, an 8th-century English Benedictine monk.

The cross on the bread represented the rebirth of the world after the winter and the four phases of the moon, as well as the four seasons and the wheel of life, which are very strong images in pagan tradition. The Christians saw the Christian cross in the buns and, as with many other pre-Christian traditions, replaced their pagan meaning with a Christian one – the resurrection of Christ at Easter. According to Elizabeth David, it took until Tudor times before the buns were permanently linked to Christian celebrations.

During the reign of Elizabeth I in the 16th century, the London Clerk of Markets issued a decision prohibiting the sale of spiced bakes, except at funerals, at Christmas, or on Good Friday, which is when spiced buns started to be linked firmly to these festivities. The first registered reference to hot cross buns can be found in Poor Robin's Almanack in the early 17th century:

"Good Friday comes this Month, the old woman runs,
With one or two a Penny hot cross Bunns."

Under the rule of Cromwell, an Act of Parliament in 1647 prohibited the preparation of special food for festivities and made it a punishable offence for nearly two decades. After Charles II was restored to the throne in 1660, people could return to their festivities and the baking of buns, cakes, and gingerbreads that came with it.

A century later, the custom surrounding the hot cross buns began to gain a superstitious rather than religious significance – buns baked on Good Friday supposedly would not spoil for the rest of the year; sometimes the buns were even taken on ships because people were convinced that they could prevent shipwrecks.

In the East End of London you'll find a pub called The Widow's Son, named after a widow who lived in a house on the site in the 1820s. The legend goes that the widow baked hot cross buns for her sailor son, who was supposed to come home from sea that Good Friday. The son must have died at sea as he didn't return home, but the widow refused to give up hope of his return and continued to bake a hot cross bun for him every year, which she then saved along with the buns she had baked in previous years. After her death, a net full of hot cross buns was discovered hanging from the ceiling of her cottage. The pub has been on the site of the widow's house since 1848, and every Good Friday, the ceremony of the Widow's Bun is celebrated and members of the Royal Navy attend the celebrations, with one of them placing a new hot cross bun in a net that is suspended above the bar. Remember, buns baked on Good Friday will never spoil!

Frederick T. Vine shows in his 1898 book, *Saleable Shop Goods*, that the addition of a separate cross to the hot cross bun is a phenomenon from the 20th century. The book contains an illustration of a pastry docker in the shape of a cross and shows that around 1900 the cross on the hot cross bun was still impressed, rather than added in a separate layer of dough like we do today. The buns in Frederick T. Vine's recipe ask for spices, but do not yet contain the dried fruit that we have come to associate with it for the last hundred years.

Today the shops sell all kinds of hot cross buns, often the whole year round, from chocolate flavored with chocolate bits added, to cranberries and banana. There are even hot cross doughnuts on offer! It's hard to say that I prefer the original, because hot cross buns have evolved over time so it's not clear what is original, but I will say that I enjoy the traditional version, a spiced bun dough studded with currants and candied peel, a cross added in plain pastry, and a shiny egg-washed, golden-brown top – just as I remember them from my childhood travels around Britain.

For 12 buns

For the buns

4¾ tsp (15 g) dried yeast

1¼ cups lukewarm whole milk

4¼ cups (500 g) strong white
  bread flour (see page 16)

¼ cup (60 g) demerara (coarse raw
  sugar), or granulated white sugar

1 tsp ground cinnamon

½ tsp ground mace

¼ tsp ground nutmeg

⅛ tsp allspice

⅛ tsp ground ginger

⅛ tsp ground coriander

5 Tbsp (70 g) butter, cubed, at room
  temperature

1 egg

1 tsp fine sea salt

1 cup (150 g) currants

⅓ cup (50 g) candied citrus peel

2 egg yolks + 2 Tbsp milk, for egg wash

For the crosses

⅔ cup water

⅔ cup (75 g) plain white flour

For a 15 x 10–inch jelly roll tin (if you don't want the buns to attach to one another while baking, use a larger sheet or bake in two batches)

Add the yeast to the lukewarm milk and stir briefly and gently to activate it. The yeast will start to foam up in clusters, which means it is ready for use. Combine the flour, sugar, and spices in a large bowl or the bowl of an electric mixer fitted with a dough hook and put the butter on top. Pour half of the yeast mixture over the butter and start kneading. When the milk and butter are completely absorbed, add the rest of the yeast mixture, along with the egg. Knead for 5 minutes, then let the dough stand for a few minutes (at this point it will be very wet). Add the salt and then the currants and candied peel and knead for 10 minutes, scraping the dough off the dough hook and sides of the bowl if needed, until the dough has come together in a smooth and elastic dough that is not too dry but also not terribly wet.

Cover the dough and set aside for 1 hour until it has doubled in quantity. Meanwhile, line the baking tin with parchment paper. For the crosses, mix the water and flour into a thick batter. Scoop it into a piping bag with a small nozzle and cover until needed.

Divide the dough into 12 equal pieces. Take a piece of dough and lightly flatten it on your work surface, then pull the outer parts in like a purse and gently squeeze together like a dumpling so that the dough can no longer split open while rising. Turn the dough over so the squeezed ends are on the bottom. It should be nice and smooth on top – if not, flatten it and start again. Place in the baking tin and continue shaping the other buns, adding them to the tin to form neat rows.

Cover the sheet of buns with a light cotton cloth and wrap it in a large plastic bag (I keep one especially for this purpose). Rest the dough for 1 hour until the buns have doubled in size. Towards the end of the resting time, preheat the oven to 400°F.

Carefully pipe a cross onto each bun, then carefully brush the buns generously with the egg wash and bake for about 20–30 minutes until golden brown.

The buns are best eaten on the day they're made. The next day they can be revived in a hot oven for a few minutes. You can also freeze the baked buns, thaw, and then pop them in a hot oven for a few minutes.

These buns are excellent halved, then toasted and spread with copious amounts of farmhouse butter. Leftover buns can be used in the Bun and Butter Pudding recipe from my book *Pride and Pudding*.

Devonshire splits

These small buns were once found in both Cornwall and Devon. The recipes are almost the same, but the splits from Cornwall are larger. A Cornish split spread with treacle (or molasses) is known as "thunder and lightning." In her 1932 book, *Good Things in England*, Florence White recommends rubbing the splits with a buttered piece of paper after baking to make them shine, and then wrapping them in a tea towel to keep them warm. The splits are best served fresh from the oven. When they cool, they lose their airiness, but then they can certainly still serve as regular white buns. The name "split" tells us that the buns must be split open for the filling.

For 16 splits

4¾ tsp (15 g) dried yeast

1¼ cups lukewarm whole milk

4¼ cups (500 g) strong white bread flour (see page 16)

2 Tbsp (30 g) demerara (coarse raw sugar), or granulated white sugar

2 Tbsp (30 g) butter, at room temperature

1 tsp fine sea salt

Add the yeast to the lukewarm milk and stir briefly and gently to activate it. The yeast will start to foam up in clusters, which means it is ready for use. Combine the flour and sugar in a large bowl or the bowl of an electric mixer fitted with a dough hook and put the butter on top. Pour half of the yeast mixture over the butter and start kneading. When the milk and butter are completely absorbed, add the rest of the yeast mixture. Knead the dough for 5 minutes, then let it stand for a few minutes (at this point the dough will be very wet). Add the salt and then knead for 10 minutes, scraping the dough off the dough hook and sides of the bowl if needed, until the dough has come together in a smooth and elastic dough that is not too dry but also not terribly wet.

Cover the dough and set aside for 1 hour until it has doubled in quantity. Meanwhile, line two baking sheets with parchment paper.

Briefly knead the dough and divide it into 16 equal pieces. Take a piece of dough and lightly flatten it on your work surface, then pull the outer parts in like a purse and gently squeeze together like a dumpling so that the dough can no longer split open while rising. Turn the dough over so the squeezed ends are on the bottom. It should be nice and smooth on top – if not, flatten it and start again. Place the bun on the baking sheet and continue shaping the other buns.

Cover the sheet of buns with a light cotton cloth and wrap it in a large plastic bag (I keep one especially for this purpose). Rest the dough for 1 hour until the buns have doubled in size. Towards the end of the resting time, preheat the oven to 400°F.

Bake the buns for about 10–15 minutes until they have a light golden blush. Eat them fresh from the oven.

These buns are best eaten straight from the oven, cut open and filled with clotted cream or whipped cream and jam, and dusted with confectioners' sugar. When cooled and left for a few hours they become perfect little buns for lunch, but less suitable as an afternoon tea treat as they become heavier as they cool. You can also freeze the baked buns, thaw, and then pop them in a hot oven for a few minutes to revive them.

Brighton rock cakes

Usually these buns appear as "rock cakes" or "rock buns" in old cookery books, but in 1854 two recipes for Brighton rock cakes appeared in George Read's *The Complete Biscuit and Gingerbread Baker's Assistant*. Read gives a recipe for Brighton rock cakes and another for Brighton pavillions. The latter are made the same way as Brighton rock cakes, but are finished with a topping of currants and coarse sugar that, he says, should be "as large as a pea."

You can still buy Brighton rock cakes in the seaside town of Brighton at the Pavilion Gardens Café. The open-air kiosk at Brighton Pavilion has been selling Brighton rock cakes since 1940, and possibly even longer if we look at Read's recipe from 1854. Rock cakes are popular throughout Great Britain and Northern Ireland, and often appear in literature. In *Harry Potter and the Philosopher's Stone*, Hagrid serves them to Harry and Ron, and Agatha Christie also mentions them in more than one novel.

This recipe for Brighton rock cakes contains candied cedro, a type of citrus, but most rock cakes contain only currants, so you can easily leave it out.

For 6 rock cakes

1¾ cups (225 g) plain white flour

½ cup (100 g) demerara (coarse raw sugar), or granulated white sugar

1 tsp baking powder

¼ Tbsp mixed spice (or pumpkin pie spice)

pinch of sea salt

5 Tbsp (75 g) chilled butter, diced

1 egg

3 Tbsp whole milk

⅓ cup (50 g) currants

¼ cup (30 g) candied cedro (see page 19; optional)

3 glacé cherries, halved, to garnish (optional)

pearl sugar nibs, to garnish (optional)

Preheat your oven to 400°F and line a baking sheet with parchment paper.

Mix the flour, sugar, baking powder, mixed spice, and salt in a large bowl. Add the butter and rub it into the flour mixture until it has the consistency of breadcrumbs. Stir in the egg, then add enough milk to bring the dough together without making it too wet. If the dough is too dry to press together, add a teaspoon more milk.

Fold the currants and candied cedro through the dough. Form six rock cakes using two forks – this will help achieve a rugged, rocky look. Place on the baking sheet and decorate with the cherries and sugar, if using. Bake in the middle of the oven for 15 minutes until the rock cakes have a golden blush.

Fat Rascals

Fat Rascals are described in historical writings as "turf cakes," and they are traditionally from Yorkshire. They were baked in a covered pan under the ashes of a peat fire, resulting in a cake resembling a flat rock cake. The famous Bettys tearoom in Yorkshire, founded by a Swiss immigrant in 1919, claims that they have been baking Fat Rascals for over 30 years. They bake three types of Fat Rascals, and the tearoom also holds the official trademark for Fat Rascals, which forbids other tearooms from offering their own version.

However, Fat Rascals are actually much older than 30 years. In the *Leeds Intelligencer* of 17 November 1860, the correspondent writes that while he was visiting Yorkshire he came upon Fat Rascals in a bakery. And in *The Cornish Telegraph* of 10 October 1889, we even find a recipe for Fat Rascals, showing that they must have been an established bake by then. I own a small handwritten cookbook from around 1907 with a recipe for Fat Rascals, and the *Yorkshire Evening Post* of 2 August 1912 states that Fat Rascals are the pride of every housewife in Goathland in Whitby.

The only thing missing from the old recipes and sources, and what Bettys seems to have invented, is the little face on top of the cake that's made with two candied cherries and whole blanched almonds. The recipe from 1889 tells the reader only to dust the cakes with white sugar before baking.

For 6 Fat Rascals

1¾ cups (225 g) plain white flour

½ cup (100 g) demerara (coarse raw sugar), or granulated white sugar

1 tsp baking powder

¼ Tbsp mixed spice (or pumpkin pie spice)

pinch of sea salt

5 Tbsp (75 g) chilled butter, diced

1 egg

3 Tbsp milk

⅓ cup (50 g) currants

1 egg yolk + 1 Tbsp milk, for egg wash

Preheat your oven to 400°F and line a baking sheet with parchment paper.

Mix the flour, sugar, baking powder, mixed spice, and salt in a large bowl. Add the butter and rub it into the flour mixture until it has the consistency of breadcrumbs. Stir in the egg, then add enough milk to bring the dough together without making it too wet. If the dough is too dry to press together, add a teaspoon more milk.

Fold the currants through the dough. Push the dough flat and form six round discs. Place on the baking sheet, brush with the egg wash, and decorate as you wish.

Bake in the middle of the oven for 15 minutes until the cakes have a golden blush.

Paris buns

These buns were once very popular in Belfast, Northern Ireland, and the west coast of Scotland, but they are hard to find today. They are similar to scones and rock cakes. I found a recipe in *The Modern Flour Confectioner* from 1891, a cookbook by Robert Wells. Why the buns were called Paris buns is unclear.

Wells does not decorate the top of the buns, but the buns people remember from the last 50 years all have either a topping of small pearl sugar nibs or currants, or a combination of the two. I prefer to decorate the buns, as they look far more interesting with the topping.

The Northern Irish women with whom I spoke reminisced about the Paris buns from their childhood. Perhaps this is also the reason the Northern Irish Van Morrison included them in his song "Cleaning Windows" from 1982: "We went for lemonade and Paris buns."

For 4 large buns

2 cups (250 g) plain white flour

¼ cup (55 g) demerara (coarse raw sugar), or granulated white sugar

1 tsp baking powder

pinch of sea salt

4 Tbsp (60 g) chilled butter, diced

1 egg yolk

6 Tbsp buttermilk

⅓ cup (50 g) currants

1 egg yolk + 1 Tbsp milk, for egg wash

small pearl sugar nibs, to garnish

currants, to garnish

Preheat your oven to 375°F and line a baking sheet with parchment paper.

Mix the flour, sugar, baking powder, and salt in a large bowl. Add the butter and rub it into the flour mixture until it has the consistency of breadcrumbs. Add the egg yolk and knead it into the dough.

Add half of the buttermilk and use a wooden spoon or spatula to mix it into the dough, then add the rest of the buttermilk and the currants.

Divide the dough into four pieces and shape them into very rough balls without kneading. Don't be tempted to roll neat balls – just pat the dough together with your hands or two forks and leave it rough to give a nice effect when the buns are baked. Place the buns on the baking sheet.

Brush the buns with the egg wash, sprinkle with the pearl sugar and/or a couple of currants, and bake for 15–20 minutes until they are lightly colored.

These buns are best when they are still a little warm, and they're best eaten on the day they're baked.

Banbury cakes

Banbury cakes are very similar to Eccles cakes but are much older. Eccles cakes are round, while Banbury cakes are oval. A Banbury cake is certainly not a cake or a bun, but rather a sweet pastry.

In *The Penguin Companion to Food*, I found that local archives show that Banbury cakes were sold in 1638 by one Bette White in 12 Parsons Street in the town of Banbury in Oxfordshire. In the early 19th century, Banbury cakes were baked and sold by two sisters, Lizzie and Lottie Brown. Florence White writes in her *Good Things in England* from 1932 that the best Banbury cakes can be found at E.W. Brown's "The Original Cake Shop" on 12 Parsons Street, the exact address where they were sold nearly 300 years earlier. Banbury cakes were sold by street vendors from wicker baskets lined with white cloths. For the town of Banbury, this meant that making these special baskets was an additional cottage industry. Eventually cardboard boxes made into the shape of the cake shop took the place of the baskets, and Banbury cakes were sent all over the country with the postal coach.

I traveled to Banbury in 2013, hoping to find Banbury cakes, but I found nothing at 12 Parsons Street, nor did I find one single Banbury cake in Banbury. The last owner, Wilfrid Brown, sold the family bakery to a project developer, who demolished the building in 1968. Although I found at least two Banbury cake shops on old postcards, there is no trace of a bakery in the current street scene. It made me feel sad, as if I were mourning the loss of something I never had. There is beauty in a town that proudly offers their local bake, just like they do in Bakewell, but unfortunately Banbury has lost its baking heritage. I wonder if the bakery would have been allowed to be demolished today.

Fortunately, there is still one last Banbury cake maker, Philip Brown, a distant cousin of Lizzie and Lottie Brown, the sisters who baked Banbury cakes in Banbury in the early 19th century. He does not have a physical store, but delivers his Banbury cakes in and around Banbury. He also descends from "The Original Cake Shop" owner, E.W. Brown, whose bakery I discovered on old postcards from around 1900.

John Kirkland says in his 1907 book, *The Modern Baker, Confectioner & Caterer*, that Banbury cakes are sold in several places, but in Banbury itself the Banbury cakes are of the best quality. A mincemeat filling is often used, but Kirkland gives a Banbury meat filling that is much more interesting – a filling with currants and cake crumb. I collect cake crumb by freezing pieces of leftover homemade cake in bags. If you never have leftover homemade cake, you can use the Madeira Cake recipe on page 44.

Eccles cakes

In the northwest of England, the town of Eccles lends its name to Eccles cakes. In the region, Eccles cakes aren't exclusively eaten as a sweet pastry, but also alongside a chunk of Lancashire cheese. Chorley cakes are similar, although they are made with shortcrust pastry and not puff pastry like Banbury and Eccles cakes.

Mrs Raffald is one of the first to give a recipe for Eccles cakes in her book, *The Experienced English Housekeeper* from 1769, but the recipe does not yet bear the name "Eccles cakes," and the filling also contains a small amount of meat, as was the case with the mince pies (see page 220) of the past.

In the year 1793, James Birch began to bake and sell Eccles cakes at his shop in today's Church Street in Eccles. It is quite possible that he used Mrs Raffald's recipe, omitting the meat. A few years later he opened a larger bakery across the street and a former employee started his own store at the old location, with a large inscription claiming that his shop, Bradburns, was the only original Eccles cake shop. Of course there was a feud, as the two Eccles cake shops were in the same street.

It's likely that these cakes, or a version of them, were at one point baked as "Wakes cakes" for the Eccles Wakes, which celebrated the feast of St Mary and the town church. In 1877 the Home Secretary, at the request of the Eccles Local Board, banned the Wakes because they had become a riotous affair that had nothing more to do with the rushbearing traditions of the past where townspeople would gather to bring bunches of rushes to spread over the church floor.

On a postcard from around 1900 I found another Eccles cake shop, and this shop also claimed to sell the one and only Eccles cakes. Yet it was Bradburns that survived the longest in the end – the shop was known until about 1953, but the building was demolished in the 1960s, in the same decade the Banbury cake shop was demolished. Why, oh why, were these shops not protected and preserved? Just as with the Banbury cakes, there is one more company that, although no longer in Eccles itself, makes Eccles cakes based on a family recipe.

Bradburns and the other Eccles cake shops are now forgotten, but Birch Eccles cake shop is still remembered by a plaque on the wall in the village. The text reads that Eccles cakes from Birch were exported as far as the West Indies and Australia.

THE OLD ECCLES CAKE SHOP, Eccles.

The Vine Series.
No. 150.

Banbury cakes

You are welcome to make traditional puff pastry, but my quick method works every time and costs you half the effort. Just make sure your butter is cut in small enough cubes and frozen, and keep the dough as cold as you can while you do the folding.

For 10 cakes

For the quick puff pastry

1 cup (240 g) butter, cut into cubes
  no larger than ½ inch

2 cups (240 g) plain white flour

½ tsp sea salt

½ cup ice-cold water

flour, for dusting

1 egg yolk + 1 Tbsp milk, for egg wash

superfine sugar, for sprinkling

For the filling

¾ cup (60 g) cake crumbs (left over
  from other baking; defrosted if frozen)

½ cup (60 g) currants

⅓ cup (50 g) candied citrus peel

¼ tsp ground nutmeg

¼ tsp ground cloves

¼ tsp ground mace

¼ tsp ground cinnamon

¼–½ cup (100 g) apple purée

Put the diced butter in the freezer for 30 minutes. Put the flour and salt in the bowl of a food processor fitted with the blade attachment and place in the fridge if you have space.

Take the butter from the freezer and the bowl from the fridge. Toss the butter in the flour so that the butter is coated with flour. This will prevent sticking.

Pulse the mixture twice for 1 second. Add half of the cold water and pulse three times, then add the rest of the water and pulse six times.

Dust your work surface with flour and take the dough out of the bowl. Push the dough flat with your hands but do not knead it – the small chunks of butter that are visible in the dough must be preserved and not blended with the flour.

Dust the dough with flour and pat it flat into a square with a rolling pin. Fold the dough in three parts like a letter, pat it down lightly with the rolling pin, and then fold it in three again, but in the opposite direction. Wrap the dough in plastic wrap and let it rest for at least 30 minutes in the refrigerator. The dough will be marbled with the butter and that is the intention. Repeat the folding and chilling step three times.

Preheat your oven to 400°F and line a baking sheet with parchment paper.

For the filling, push the cake crumbs through a fine sieve using a spatula or the back of a spoon. Combine the cake crumbs, currants, candied peel, and spices in a bowl and stir in the apple purée until everything is well combined.

Roll out the dough until it is ¹⁄₁₆ inch thick (or as thin as possible). Cut out circles from the dough using a 3½-inch cutter and brush them with the egg wash. Place a tablespoon of the filling on each round and fold the outer edges inwards over the filling as with a Cornish pasty. Push the dough together with your fingers to seal it, then turn the parcels over with the seam underneath. The tops should look perfectly smooth.

Place the parcels on the baking sheet and cut three slashes in the top of each. Brush the tops with the egg wash and sprinkle with the superfine sugar.

Bake for 20–25 minutes until the Banbury cakes are golden. Serve them warm or cooled – they will keep for a few days because of the rather moist filling.

135

Eccles cakes

Eccles cakes are traditionally 4 inches wide. I've given the option to make a small version that is half the size, but feel free to make larger ones.

For 10 small or 5 large cakes

For the quick puff pastry

1 cup (240 g) butter, cut into dice
   no larger than ½ inch

2 cups (240 g) plain white flour

½ tsp sea salt

½ cup ice-cold water

flour, for dusting

1 egg yolk + 1 Tbsp milk, for egg wash

coarse white sugar or demerara (coarse
   raw sugar)

For the filling

7 oz (200 g) mincemeat (see page 221)

Put the diced butter in the freezer for 30 minutes. Put the flour and salt in the bowl of a food processor fitted with the blade attachment and place in the fridge if you have space.

Take the butter from the freezer and the bowl from the fridge. Toss the butter in the flour so that the butter is coated with flour. This will prevent sticking.

Pulse the mixture twice for 1 second. Add half of the cold water and pulse three times, then add the rest of the water and pulse six times.

Dust your work surface with flour and take the dough out of the bowl. Push the dough flat with your hands but do not knead it – the small chunks of butter that are visible in the dough must be preserved and not blended with the flour.

Dust the dough with flour and pat it flat into a square with a rolling pin. Fold the dough in three parts like a letter, pat it down lightly with the rolling pin and then fold it in three again, but in the opposite direction. Wrap the dough in plastic wrap and let it rest for at least 30 minutes in the refrigerator. The dough will be marbled with the butter and that is the intention. Repeat the folding and chilling step three times.

Preheat your oven to 400°F and line a baking sheet with parchment paper.

Roll out the dough until it is ¹⁄₁₆ inch thick (or as thin as possible). Cut out circles from the dough using a 3½-inch cutter (for small cakes) or a 7-inch cutter (for large cakes). Brush the dough circles with the egg wash and place a teaspoon of the filling in the middle of each small round or 2 teaspoons in the middle of each large round. Fold the edges of the dough over the filling like a purse. Push the dough together with your fingers to seal it, then turn the parcels over with the seam underneath. The tops of the parcels should look perfectly smooth.

Place the parcels on the baking sheet and cut three slashes in the top of each. Brush the tops with the egg wash and sprinkle with the sugar.

Bake the Eccles cakes in the middle of the oven for 15–20 minutes until golden.

Serve as a sweet cake or with cheese. Lancashire cheese is traditional, but blue cheeses work wonderfully as well.

Isle of Wight doughnuts

Fritters are another example of how people baked sweets without or before the wider use of the oven.

The first reference and recipe for Isle of Wight doughnuts appeared in *Modern Cookery for Private Families* by Eliza Acton in 1845. She explains that when the "doughnuts are made in large quantities, as they are at certain seasons in the island, they are drained upon very clean straw." This tells us that these doughnuts were indeed popular on the island, although the first time they appear in a newspaper is 33 years later in the *Portsmouth Evening News* of May 1878, in an advertisement for a confectioner in Portsmouth (which is close to but not actually on the Isle of Wight) advertising the sale of "The Isle of Wight Dough Nut" in their shop.

The Isle of Wight doughnut must have been around much earlier, as Rosa Raine mentions remembering them from her childhood in her book *The Queen's Isle: Chapters on the Isle of Wight*, published in 1861. Raine writes that they are peculiar to the island and that she was given these buns as a child. She tells us they are locally known as "birds' nests,-----" and when torn open they are filled with a "little cluster of plums," which would've been raisins.

Eliza Acton uses lard in her pastry and for frying, and while I enjoy using lard when I can use homemade lard or an organic brand, I understand it's not everyone's cup of tea. Feel free to use butter for the pastry and oil for frying.

For 16 doughnuts

4¾ tsp (15 g) dried yeast

1¼ cups lukewarm whole milk

4¼ cups (500 g) strong white bread flour (see page 16)

¼ cup (50 g) dark brown sugar

½ tsp ground cinnamon

¼ tsp ground cloves

¼ tsp ground mace

2 Tbsp (30 g) lard or butter, at room temperature

1 tsp fine sea salt

currants

lard, beef tallow, or oil, for deep-frying

confectioners' sugar, for dusting

Add the yeast to the lukewarm milk and stir briefly and gently to activate it. The yeast will start to foam up in clusters, which means it is ready for use. Combine the flour, sugar, and spices in a large bowl or the bowl of an electric mixer fitted with a dough hook and put the lard or butter on top. Pour in half the yeast mixture and start kneading. When the milk and lard or butter are completely absorbed, add the rest of the yeast mixture. Knead the dough for 5 minutes, then let it stand for a few minutes (at this point the dough will be very wet). Add the salt and then knead for 10 minutes, scraping the dough off the dough hook and sides of the bowl if needed, until the dough has come together in a smooth and elastic dough that is not too dry but also not terribly wet.

Cover the dough and set aside for 1 hour until it has doubled in quantity. Meanwhile, cover a baking sheet with parchment paper.

Briefly knead the dough and divide it into 16 equal pieces. Take a piece of dough and lightly flatten it on your work surface. Put a couple of currants in the middle, then pull the outer parts in like a purse and gently squeeze the dough together like a dumpling so that it can no longer split open while rising. Turn the dough over so the squeezed ends are on the bottom. It should be nice and smooth on top – if not, flatten it and start again. Place the doughnuts on the baking sheet and set aside to rise for 30 minutes.

Heat the lard, beef tallow, or oil in a deep-fryer or a deep flameproof casserole dish to 350–375°F. Use a slotted spoon to carefully immerse the doughnuts in the hot oil and cook in batches until golden brown. Remove and drain on paper towels while you cook the remaining doughnuts. Serve dusted with confectioners' sugar.

Aberdeen crulla

Many sources claim that the Abdereen crulla comes from Dutch *krulla* or *krullers*, but I haven't been able to find a similar twisted bake with that name anywhere in my historical Dutch cookbooks.

The US and Canada have twisted fritters called "crullers," which could explain the name, as many Dutch words were adapted and used in a context different to how Dutch people would use them. A "cruller" would be someone who curls things, not a pastry that is curled. In Southern Sweden and Denmark, *klenäter* – which means "small, expensive, and finely created objects" – are baked for Christmas. They look a lot like the aforementioned crullers and the Jersey wonders from the Isle of Jersey, which are published in my book *Pride and Pudding*.

The earliest recipe I could find for an Aberdeen crulla creates a near-identical bake to the three twisted fritters I mentioned above. The recipe appears in Mrs Dalgairns' *The Practice of Cookery* from 1829, and instructs the reader to create an oblong shape and to divide the center into three or four strips, and then plait one bar over another, so as to meet in the center. A century later, Scottish cookery author Florence Marian McNeill copied this recipe word for word in her book *The Scots Kitchen*.

While crullers and *klenäter* still exist today, Aberdeen crulla have disappeared completely.

For 12–14 crullas

7 Tbsp (100 g) butter, at room temperature

½ cup (100 g) demerara (coarse raw sugar), or granulated white sugar

2 eggs, lightly beaten

2½ cups (300 g) strong white bread flour (see page 16)

flour, for dusting

lard, beef tallow, or oil, for deep-frying

confectioners' sugar or superfine sugar, for dusting

Beat the butter and sugar together until creamy. Gradually add the beaten eggs, whisking constantly.

Add the flour bit by bit and, once the dough forms a ball, turn it out onto a lightly floured work surface and knead for about 10 minutes. Wrap the dough in plastic wrap and chill in the fridge for 30 minutes.

Cut off a 1½-oz (42-g) piece of dough. Roll the dough into a ball and then use a rolling pin to flatten it into an oval shape about 4½ inches long and ¼ inch thick.

Use a small sharp knife to cut the dough lengthwise into three even strips, leaving the top part joined so that you can plait the dough and then crimp the ends together.

Line a baking sheet with paper towels. Melt some lard, tallow, or oil in a deep-fryer or a heavy-based frying pan, making sure you have enough to cover the crullas, and heat it to 375 °F. Carefully lower a crulla into the fat and fry for 4 minutes until browned but still blushing golden on both sides. You can fry a couple of crullas at the same time, but make sure they don't stick together, or stick to the frying basket, if you are using one. Carefully remove with a slotted spoon or tongs and drain on the paper towels.

Dust the crullas with sugar and serve immediately.

Yum-yums

These aptly named confections were originally a Scottish treat but are available all over Britain. Just like the Aberdeen Crulla (page 141), most sources claim that yum-yums came to Scotland via the Dutch, who supposedly eat this kind of fried dough for Christmas. However, this is not true, as knotted fritters are not traditional in the Netherlands at all. I believe these deep-fried knots were born as Aberdeen crullas and evolved into what they are today. The earliest record I managed to find was in an *Aberdeen Press and Journal* article from 1978 that describes them as if they were already a classic Scottish treat at that time.

Yum-yums are made of a laminated style of dough with yeast, which is twisted and deep-fried and covered in a thin layer of icing. Make sure the fat is hot enough, because otherwise these pastries soak up the fat and become too fatty. It's best to fry just one or two at a time in order to keep the fat as hot as possible, which will give the best result.

For 18 twisted and 36 fingers

1½ tsp (5 g) dried yeast

⅓ cup lukewarm water

¼ cup lukewarm milk

2 cups (240 g) strong white bread flour (see page 16)

1 Tbsp granulated white sugar

½ tsp salt

1 cup (240 g) butter, cut into ½-inch cubes, frozen

1 egg, whisked

flour, for dusting

lard, beef tallow, or oil, for deep-frying

For the icing
heaping 1 cup (130 g) confectioners' sugar

3 Tbsp water

Add the dried yeast to the lukewarm water and milk and stir briefly and gently to activate it. The yeast will start to foam up in clusters, which means it is ready to use.

Combine the flour, sugar, and salt in the bowl of a food processor. Add the butter and pulse twice for 1 second to coat the butter in flour. Add half the yeast mixture with the egg, pulse twice for 1 second, then add the rest of the yeast mixture and pulse six times.

Dust your work surface generously with flour and take the dough out of the bowl. Coat the dough in flour and push it flat with your hands but do not knead it – the small chunks of butter that are visible in the dough must be preserved and not blended with the flour. Place the dough in a bowl and put it in the fridge for a few hours, but ideally overnight because the yum-yums will color faster when the dough has rested longer.

Generously flour your work surface and dough and use a rolling pin to pat the dough into a rectangle. Roll out the dough to a12 x 16–inch rectangle. Fold the dough in three parts like a letter, pat it down lightly with the rolling pin, and then fold it in three again, but in the opposite direction. Wrap the dough in plastic wrap and let it rest for at least 30 minutes in the refrigerator. The dough will be marbled with the butter and that is the intention. Repeat the folding and chilling step three times and then roll out the dough again to a 12 x 16–inch rectangle.

Cut out 2 x 6–inch rectangles from the dough, then cut a line down the middle of each, leaving about ½ inch of dough at each end. Twist each strip and place on a baking sheet lined with parchment paper. To make fingers instead of twists, cut each rectangle in half. Cover and leave to rise for 30 minutes.

Meanwhile, make the icing by combining the sugar and water.

Line a baking sheet with paper towels. Melt some lard, tallow, or oil in a deep-fryer or heavy-based frying pan, making sure you have enough to cover the yum-yums, and heat it to 375°F. Carefully lower the yum-yums into the fat and cook in batches, turning, for 1½–2 minutes until golden brown. Remove with a slotted spoon or tongs and transfer to the sheet. Pat dry with the paper towels, then transfer to a wire rack and brush them all over with the icing while hot. Allow to cool before serving. Store the yum-yums in an airtight container.

Botallack mine engine houses, West Cornwall

Winnats Pass, Peak District, Derbyshire

Oatcakes & griddle cakes

Oats and barley were historically the principal crops in the North where wheat was hard to grow because of the colder, wetter summers and longer winters. The mountains and glens in the Scottish Highlands can be covered by a blanket of snow while the wheat growing in the South is getting out the picnic blanket in early spring. While the mid and south of Britain harvest in July, the north of Scotland often harvests at the end of September. In some areas with a more changeable climate, different crops would even be sown together on the same land to ensure a harvest. If they all grew, the bakes would be made with a multi-cereal mix, but if the weather was wet, only the hardier grains would survive. Peas and beans would also be added to bakes when grain was expensive.

The rougher climate is the reason that flatcakes or flatbreads made from the more resistant oats and barley are more prevalent in the cuisine of the northern English counties, Wales, Northern Ireland, and Scotland, just as they are in Scandinavia. Oats and barley don't contain a lot of gluten-forming protein, which makes them unsuitable for making a large loaf of bread. This is a great example of how regionality and climate influences the development of a cuisine.

"A grain, which in England is generally given to horses, but in Scotland supports the people."
Samuel Johnson on oats, in A Dictionary of the English Language, *1755*

The earliest oatcakes, griddle cakes, and flatbreads were made on a griddle or bakestone: a heavy cast-iron disc that hung or lay over an open-hearth fire, a small purpose-built fire, or later a stove, where they were often a standard built-in feature. Today you can use a heavy-based cast-iron pan instead to mimic the effect, but you are also welcome to use the oven. People made these typical bakes at home without an oven and before the advent of leavening agents that would make people obsessed with risen loaves.

There are many different kinds of oatcakes, depending on the region. Bannocks were baked all over Scotland. This ancestor of the modern scone was cooked as small, flat oat patties or one large one divided into four as "farls." In Scotland, wheat bannocks are today referred to as griddle scones and sold next to the oven-baked scones that we have come to associate with the West Country.

Scottish oatcakes are unsweetened, biscuit-like oat crispbreads that are thin, round, or farl-shaped. In a Scottish bakery on the Isle of Skye, I had the choice between fine oatcakes and oatcakes made with oat groats rather than oat flour or rolled oats. There is also the choice between oatcakes with roasted oats, which are honey colored, and oatcakes made without first roasting the oats, which are very pale, as if they haven't been baked long enough.

In Wales, Cumbria, and Scotland, there was once an ancient form of oatcake that has been largely forgotten. The clapcake is rolled out as thinly as possible or pressed flat with the hands. After baking, the thin, crisp cakes were often dried over the stove or in racks in front of the fireplace to help preserve them. These oatcakes were very much like the crispbreads from Scandinavia, which isn't surprising as Scandinavia and the northern counties share a similar climate where oats thrive while wheat fails.

In Staffordshire, oatcakes are large round pancakes that consist of oats, water or milk, and yeast – formerly sourdough. They used to be the main meal of the workers in the potteries that are so typical of the region. The dough has the consistency of a thick pancake batter and is poured or spooned onto a hot griddle or into a cast-iron pan. In the nearby county of Derbyshire, the oatcakes were made up to three times thicker than the Staffordshire oatcakes, and were mainly eaten by local miners.

Lancashire and Yorkshire oatcakes are not round but oval. The dough is thicker and contains no wheat flour, just oats. They were dried, much like the Welsh oatcakes, but hanging over a stick, which gave them a shape similar to that of a taco. These oatcakes are impossible to find today.

Oats release energy slowly and keep you feeling full for longer. It's quite extraordinary that in a region where people need more substantial meals, the crops that grow best are the ones that provide the right nourishment. Nevertheless, Scotland was heavily affected by famine in the 17th and 18th centuries. Many Scottish families were forcibly evicted, but sometimes they also decided freely to emigrate to places with a better, more mild climate, such as America, Australia, and Canada. Others stayed closer to home in the Lowlands or the South of England, where they introduced the scone.

Staffordshire oatcakes

These oatcakes were the traditional breakfast for people who worked in the potteries of Stoke-on-Trent and the surrounding area. Unlike Scottish oatcakes, which are biscuits, these oatcakes are floppy like pancakes and vary in thickness from region to region in the North of England. They were eaten while still hot, filled with bacon or any other savory filling, or dried in front of the fire so they became hard as a crispbread and sometimes even toasted.

Staffordshire oatcakes were bought by the workers early in the morning at a hole-in-the-wall oatcake shop, which was no more than a window in a house from which the oatcakes were baked and sold. The last hole-in-the-wall closed its window in 2012, and with its closure this tradition is sadly lost. In some cafés, B&Bs, and pubs in the Peak District and Derbyshire, you can still get oatcakes for breakfast, and you will also find them in local shops and bakeries, where you can buy them individually for a few pence each.

Today, a small portion of wheat flour is usually added to the batter of Staffordshire oatcakes. That was not the case in the past, as we learn in Florence White's book *Good Things in England* from 1932. Adding wheat flour makes the oatcakes more resilient so they don't tear so easily after you have filled them.

Need some help choosing the perfect type of oats or oatmeal? Read all about oats on page 16.

For 10–12 oatcakes

2½ cups (225 g) oat flour

¾ cup (100 g) whole-wheat flour or whole-grain spelt flour

¾ cup (100 g) plain white flour

1 tsp granulated white sugar

½ tsp sea salt

2¼ tsp (7 g) dried yeast

2 cups lukewarm whole milk

2 cups lukewarm water

butter, lard, or oil, for cooking

Mix the flours, sugar, and salt in a large bowl. Add the yeast to the lukewarm milk and stir briefly and gently to activate it. The yeast will start to foam up in clusters, which means it is ready to use.

Add the yeast mixture and water to the dry ingredients and mix well. Cover the bowl with plastic wrap or a damp tea towel and let the batter rest for 1 hour.

Heat a cast-iron pan or heavy-based frying pan (or on an old-fashioned griddle if you have one) and grease it with some butter, lard, or oil. Cook the oatcakes on both sides. The easiest way is to pour a soup ladle of the batter into the middle of the pan and then spread it outwards with the back of a tablespoon or a spatula.

I like to cook a batch of oatcakes and freeze them. They are easily revived in a hot pan when thawed an hour or two before you want to serve them. Serve with savories like bacon, sausages, eggs, and sautéed mushrooms, any sweet condiment you like, or just plain sugar. These oatcakes are quite filling so you only need to eat one or maybe two, depending on your appetite.

Clapcake

Clapcake, clapbread, or havercake from Cumbria, northern England, and clap scones from Scotland, resemble the thin crispbread we usually associate only with Scandinavia. *The diary of Celia Fiennes* from 1698 tells us how these clapcakes were made in Cumbria:

They mix their flour with water, so soft as to rowle it in their hands into a ball, and then they have a board made round and something hollow in the middle riseing by degrees all round to the Edge a little higher, but so little as one would take it to be only a board warp'd, this is to Cast out the Cake thinn and so they Clap it round and drive it to ye Edge in a Due proportion till drove as thinn as a paper and still they Clap it and drive it round, and then they have a plaite of jron same size with their Clap board, and so shove off the Cake on it and so set it on Coales and bake it...

After being baked, the clapcake was dried in front of a fire on a special wooden rack called a "havercake maiden," which looks like a miniature bench. Celia also writes that people dipped it in milk, ate it with meat, or simply smeared it with butter, and that it was the only bread eaten in this region unless you lived close to a market town where there were regular markets.

Novelist Elizabeth Gaskell described the drying of clapcakes in 1863: "The great rack of clap-bread hung overhead, and Bell Robson's preference of this kind of oat-cake over the leavened and partly sour kind used in Yorkshire was another source of her unpopularity." Historian Peter Brears found a later reference to clapcake in the 1940s, when a Dr Henry Bedford recorded them still being made in the Lake Counties.

Today clapcake is, unfortunately, largely forgotten. It's a shame, because it is a versatile oatcake suitable for various applications, great for breakfast or lunch with cheese, jam, or even chocolate spread, but it's also perfect to serve with a cheese platter or dips. I regularly bake a batch of clapcakes, and they keep for up to a month in a sturdy brown paper bag – they become rather like cardboard when kept in an airtight container. Clapcakes can be revived by putting them in a hot oven for a few minutes. Although not traditional, rolling different types of seeds, such as caraway, into the dough as they do in Scandinavia makes for a nice variation. I add a little regular flour to this batter because it makes for an easier batter, but feel free to use all oat flour.

For 4 individual 8-inch clapcakes,
or 1–2 larger ones

1½ Tbsp (20 g) lard
1 cup boiling water
1¾ cups (170 g) oat flour
½ cup (60 g) plain white flour
  or superfine oat flour
pinch of baking powder
½ tsp fine sea salt
oat flour, for dusting

Preheat your oven to 450°F.

Melt the lard in the boiling water. Mix in the flours, baking powder, and salt to make a smooth dough. Mix with a wooden spoon and, once it is cool enough, knead well by hand. If the dough remains too wet (this will depend on the age of your flour), add a little more flour until the dough is no longer sticky.

Divide the dough into portions or leave it whole if you are making one large clapcake. On a sheet of parchment paper generously dusted with oat flour, roll out the dough to a thickness of 1/16 inch (or as thin as possible). Use a Scandinavian knobbly rolling pin if you have one.

Using the parchment paper, slide the clapcake(s) onto a baking sheet. Bake in the middle of the oven for 15 minutes, then turn and bake for another 5 minutes. Let the clapcakes cool on a wire rack. Clapcakes keep for a very long time in a sturdy brown paper bag.

Bannocks

Bannocks come from the northern parts of Great Britain: Northern England, Northern Ireland, and Scotland. They are flat, scone-like buns or quick breads that are baked on a griddle and made with barley, oats, and sometimes a proportion of rye – whatever grew to harvest. Before baking soda was invented, they were also made by saving a proportion of dough from the previous bake, thus creating sourdough bannocks.

A bannock made with rye and barley was called "Brown George." If no oats, barley, or rye were available, pea flour was sometimes used. Peas were dried and often served as a substitute for other flours if harvests failed. They were planted around the edges of fields, separately, or on rotation with other crops because pea plants have the ability to improve the soil to benefit future crop yields.

In her 1929 book, *The Scots Kitchen*, Florence Marian McNeill says that bannocks must be baked in small circles, but nowadays they are often baked in a large round cake and cut into four wedges called farls. You can choose whether you want bannocks or farls. Eat them while they're still hot; if you let them cool, they become tough and tasteless.

For 4 bannocks

2½ cups (225 g) barley flour or
  oat flour, or 2⅔ cups (225 g)
  chickpea flour or pea flour
½ cup (55 g) plain white flour
¼ tsp fine sea salt
1 tsp baking soda
2 cups buttermilk
oat flour or plain white flour,
  for dusting

Put the barley or oat flour, plain flour, and salt in a bowl and mix well.

Add the baking soda to the buttermilk and beat well with a whisk until bubbles form. Pour into the bowl with the flour mixture and mix well.

Pat the dough into a ball and place it on a floured work surface. If the dough remains too wet (this will depend on the age of your flour and the conditions you're baking in), add a little more flour. Pat the dough out to a circle ½ inch thick and cut it into four wedges or shape it into small round cakes.

Place a griddle, cast-iron pan, or spun-iron pan on the stove to heat up. Use a pinch of flour or a bit of dough to test the heat of the pan. If the flour burns immediately, it is too hot; if it takes a few minutes to brown, it is perfect. Cook the bannocks for a few minutes on each side until they are light brown. Eat them while they're still hot.

When using barley or oat flour, it's nice to fold ¾ cup (100 g) dried cranberries or blueberries, or 1 tsp caraway seeds, through the dough.

Scottish oatcakes

These biscuit-like oatcakes can be considered a crispbread, as they were traditionally made as a long-lasting, easy-to-bake alternative to bread. Before the advent of ovens they were baked on a griddle – a flat iron disc suspended over or placed over a fire.

Scottish oatcakes are usually round, but sometimes they are made into large rounds and then cut into four to create farls. Florence Marian McNeill, who wrote *The Scots Kitchen* in 1929, uses medium oatmeal. She was from the Isle of Orkney, where today Orkney oatcakes are made into farl shapes. The bakery on Orkney also makes an oatcake with a portion of barley or beremeal flour (beremeal being an ancient form of barley indigenous to this region).

In Scotland, you can find many varieties of oatcakes. There is a fine version made with oat flour, a rougher variety made partly with oatmeal, and one made partly with steel-cut oats for extra texture. Oatcakes can range from very brittle and fragile to hard and sometimes even chewy, depending on the choice of oats, the amount of water used, and how long they were baked. Sometimes they are made by roasting the oats and oatmeal first to create a darker oatcake. Lard used to be traditional but has now been replaced by vegetable oils. While butter is an option, I find it is very rich, creating almost a digestive biscuit.

Today oatcakes are often served with a cheese board. I think they're the perfect partner for haggis – spread the haggis onto the oatcakes like a pâté, and wash it down with a wee dram. I personally like any kind of oatcake, and my larder is always stocked with them. They're my favorite thing to take with me for those little bursts of hunger during long and busy days. When you have oatcakes, you have a meal.

Makes about 20 oatcakes

1⅔ cups (150 g) porridge oats or oatmeal (see page 16)

1⅔ cups (150 g) oat flour

½ tsp sea salt

⅓ cup vegetable oil, melted lard, or melted butter

¼ cup hot water

oat flour, for dusting

Preheat your oven to 375°F and line two baking sheets with parchment paper.

Mix the oats, oat flour, and salt together, then mix with the oil, melted lard, or butter. Add the hot water and mix well. Let the dough rest for 10 minutes so that the oats can swell.

Knead the dough, but if it is still too crumbly, add more hot water and let it rest again – one type of oats can be drier than another.

Roll out the dough on a work surface dusted with oat flour until it is about ¼ inch thick. Use a 2½- to 2¾-inch cutter to cut out the oatcakes.

Transfer the oatcakes to the baking sheets and bake for 10–15 minutes.

Tattie scones

Tattie scone, potato farl, potato scone, or boxty is a thick pancake made with potato, flour, and sometimes buttermilk. It is part of the Ulster fry, the traditional Northern Irish breakfast, served with bacon, eggs, sausages or black pudding, tomatoes, and perhaps also mushrooms and beans. In Scotland, tattie scones are sold in bakeries and also eaten with breakfast. My favorite combination when in Scotland is a tattie scone, a slice of haggis, and a fried egg, washed down with a cup of builder's tea. It's a perfect way to start a day in the Highlands.

Potato flatbreads exactly like these are also part of the food culture in Iceland as *kartöfluflatbrauð* and in Norway as *mjukbrød*, which is eaten with fermented trout.

Although they are excellent for breakfast, I also like to eat tattie scones as a side with a salad or to mop up the colorful juices of an Indian curry.

For 1 scone divided into 4 farls

8 oz (225 g) floury potatoes, such as
   Maris Piper, Russet Burbank, or
   Kennebec, peeled and cut into chunks
2 Tbsp (25 g) butter
⅔ cup (80 g) plain white flour
½ tsp fine sea salt
⅛ tsp baking powder
flour, for dusting
butter, for greasing

Boil the potatoes, then drain and shake the pot to let the potatoes dry. Add the butter, flour, salt, and baking powder and knead into a dough.

Dust an 8-inch cast-iron pan with flour. Push the dough into the pan to create a flat, round shape. Remove the dough from the pan by carefully flipping it over, then cut it into four equal wedges – this makes it easier to cook the farls.

Heat the pan and grease it with some butter. Dust the farls on both sides with flour. Cook the farls, one at a time, for 3 minutes on each side, or fry them all together in one go. You can use some excess dough to test how hot the pan is. If the pan is too hot, the farls will burn instead of slowly cooking.

Crumpets and pikelets

Traditionally baked on a griddle or straight onto the hotplate of the stove range, crumpets and pikelets can be made from the same dough with the addition of a little more water for the pikelets, but the method is a bit different. Pikelets are baked like thick pancakes and crumpets are baked in a ring so that you get higher, pillowy cakes. They are both often baked in advance and sold per piece or per stack so that you can heat them up at home. The British like to toast crumpets, either in a toaster for which they are the perfect size, or impaled on a toast fork over an open fire.

The thing that defines both cakes is the pale baked top with many holes, in contrast to the well-baked, brown bottom. Personally, I prefer a pikelet or crumpet that is re-fried in a pan or toasted. I know that sounds strange, but when I am in London for work I always buy a packet of crumpets or pikelets in Marks & Spencer on the way home, with the prospect of an easy and quick breakfast the next day. That also means that you can easily bake and freeze them yourself. Simply defrost for a few minutes on the radiator or overnight in the refrigerator, and you're done!

You can eat both of these griddle cakes either sweet or savory. For example, think of golden or maple syrup that makes the holes on top of the pale cakes into little pools of syrup. Or with an egg and bacon, the runny egg yolk perfectly caught in the holes.

For 18–20 crumpets

1⅔ cups (200 g) strong white bread flour (see page 16)

¼ cup (25 g) rye flour

¾ cup buttermilk

½ cup + 2 Tbsp water

1 tsp (3 g) dried yeast

1 tsp fine sea salt

½ tsp baking powder

olive oil, for greasing

You can also make these with sourdough. Preferably use a rye flour starter and replace the ¼ cup (25 g) of rye flour with 2 Tbsp (25 g) of starter.

Mix the flours, buttermilk, and water together and whisk until you no longer have any lumps. Add the yeast, mix well, cover and let rest for an hour. You can also make the batter the night before and let it rise, covered, in the fridge, then add the salt and baking powder on the day of cooking.

When you are ready to bake the crumpets, add the salt and baking powder to the batter. Heat a griddle or a cast-iron pan. Grease the pan by spreading over some olive oil with paper towels. Test the heat of the pan with half a teaspoon of batter. If it immediately colors, the heat is too high.

Grease 3¼-inch (8-cm) crumpet rings with olive oil. Place the rings in the pan, spoon 2 tablespoons of batter into each, spread out, and cook for 6–8 minutes. The characteristic holes should now slowly appear on the top. It's a mesmerizing sight to see the holes pop!

When the top starts to appear drier, you can turn the crumpet over, along with the ring, and bake for another minute, making sure the top remains as pale as possible. If you turn the crumpet too soon, the batter will pour out of the ring. Don't be surprised if your first crumpets are a disaster – you will get the hang of judging when the moment is right to turn them over.

Serve the crumpets immediately or freeze once cooled. Reheat in a hot pan or in the toaster.

Toasted crumpets with lots of butter to fill the little holes is very traditional. Golden syrup is a classic accompaniment (or, try maple syrup), but crushed raspberries and cream are a real treat too and will get you one of your "five a day." One to two crumpets per person are sufficient for breakfast, depending on what you serve with them.

For 18–20 pikelets

1⅔ cups (200 g) strong white bread
   flour (see page 16)

¼ cup (25 g) rye flour

¾ cup buttermilk

1 cup water

1 tsp (3 g) dried yeast

1 tsp fine sea salt

½ tsp baking powder

olive oil, for greasing

Mix the flours, buttermilk, and water together and whisk until you no longer have any lumps and your batter has the consistency of plain yogurt. Add the yeast, mix well, cover, and let rest for an hour. You can also make the batter the night before and let it rise, covered, in the fridge, then add the salt and baking powder on the day of cooking.

When you are ready to bake the pikelets, add the salt and baking powder to the batter. Heat a griddle or a cast-iron pan. Grease the pan by spreading over some olive oil with paper towels. Test the heat of the pan with half a teaspoon of batter. If it immediately colors, the heat is too high.

Spoon 2 tablespoons of batter into the hot pan and spread it out using the back of your spoon in a circular motion. Each pikelet should be 4 inches (10 cm) wide. The characteristic holes should now slowly appear on the top. Use a spatula to judge when the pikelet is sufficiently baked and then turn it over for just a few seconds to cook the top, making sure the top remains as pale as possible.

Serve the pikelets immediately or freeze once cooled. Reheat in a hot pan or in the toaster.

Golden syrup is a classic accompaniment (or, try maple syrup), but crushed raspberries and cream are a real treat too and will get you one of your "five a day." Two to four pikelets per person is usually sufficient for breakfast, depending on what you serve with them.

Crumpets (page 158) and Pikelets (page 159)

English muffins

English muffins are griddle-baked yeast buns, cooked until golden brown on both the top and bottom, while the sides remain delicately pale and ideal for tearing open. Tearing open the muffin rather than using a knife was stressed by Hannah Glasse in *The Art of Cookery Made Plain and Easy*, published in 1747. In what is one of the earliest recipes for English muffins, she writes that when you halve a muffin with a knife instead of tearing it, it becomes as heavy as lead, and this is true. A muffin is indeed fluffier when torn open, but not as easy to serve with a poached or fried egg. It therefore depends on what I'm serving with them as to whether or not I will tear or cut through the pale, barely cooked belly of this bun.

Bake these muffins in a larger quantity and freeze them for easy breakfasts to come. It's so rewarding to take them out of the freezer, let them thaw for 10 minutes and then just put them in the pan to warm. Or cut them – sorry, Hannah – for fewer crumbs, and pop the halves into the toaster. They're delicious toasted on the outside and soft as a cushion on the inside, covered with butter or jam.

English muffins are an integral part of the iconic eggs Benedict, which consists of a base of toasted muffin halves, a poached egg, bacon or ham, and hollandaise sauce. But plain fried or scrambled eggs are perfect too – a toasted muffin makes any breakfast into a feast. It's a joy on the plate and to the nose as it fills the house with that seductive smell of freshly toasted baked goods.

For 10 muffins

3½ tsp (11 g) dried yeast

1¼ cups lukewarm whole milk

5 cups (600 g) strong white
  bread flour (see page 16)

2 Tbsp (30 g) demerara (coarse raw
  sugar), or granulated white sugar

2 Tbsp (30 g) lard or butter,
  at room temperature

2 eggs, beaten

1¾ tsp fine sea salt

semolina or polenta, for dusting

flour, for dusting

Add the yeast to the lukewarm milk and stir briefly and gently to activate it. The yeast will start to foam up in clusters, which means it is ready for use. Combine the flour and sugar in a large bowl or the bowl of an electric mixer fitted with a dough hook and put the lard or butter on top. Pour in half of the yeast mixture and start kneading. When the milk and lard or butter are completely absorbed, add the rest of the yeast mixture, along with the eggs. Knead for 5 minutes, then let the dough stand for a few minutes (at this point it will be very wet). Add the salt and knead for 10 minutes, scraping the dough off the dough hook and sides of the bowl if needed, until the dough has come together in a smooth and elastic dough that is not too dry but also not terribly wet.

Cover the dough and set aside for 1 hour until it has doubled in quantity. Meanwhile, line two baking sheets with parchment paper and sprinkle with semolina or polenta.

Gently roll out the dough on a floured work surface until it is 1¼ inches thick. Use a 3¼-inch cutter to cut out your muffins. Place the muffins on the sheets, leaving enough room so they have space to expand. Sprinkle the muffins with more semolina or polenta.

Cover the sheet of muffins with a light cotton cloth and wrap it in a large plastic bag (I keep one especially for this purpose). Rest the dough for 30 minutes–1 hour. Towards the end of the resting time, preheat the oven to 350° F.

Heat a griddle or cast-iron pan over low heat so that it does not become too hot. You can test the heat of the pan with an excess piece of dough. Cook the muffins on both sides for 5–6 minutes until golden brown. At this point they will be undercooked on the inside, so place them in the oven for 5 minutes to continue cooking. Let the muffins cool on a wire rack, or immediately devour them with a lot of butter. You can also freeze them in bags for later.

Welsh cakes

These griddle cakes come from Wales, but are commonly eaten throughout Britain. In Welsh they have a couple of names: *picau ar y maen, pice bach,* and *cacen gri.* The word "*maen*" means bakestone, referring to the fact that Welsh cakes are baked on a griddle. Welsh cakes were sometimes called "bakestones." The *Yorkshire Evening Post* from 15 April 1935 reported: "The other day I gave a recipe for Welsh bakestone cakes…"

For 8–10 small Welsh cakes

1¼ cups (150 g) plain white flour

2 Tbsp (25 g) granulated white sugar

½ tsp baking soda

½ tsp baking powder

pinch of sea salt

2 Tbsp (25 g) chilled butter

2 Tbsp (25 g) lard (or more butter)

1 Tbsp golden syrup, maple syrup, or honey

1 egg

1 Tbsp milk

¼ cup (35 g) currants

flour, for dusting

superfine sugar, for sprinkling

Mix together the flour, sugar, baking soda, baking powder, and salt, then rub in the butter and lard, if using. Add the golden syrup, egg, and milk and use a wooden spoon or spatula to combine everything. If the mixture is too dry, add a little more milk. You're aiming for the consistency of scone dough.

Finally, knead in the currants and roll out the dough on a floured work surface to a thickness of ⅝ inch. Use a 2½- to 2¾-inch cutter to cut out circles. Re-roll the remaining dough and continue cutting out circles until you have used all of the dough.

Place a cast-iron pan on the stove to heat up. Use a pinch of flour or a bit of the dough to test the heat of the pan. If it burns immediately, it is too hot. When it takes a few minutes to brown, it is perfect.

Bake the cakes for 2–3 minutes on each side until golden brown. Generously sprinkle with superfine sugar while still warm.

The perfect afternoon tea

It is not certain exactly when the afternoon tea ritual was introduced. The most popular story tells us that the Duchess of Bedford invented it around 1840 to fight a sinking feeling in the afternoon. Since people in the 18th century had to wait until eight in the evening for dinner, you can imagine that they had the munchies in the afternoon. The duchess is said to have had a tray with tea and bread and butter in her room in the afternoon. Soon she started inviting friends to participate in this ritual. By 1880, it became a social event, and soon the etiquette of afternoon tea was born.

The rules
There are rules when it comes to afternoon tea: there must be fresh water in the teapot at all times, and loose tea is considered the best. The tea caddy, a richly decorated wooden tea box, must always be placed closest to the host, who also has the key. This shows that he or she is in charge. The tray always holds a teapot, tea strainer with saucer, sugar bowl with loose sugar, milk jug, dish with lemon slices, lemon fork, and a jug of hot water to dilute the tea when a guest so wishes. The table holds teacups and saucers, forks and teaspoons, small cake plates, and preferably linen napkins. And then there are the sandwiches, warm scones, and small tarts and cakes. Furthermore, there is a bowl with the best jam and thick cream or clotted cream, each with a spoon.

On the issue of cream
Devon and Cornwall have been embroiled in a "cream first or jam first" debate for decades. I think it is not about what is the proper way, but how someone prefers to have their scone. I like to break my scone into pieces, little by little. Then I put a generous blob of clotted cream on a chunk, followed by a little bit of jam, preferably homemade from raspberries or strawberries. A scone should not be too sweet, so that you can spread it generously with cream and jam without wondering whether you'll end up in a sugar coma after one scone. For me, a scone is partly an excuse to eat as much clotted cream as I can manage. You'll find a recipe to make your own clotted cream in my book *Pride and Pudding*, but nothing beats Trewithen or Rodda's clotted cream.

The procedure
According to etiquette, you start with the thinly sliced, dainty, triangular sandwiches with cucumber and butter, egg salad, salmon, and maybe ham. Next come the scones, so that they do not cool completely yet are not warm enough to melt the cream. Scones may never be cut with a knife. If they are baked correctly, they have a crack in the middle so that you can break the scone in two. The small cakes are kept for the end. By then you will be almost full, and you can ask for your cakes to be wrapped to take home.

The head of the table or the family, or the host, is the one who pours the tea. This is traditionally called "being mother" because pouring the tea is usually the job of the mother of the house. According to tradition, you first put milk in your cup. This dates back to the time when teacups were made of ultra-fine porcelain that could break due to the heat of the tea. Today you can do this the other way around – if nobody is watching. You hold your cup elegantly in your hand – without a little finger in the air – and your saucer may never leave the table. The rudest thing you can do is leave your spoon in your cup.

The importance of tea
Britain is a nation of tea drinkers. Tea was introduced to court in England in the mid-17th century by Catherine of Bragança, the Portuguese wife of Charles II. Her dowry consisted of, among other things, a box of tea.

Tea used to be a privilege only available to the most well-to-do of society and so important that it was high on the political agenda. The *Commutation Act* of 1784 lowered tea taxes and made tea affordable to all those who wanted it in their cup. This finally made tea a part of everyday life. In Victorian times, sugary tea kept the workers going in the factories and on the fields. Tea became the most consumed beverage in Britain, and remains so to this day.

The British love to get completely absorbed in afternoon tea. For special occasions, they head to posh hotels and tearooms. I'm told by the landlady of the B&B that has become our second home in the last 10 years that British people love to plan a day off spending the night at a B&B in a quaint location, waking up to a full English breakfast in the morning, fasting through lunch, and then heading out for a proper afternoon tea after a countryside walk.

Scones

While we would quickly assume that scones originated in the South-west where they are an integral part of the "cream tea," they are actually quintessentially Scottish. Scones are closely related to bannocks and other quick breads like soda bread and griddle cakes. Originally scones were baked on a griddle over a fire, and although I still found griddle scones being sold in a bakery on the Scottish Isle of Skye, nowadays scones are usually baked in an oven.

Florence Marian McNeill explains in her 1929 book, *The Scots Kitchen*, that the names "scone" and "bannock" are used loosely and that a bannock is a large round scone that you can divide into four or more wedges, or farls. When the dough is cut into small rounds, it is a scone. She claims the name derives from the Gaelic word "*sgonn*," and translates it as a "shapeless mass."

McNeill gives various recipes for scones and bannocks, but her recipe that she describes as the "old method" and the one after it that she describes as the "modern method" clearly show us that scones were indeed made before the invention of baking powder in the early 19th century. Baking powder made them lighter and more like the scone we know today. Scones became increasingly more popular in the Edwardian period, as we can clearly see from tearoom advertisements in newspapers from that era.

In the South-west, another bake was popular at teatime and that was the split (see page 126), a small, soft white bun that is split and filled with cream and jam. Somehow the splits fell out of favor and scones took over to become the icon of a Cornish and Devonshire cream tea. It is possible that Scottish Highland folk emigrating south in search of better living conditions and work in the 18th century introduced the scone to the rest of the country.

For 16 small or 10 large scones

3½ cups (430 g) plain white flour

2 Tbsp baking powder

3 Tbsp (40 g) demerara (coarse raw sugar), or granulated white sugar

pinch of fine sea salt

⅔ cup (150 g) butter, cubed, at room temperature

2 eggs, beaten

1 tsp lemon juice

6 Tbsp whole milk

flour, for dusting

1 egg yolk + 1 Tbsp milk, for egg wash

thick cream, clotted cream, and/or jam, for serving

Preheat your oven to 425°F and line two baking sheets with parchment paper.

Put the flour, baking powder, sugar, and salt in a bowl and rub in the butter with your fingers until the mixture resembles breadcrumbs. Add the eggs and then the lemon juice. Add the milk, a little at a time, and mix with a spatula until you have a soft and slightly sticky dough.

Place the dough on a generously floured work surface and gently knead it together until all the flour is incorporated and the dough no longer sticks but still feels soft. This takes around 1 minute. Flatten the dough with your hands until it's about ¾ inch (2 cm) thick. Use a piece of parchment paper to smooth the top of the dough to give the scones a nice finish.

Using a 2-inch (5-cm) round cutter for small scones or a 2¾-inch (7-cm) cutter for large scones, cut out the scones by pushing the cutter straight down. Don't twist the cutter, as this will affect how much the scones rise. Pat the remaining dough back together and cut out more scones until you have used all the dough.

Place the scones on the sheets and brush with the egg wash. Bake in the middle of the oven for 10–15 minutes until the scones have risen and are golden in color.

Transfer the scones to a wire rack to cool slightly. Cover them with a tea towel to keep them warm and soft. Scones must be eaten the same day they are made or reheated in the oven. They can also be frozen, thawed and revived in a hot oven. Serve with thick cream or clotted cream and your favorite jam.

Rye, East Sussex

Sultana scones

For 16 small or 10 large scones

3½ cups (430 g) plain white flour

2 Tbsp baking powder

3 Tbsp (40 g) demerara (coarse raw sugar), or granulated white sugar

pinch of fine sea salt

⅔ cup (150 g) butter, cubed, at room temperature

2 eggs, beaten

1 tsp lemon juice

6 Tbsp whole milk

½–⅔ cup (70–100 g) sultanas (golden raisins) or currants

flour, for dusting

1 egg yolk + 1 Tbsp milk, for egg wash

Preheat your oven to 425°F and line two baking sheets with parchment paper.

Put the flour, baking powder, sugar, and salt in a bowl and rub in the butter with your fingers until the mixture resembles breadcrumbs. Add the eggs and then the lemon juice. Add the milk, a little at a time, and mix with a spatula until you have a soft and slightly sticky dough.

Place the dough on a generously floured work surface and gently knead in the sultanas or currants, bringing the dough together until all the flour is incorporated and the dough no longer sticks but still feels soft. This will take around 1 minute. Flatten the dough with your hands until it's about ¾ inch (2 cm) thick. Use a piece of parchment paper to smooth the top of the dough to give the scones a nice finish.

Using a 2-inch (5-cm) round cutter for small scones or a 2¾-inch (7-cm) cutter for large scones, cut out the scones by pushing the cutter straight down. Don't twist the cutter, as this will affect how much the scones rise. Pat the remaining dough back together and cut out more scones until you have used all the dough.

Place the scones on the baking sheets and brush with the egg wash. Bake in the middle of the oven for 10–15 minutes until the scones have risen and are golden in color.

Cheese scones

For 16 small or 10 large scones

3½ cups (430 g) plain white flour

2 Tbsp baking powder

3 Tbsp (40 g) demerara (coarse raw
  sugar), or granulated white sugar

pinch of fine sea salt

⅔ cup (150 g) butter, cubed, at room
  temperature

2 eggs, beaten

1 tsp lemon juice

6 Tbsp whole milk

7 oz (200 g) aged Cheddar cheese,
  Red Leicester cheese, or similar,
  grated or crumbled

flour, for dusting

1 egg yolk + 1 Tbsp milk, for egg wash

Preheat your oven to 425°F and line two baking sheets with parchment paper.

Put the flour, baking powder, sugar, and salt in a bowl and rub in the butter with your fingers until the mixture resembles breadcrumbs. Add the eggs and then the lemon juice. Add the milk, a little at a time, and mix with a spatula until you have a soft and slightly sticky dough. Add two-thirds of the cheese and mix well.

Place the dough on a generously floured work surface and gently knead it together until all the flour is incorporated and the dough no longer sticks but still feels soft. This takes around 1 minute. Flatten the dough with your hands until it's about ¾ inch (2 cm) thick. Use a piece of parchment paper to smooth the top of the dough to give the scones a nice finish.

Using a 2-inch (5-cm) round cutter for small scones or a 2¾-inch (7-cm) cutter for large scones, cut out the scones by pushing the cutter straight down. Don't twist the cutter, as this will affect how much the scones rise. Pat the remaining dough back together and cut out more scones until you have used all the dough.

Place the scones on the baking sheets and brush with the egg wash. Cover the scones with the reserved cheese. Bake in the middle of the oven for 10–15 minutes until the scones have risen and are golden in color.

Transfer the scones to a wire rack to cool slightly. Cover them with a tea towel to keep them warm and soft. Scones must be eaten the same day they are made, or reheated in the oven. They can also be frozen, thawed, and revived in a hot oven.

These scones are also very tasty with a blue-vein cheese, such as Stilton or Fourme d'Ambert. Just use all of the cheese in the dough instead. Serve the scones plain or with butter.

The daily bread

The earliest bread was made with grain that had to be ground using a labor-intensive, manual grindstone called a hand quern. Grinding even a small amount of grain was a time-consuming and tedious task that made a very gritty, dense bread that wreaked havoc on people's teeth. With the advent of grain mills in medieval times, powered by animals, water, or wind to grind the grain between two large stones, people could buy flour or take their grain to the mill to be milled into flour in exchange for a fee or a portion of their harvest. These mills were usually maintained by a monastery or feudal lords. The Domesday Book lists around 6000 mills in England in 1086.

Bread was the cornerstone of the diet of ordinary people for centuries. As a symbol of life, bread was central to rural, often pagan, religious festivities. While breads indented with a cross were baked by pagans for the goddess Eostre, Christians saw bread as the body of Christ. The harvest loaf (see page 15) in the shape of a wheat sheaf is a large ceremonial bread that still exists today. It was traditionally baked for the harvest festival from the first grain of the season.

The kind of bread people ate in the past depended on their status and the region they were from. While in the South bread was made with a combination of wheat, rye, and barley that was often cropped together and oats were grown solely for animal fodder, in the wetter climate of the North, oats were sometimes the only crop that grew and people depended on it for their survival.

The class difference in bread

Gervase Markham lists three types of bread in his tome, *The English Huswife*, published in 1615. Manchet bread was the bread for the rich and was made from the finest sifted whole-wheat flour, which almost looked white and was leavened with ale barm. Cheat bread was considered bread of middle grade and was made with coarser sifted wheat and leavened with sourdough. It was browner than manchet bread but still not brown, and still bread for the well-to-do. The third category Markham lists is brown bread for servants. This bread was made with barley, malt, rye or wheat, and peas, and leavened with sourdough. It was the coarsest type of bread and would remain the bread of the working class up until the end of the 19th century. A fourth type of bread Markham doesn't list in his cookbook but does give recipes for in another publication is horse-bread, a dense, dark bread made of pulses and a portion of oat flour, barley flour, and/or bran. Even in times of plenty, the poor would have to sustain themselves with the unpalatable yet nutritious bread that was baked for the animals of the rich.

In the 19th century, bread continued to be the most important source of calories, along with the jam or treacle that was spread on top. Eliza Acton states in her book, *Modern Cookery for Private Families*, in 1845 that bread is "the first necessity of life to the great mass of the English people" and it is not unusual "for the entire earnings of a poor hard-working man to be expended upon bread only, for himself and family." The working class still ate brown bread and dreamed of white bread, which was considered a superior product. Because white bread was made from the more expensive wheat flour, things were often added to whiten inferior flour and to stretch it for longer. Chalk, potassium aluminum sulphate, ground-up bones, and other more harmful additions were not uncommon. *The Sale of Food and Drugs Act* prevented this and other adulterations in 1875, but many poor people would have eaten adulterated bread and, in dire need, bread baked for animal fodder for many years of their lives until their early deaths.

Baking the bread

Medieval bread ovens were beehive ovens made of stone and clay, with the name derived from its domed shape, which resembles that of an old-fashioned beehive. From the 16th century up until the end of the 19th century, Devon was well known for its gravel-tempered clay beehive or stone ovens, which were made to be enclosed in raised brickwork or set into fireplaces, leaving the mouth open to the front. They have been found in Wales and Cornwall, and there is evidence some were even exported by new settlers to America. Coal-fired cast-iron kitchen ranges built into the open hearth and including an oven came into use by the end of the 18th century, but even in the 19th century contemporary cookery writers expressed their preference for a brick oven for baking.

These beehive brick ovens were fueled with wooden twigs called faggots, followed by larger logs of wood, and, in later years, coals. When the wood had burnt to ash, the oven would be swept out and the heat inside would be hot enough for baking. When fueled properly, an oven like this could retain heat for at least nine hours. My friend Giulia's brick beehive oven, when fired at five the day before, still gives enough heat the next morning at nine to make it perfect for cooking breakfast.

Only the well-to-do had ovens built into their homes or a separate bakehouse. Working-class people depended on the communal village oven, the local baker, or the ovens from the landlord or monastery. Communal ovens were also integrated into housing developments in new industrial settlements in the late 18th century. People would take their bread dough and even a joint of meat, pies, or cakes and puddings to be baked for either a fee or, in rural areas, a portion of grain. This was often done on the way to church and the baked goods picked up after service.

An actual oven wasn't, and still isn't, the only way to bake a good bread. The Dutch oven is a primitive method where the dough is placed in a heavy, hot cast-iron pot or skillet over a fire and covered with a lid that is then covered with the embers of the fire. Eliza Acton often recommended its use in her *Modern Cookery for Private Families,* and many people still put their bread dough into a cast-iron pot before baking the loaf in a modern oven. The sealed interior traps steam, which mimics a professional steam-injected oven. The surface of the dough stays cooler, actually baking slower, and makes for a crunchier, more flavorsome crust that is beautifully blistered with bubbles and a deeper and more even color. This browning of the crust is called the Maillard reaction.

Baking bread in brick ovens was common until the late 19th century. At the start of the 20th century, gas ovens and electric mixers came into use, and bakers also became confectioners and biscuit makers – previously separate professions. Bakeries now had a shopfront for the first time to fit into the first shopping streets in cities. The people demanded options and the baker gave those options, selling an array of sweet cakes and confections along with a growing range of breads and buns.

"The best thing since sliced bread."

A new type of leaven
Baking soda arrived in kitchens in the 1840s. Unlike the reaction of yeast and sourdough, which needs time and warmth to work, baking soda acts quickly, which is why the breads it produces are called "quick breads." It is usually used for bakes made with flour with a low protein or gluten content like rye, oats, and barley, but today often also with wheat. A bread like this needs to be eaten straight out of the oven because when it cools and sits for a few hours it becomes heavy like a block of clay, as is the case with soda bread. While in the rest of Britain people became obsessed with large white loaves of bread, in the northern regions that depended on the hardier, low-gluten grains like oats and barley, a culture of soda bread and other quick breads or griddle cakes remained the custom.

Industrial bread
The wheat that traditionally grew in Great Britain is a soft wheat with a low protein or gluten content that is unsuitable for large, airy loaves of bread. As a result, harder wheat was imported from Canada and America very early on, but this made bread expensive. After the war years, the British were tired of the brown war bread and craved soft white bread. To meet this demand, Chorleywood research bakers in 1961 developed a method that could make use of British soft wheat and that was ready to bake in a fraction of the time normally required to make a decent bread. Adding hard fats, extra yeast, and a number of chemicals and then mixing the dough at high speed created the iconic British bread: rectangular like a brick, spongy, and presliced into neat square slices. This made the bread cheap, but it also made the bread British. Today the Chorleywood method is used in industrial bakeries worldwide. It meant the end of many small artisan bakeries who had to charge more money for their higher-quality artisan breads.

Britain is experiencing a bread renaissance, with people baking at home and bakeries offering high-quality tin loaves and bloomers and the brown rye sourdoughs we have now come to associate with France. Every bread has its place. The dense brown loaf of the working class is now favored for its nutritional benefits, and the spongy, presliced industrial bread with its neutral flavor is the preferred bread for bacon, sausage, prawn, or crisp sarnies (sandwiches) because it is pliable and has the ability to wrap itself around the filling.

Many people used to think it was great progress to be able to buy a cheap, presliced bread that comes in neat square slices and keeps for a very long time. The phrase "the best thing since sliced bread" is therefore used to refer to a fantastic development or progress.

Cottage loaf

The most widespread forms of British bread today are the bloomer and the tin loaf. Both can be made from the same dough, but the tin loaf is made in a loaf tin (see opposite). An older form of bread is the cottage loaf. This bread is made by stacking two balls of dough, one on top of the other, and perforating the top one, which is smaller, with a stick the width of a thumb to attach it to the larger ball below. According to historians, it's possible that this form became popular because the bakers saved space in their ovens by making higher loaves. In those days, people did not yet have loaf tins that could make it even easier to bake the bread.

The cottage loaf is an old-fashioned shape of bread that fell out of favor with the advent of bread tins, but also because people prefer a loaf that creates tidy, even slices for sandwiches. Slow Food UK reports that this shape of bread was the most popular until the Second World War. In pictures of Victorian and Edwardian bakeries, you'll spot the cottage loaves stacked high in the shop window.

Victorian recipes always call for creating a "sponge" dough with brewer's yeast, water, and flour to ferment before the bread dough is made. This was because the brewer's yeast was much weaker than the commercial yeast strains we know today, and it had to rest for longer in order to do its work properly.

For 1 large loaf

5¾ tsp (18 g) dried yeast

2 cups lukewarm water

6¼ cups (750 g) strong white
  bread flour (see page 16)

2 Tbsp (30 g) butter, lard, or olive oil

2½ tsp fine sea salt

flour, for dusting

Follow the preparation for the classic white tin loaf (see opposite) until after the first rise.

Briefly knead the dough by pulling it from the outside inwards; this will encourage the dough to rise higher instead of expanding wider.

Keep one-third of the dough aside. Shape the rest of the dough into a ball and place it on a baking sheet lined with parchment paper. Now shape the smaller dough portion into a ball and place it on top of the larger ball.

Dust the dough all over with flour. Use a dowel the thickness of your thumb to push a hole down through the upper ball, pressing all the way through the two balls until you feel the sheet underneath.

Cover the bread with a light cotton cloth and wrap it in a large plastic bag (I keep one especially for this purpose). Rest the dough for 1 hour. Towards the end of the resting time, preheat the oven to 450°F.

Leave the top ball as it is or make eight slashes with a sharp knife (this does take some practice). For a nice crust, you can put a heatproof bowl with water in the oven to create steam during baking.

Place the bread in the lower part of the oven. Bake for 15 minutes, then reduce the oven to 375°F and bake for a further 20–25 minutes until your bread is beautifully golden brown. Your bread is ready when it sounds hollow when you tap it on the bottom. Let the bread cool on a wire rack. As long as it is warm, it is still baking.

Classic white tin loaf

It is always my mission to get the best toast, and that is why I add fat to my bread dough. A study by the Good Housekeeping Institute into the best bread for toast showed that a supermarket bread came out as the best and this bread contained fat. The fat ensures that the bread colors nicely and doesn't dry out during toasting, so you get crisp toast with a wonderfully soft interior.

According to Elizabeth David, the tin loaf is a British invention. It allowed bakeries to bake more loaves at once, and at its early inception it was also a very clean alternative to the bread baked straight onto the coal- and wood-fired bread ovens.

For 1 large loaf

3¾ tsp (12 g) dried yeast

1⅓ cups lukewarm water

4¼ cups (500 g) strong white bread flour (see page 16)

1½ Tbsp (20 g) butter, diced

1¾ tsp fine sea salt

butter, for greasing

Variation: You can also bake this bread without using the tin to create a bloomer. Shape the dough into an oval and add diagonal slashes to the top of the loaf before baking.

For a 9 x 5–inch loaf tin

Add the yeast to the lukewarm water and stir briefly and gently to activate it. The yeast will start to foam up in clusters, which means it is ready to use. Put the flour in the bowl of an electric mixer fitted with a dough hook and put the butter on top. Pour half of the yeast mixture over the butter and start kneading. Add the rest of the yeast mixture, little by little. You may not need all of the liquid if your flour is very fresh. If your flour has been in your cupboard for a while, then you definitely need all the liquid.

Knead the dough for 5 minutes, then let it stand for a few minutes. Add the salt and then knead for 10 minutes. Remove the dough from the bowl and knead by hand for a few minutes. (You can, of course, do the entire process by hand.) Put the dough back into the bowl, cover, and set aside to rise until it has doubled, which can take 1–2 hours, depending on how warm the room is.

Briefly knead the dough by pulling it upwards and then pressing it back in again. This prepares the gluten to expand upwards during proofing and baking. Roll the dough into a sausage and tuck the corners underneath. Grease the loaf tin and place your dough in it. Cover the tin with a large plastic bag (I keep one especially for this purpose). Let the dough rise again for 1 hour. Towards the end of the rising time, preheat the oven to 450°F.

Leave the loaf as it is or slash the top with a sharp knife (this takes some practice). For a nice crust, you can put a heatproof bowl with water in the oven to create steam during baking.

Place the tin in the middle of the oven and lower the temperature to 425°F. Bake for 25–30 minutes until your bread is beautifully golden brown. Remove the bread from the tin and bake for another 5 minutes. Your bread is ready when it sounds hollow when you tap it on the bottom. Let the bread cool on a wire rack. As long as it is warm, it is still baking.

Cottage loaf (page 174)

Classic white tin loaf (page 175)

Tea and toast

The British love their toast. In British households, there can be toast at any given time of the day. Toast can be breakfast, spread with butter or jam, accompanied by a cup of steaming tea and a conversation around the kitchen table. Toast can also be snatched out of the toaster and clamped firmly between your teeth while putting on your shoes and rushing out the door in the morning. Toast can be a three-course meal: buttered toast is followed by eggs on toast, baked beans, baked tomatoes, sautéed mushrooms, Marmite for the lovers or avocado for the Millennials. Finally, toast can be dessert, spread with marmalade or jam.

The oldest way to toast bread was with the help of a toaster fork. The slice of bread was punctured onto the toaster fork and turned around in front of an open fire until it was sufficiently toasted. Toasted bread may well be an English invention. In 1748, the Scandinavian visitor Pehr Kalm wrote a theory in his diary about how toasting bread became popular in England:

"The cold rooms here in England in the winter, and because the butter is then hard from the cold, and does not admit of being spread on bread, have perhaps given them the idea thus to toast the bread, then spread butter on it while it is still hot."

Another traveler in England, M. Grosley, wrote the following about the abundant amount of toast in *A Tour to London* from 1772:

"The butter and tea which the Londoners live upon from morning until three or four in the afternoon, occasions the chief consumption of bread, which is cut in slices, and so thin, that it does as much honour to the address of the person that cuts it, as to the sharpness of the knife."

Toast is usually toasted in a toaster today, but a slice of bread can also be sandwiched between two wire frames and toasted on the hob of British traditional stoves such as Esse and Aga. There is really no toast like it – crunchy outside and soft within, especially when the cooker is still running on coals like in the little B&B where we like to stay near Stonehenge.

A much richer version is fried toast, deep-fried or fried in large quantities of butter or lard in a frying pan. This version is reserved for fry-ups (English breakfast) on special occasions when the extra calories and fat are not counted. However, there is a decline in the fried toast that was never missing from a breakfast plate when my parents and I traveled around Britain when I was a child. Fry-ups have become more health conscious, organic at times, with toast no longer immersed in fat, and bacon and sausages coming from happy pigs.

In the *Evening Telegraph* of 1937 an advertisement appeared to popularize toast:
"Eat toasted bread for energy."

Toast can indeed strengthen someone and offer comfort. Heartache and other dramas are also solved by serving the tormented soul a plate of toast and bottomless cups of milky tea with sugar. The British believe that an extra spoonful of sugar in tea is needed to calm the nerves.

Tea is restorative, my English friends have all said more than once – there's nothing a cup of tea can't fix. The first thing offered to you when you come out of surgery in Britain is tea and toast. While in the rest of Europe small children receive a biscuit to chew on, British children are given a slice of toast. Many children get toast with jam as a snack when they return home from school in the afternoon. It is no exaggeration to state that the British are born with a slice of toast in one hand and a cup of tea in the other. For the British, toast is part of their identity.

Soda bread

Soda bread is traditionally made in Scotland and Ireland. It's an unfermented bread that's leavened with baking soda instead of the traditional yeast. It originated from the farl-and-bannock type of quick breads and it was baked on a griddle just like other griddle cakes and quick breads. Soda bread used to be shaped into a flat disc and quartered into farls, but today it is usually baked into loaves.

Eliza Acton explains in her magnificent 1857 book, *The English Bread Book*, how the knowledge of unfermented bread and any other easy method for bread-making was invaluable to people living in remote northern areas, and remarks how the islanders of the Scottish Isle of Skye depended on supplies brought in from Glasgow by steamer boats, often leaving them without when adverse weather prevented the boats from going out to sea. Buttermilk and baking soda are things they would have had in their pantries to make soda breads, scones, and bannocks, which, lacking ovens in their cottages, they would bake on griddles. Acton also suggests that adding a very small amount of sugar improves the bread, and indeed a teaspoonful of dark brown sugar does soften the flavor of the baking soda.

The bread should be eaten as fresh out of the oven as possible, as it becomes rather heavy after it's been left for a while.

For 1 loaf

3⅓ cups (400 g) whole-wheat flour or
  whole-grain spelt flour

1 cup (100 g) oat flour

1 tsp baking soda

1 tsp dark brown sugar

1 tsp sea salt

2 Tbsp (25 g) butter

1½ cups buttermilk or
  ¾ cup yogurt and ¾ cup milk

flour or oat flour, for dusting

butter, for serving

Preheat your oven to 400°F and line a baking sheet or baking tin with parchment paper.

Mix the flours, baking soda, brown sugar, and salt well in a bowl. Rub in the butter, then create a well in the mixture.

Pour the buttermilk or yogurt and milk into the well and stir into the dry ingredients using a wooden spoon. (Once the buttermilk or yogurt is added, it begins to react with the baking soda so from then on you need to work swiftly and get the bread into the oven as quickly as possible or it will become heavy.) When the liquid is incorporated, tip the dough out onto a well-floured work surface. Shape it into a ball with your hands and flatten it slightly.

Transfer the dough to the baking sheet or tin, generously dust the top with flour or oat flour, and score a deep cross in the top with a knife, all the way down but not cutting all the way through.

Bake for 35–40 minutes until the loaf sounds hollow when tapped on the bottom. Leave to rest for a few minutes, but eat while there is still some warmth left in the bread. A lot of butter is essential!

For a variation, instead of just milk or yogurt, you can also add ¾ cup of stout beer with ¾ cup of buttermilk to the dough.

Soft white baps

It is often said mockingly by people from other nations that the British do not have a food culture. However, the people from these isles have more than seven names for a plain soft white bread roll, depending on which region they're from.

A tea cake in West Yorkshire is a plain white roll, but in the rest of the country it contains currants. In other regions you'll find the names cob, bap, morning roll, soft roll, buttery Vienna, oven bottom, Coventry batch, breadcake, scuffler, and muffin, the latter also meaning something entirely different elsewhere. My friend Jo from Lancashire passionately insists that it should be referred to as a barm cake and nothing else.

I've always known these particular buns as baps. The rolls were usually elongated, often with a visible swirl on each end where the dough had been rolled up. These rolls were the type served warm with soup when I was little.

These baps are the ultimate vessel for a bacon butty – a bap filled with fried bacon and sometimes also egg. Fish finger butties are also very tasty because the bap wraps itself well around the fingers, delicious with mayonnaise flavored with chives, tarragon, or pickles and capers. The crispy fish fingers contrast nicely with the soft bun.

For 12 baps

4¾ tsp (15 g) dried yeast

1¼ cups lukewarm water

4¼ cups (500 g) strong white
  bread flour (see page 16)

2 Tbsp (25 g) demerara (coarse raw
  sugar), or granulated white sugar

5 Tbsp (75 g) soft butter or lard,
  in chunks

1 tsp fine sea salt

flour, for dusting

Add the yeast to the lukewarm water and stir briefly and gently to activate it. The yeast will start to foam up in clusters, which means it is ready for use. Combine the flour and sugar in a large bowl or the bowl of an electric mixer fitted with a dough hook and put the butter or lard on top. Pour in half of the yeast mixture and start kneading. When the water and butter or lard have been completely absorbed, add the rest of the yeast mixture. Knead the dough for 5 minutes, then let it stand for a few minutes (at this point the dough will be very wet). Add the salt and then knead for 10 minutes, scraping the dough off the dough hook and sides of the bowl if needed, until the dough has come together in a smooth and elastic dough that is neither too dry nor terribly wet.

Cover the dough and set aside for 1 hour until it has doubled in quantity.

Briefly knead the dough and divide it into 12 equal pieces. Take a piece of dough and lightly flatten it on your work surface, then pull the outer parts in like a purse and gently squeeze together like a dumpling so that the dough can no longer split open while rising. Turn the dough over so the squeezed ends are on the bottom. It should be nice and smooth on top – if not, flatten it and start again. Place on a baking sheet and continue shaping the other baps.

Cover the sheet of baps with a light cotton cloth and wrap it in a large plastic bag (I keep one especially for this purpose). Rest the dough for 1 hour until the baps have doubled in size. Towards the end of the resting time, preheat the oven to 400°F.

Lightly sprinkle the baps with flour and gently flatten them. Bake the buns for about 8–10 minutes until they have a light blush. The baps should be very pale. Cool the baps on a wire rack.

The next day, the baps can be revived in a hot oven for a few minutes. You can also freeze them, thaw, and then pop in a hot oven for a few minutes so your baps are just as they were when they were first baked.

Stottie cakes

A stottie cake, or stotty, is a large, round, dense white loaf that was traditionally about 12 inches in diameter and baked on both the top and bottom sides. It is a working-class staple, particularly in Newcastle, as my friend Emma noted. She never encountered them until she moved to Newcastle in the 1980s.

The first published reference to a stottie cake dates from the *Daily Mirror* of 9 December 1949. The article notes that there is no recipe and, "To make it you simply roll a piece of dough out to about the thickness of one inch, prick it all over with a fork and put it in the bottom of a hot oven." Today some bakers puncture the dough with their thumb to create a dimple, while others still prick the stotties all over with a fork before baking.

To "*stot*" means to bounce in Scottish and in Geordie, which is the vernacular of the Geordies – people from the Tyneside area of north-east England. Some sources claim the bake was tested by bouncing the bread on the floor, which could explain its name, but it could also mean that the bread is so heavy it would "stot" or bounce if you threw it on the floor. Others explain that the stottie was used to test the oven temperature, although why would you bake them in quantity to sell if the stottie's sole use was to test the oven?

The bread's characteristics also match those of "oven-bottom breads," the flat, dense bread buns that are baked on the bottom of the bread oven with the leftover dough. However, those were hardly ever baked on both sides as stotties are. From testing the bake, it is my belief that stotties are a type of griddle cake or flatbread, made with the soft wheat available in England and ale barm, and baked on a very hot surface that would have created a heavy, doughlike bread with a pale, barely baked rim. It could have been baked in a skillet or on a griddle and turned mid-baking, just like a Scottish bannock or an English muffin. Or it may have been baked on the bottom of the hot baking oven like oven bottom breads or Indian naan, then turned over and left to bake on the other side in the falling oven temperature.

Highstreet bakery Greggs, which started as a small Tyneside bakery in 1939, has been baking stotties in the region for nearly 50 years. That isn't surprising, since the company is headquartered in North Tyneside, near Newcastle where the

stottie originated. In 2010, "Ham and Pease pudding Stotties," which are the traditional sandwich combination, were briefly taken out of the shop window, causing outrage from local people. Pease pudding is a spread made of cooked peas – the English answer to hummus (see my book, *Pride and Pudding*, for a pease pudding recipe).

The stottie cake was immortalized by a local newspaper photographer who photographed Muhammad Ali devouring a dinner plate–sized stottie cake topped with seeds and stuffed with lettuce, onion, cucumber, and tomato during a visit to Newcastle in 1977. To create the most authentic possible recipe for a stottie (as there are none in my old cookbooks), I enlisted my friend Emma. She showed the pictures of my test bakes to her Geordie friends and in particular to a woman who had Muhammad Ali over for afternoon tea when he visited in that year he was photographed with the stottie. It turns out that the pale-rimmed, dimpled stottie is what most people remember. The dinner plate–sized stottie is more modern and baked for longer, less dense, and usually sold halved or quartered as a sandwich.

This recipe makes two large stotties that serve two or four, or four individual ones. The stottie's dense nature makes it a perfect partner to a bowl of soup. They also make perfect sandwiches and the next day they are great halved, toasted, and topped with scrambled or poached eggs.

For 2 large or 4 individual stotties

4¾ tsp (15 g) dried yeast

1½ cups lukewarm water

4 cups (500 g) plain white flour

1 tsp (5 g) demerara (coarse raw sugar),
   or granulated white sugar

4 Tbsp (60 g) lard or soft butter,
   in chunks

1¾ tsp fine sea salt

flour, for dusting

Stotties keep best in an airtight container or a plastic bag. Individual stotties stay soft and fresh for up to 3 days, while the larger ones become harder and are best eaten within 2 days. They are easily revived by popping them in a hot oven the next day or by toasting them. They make a very filling sarnie (sandwich), but you do need to get used to their wonderfully pillowy doughiness.

Add the yeast to the lukewarm water and stir briefly and gently to activate it. The yeast will start to foam up in clusters, which means it is ready for use. Combine the flour and sugar in a large bowl or the bowl of an electric mixer fitted with a dough hook and put the lard or butter on top. Pour in half of the yeast mixture and start kneading. When the water and lard or butter are completely absorbed, add the rest of the yeast mixture. Knead the dough for 5 minutes, then let it stand for a few minutes (at this point the dough will be very wet). Add the salt and then knead for 10 minutes, scraping the dough off the dough hook and sides of the bowl if needed, until the dough has come together in a smooth and elastic dough that is neither too dry nor terribly wet.

Cover the dough and set aside for 1 hour until it has doubled in quantity. Meanwhile, line a tray or board with parchment paper and dust with flour.

Briefly knead the dough and divide it into two or four equal pieces. Take a piece of dough and lightly flatten it on your work surface, then pull the outer parts in like a purse and gently squeeze together like a dumpling so that the dough can no longer split open while rising. Turn the dough over so the squeezed ends are on the bottom. It should be nice and smooth on top – if not, flatten it and start again. Place the buns on the tray or board, dust with flour and press them down to a flat disc with a thickness of ½ inch.

Cover the tray and buns with a light cotton cloth and rest for just 10 minutes while you preheat the oven to 500°F. Pop a well-greased baking sheet, baking stone, or griddle into the oven to heat up.

Push your finger into the center of each stottie until you feel the bottom, or prick all over with a fork. Carefully transfer the stotties onto the hot baking sheet – you might have to bake them in batches. Bake for 3 minutes, then turn with a spatula and bake for another 10–12 minutes until the middle of the stotties are golden brown. If you're making large stotties, bake them for 20 minutes on each side.

Kentish huffkin

Legend has it that the baker's wife, who was in a bad mood or a "huff," walked into the bakery and angrily stuck her finger in the buns that were ready to go into the oven. The baker stubbornly baked them like that, and it turned out that the dimpled buns were very popular!

For 12 huffkins

4¾ tsp (15 g) dried yeast

¾ cup lukewarm whole milk

4¼ cups (500 g) strong white bread flour (see page 16)

1½ Tbsp (20 g) demerara (coarse raw sugar), or granulated white sugar

4 Tbsp (60 g) soft butter or lard, in chunks

½ cup + 2 Tbsp lukewarm water

1 tsp fine sea salt

flour, for dusting

Add the yeast to the lukewarm milk and stir briefly and gently to activate it. The yeast will start to foam up in clusters, which means it is ready for use. Combine the flour and sugar in a large bowl or the bowl of an electric mixer fitted with a dough hook and put the butter or lard on top. Pour in half of the yeast mixture and start kneading. When the milk and the lard or butter are completely absorbed, add the rest of the yeast mixture, followed by the lukewarm water. Knead the dough for 5 minutes, then let it stand for a few minutes (at this point the dough will be very wet). Add the salt and then knead for 10 minutes, scraping the dough off the dough hook and sides of the bowl if needed, until the dough has come together in a smooth and elastic dough that is neither too dry nor terribly wet.

Leave the dough covered for 1 hour until it has doubled in quantity.

Briefly knead the dough and divide it into 12 equal pieces. Take a piece of dough and lightly flatten it on your work surface, then pull the outer parts in like a purse and gently squeeze together like a dumpling so that the dough can no longer split open while rising. Turn the dough over so the squeezed ends are on the bottom. It should be nice and smooth on top – if not, flatten it and start again. Place on a baking sheet and continue shaping the dough.

Cover the sheet of buns with a light cotton cloth and wrap it in a large plastic bag (I keep one especially for this purpose). Rest the dough for 1 hour or until the buns have doubled in size. Towards the end of the resting time, preheat the oven to 400°F.

Dust the huffkins with flour and gently pat them down a little to flatten them. Push your finger into each bun until you feel the sheet. I can never get enough of the sensation of making dimples in the dough! Bake the buns for about 15–20 minutes until golden brown.

The next day, the buns can be revived in a hot oven for a few minutes. You can also freeze the baked buns, thaw, and then pop in a hot oven for a few minutes so your buns are just as they were when they were first baked.

Aberdeen buttery rowie

In the winter of 2017, I was invited to give a talk about British puddings at the University of Aberdeen. It was minus 10 degrees, so I warmed the attendees who had braved the snow with hot steamed plum pudding. On my walk across the great "Granite City" the next day in search of the local fare, the Scottish photographer Del Sneddon pointed me towards the Aberdeen buttery. It brought me to a bakery in a side street that I probably wouldn't have walked into if not for my search for rowies. The elderly shoplady was proud to tell me all about rowies, for which the bakery was famous.

At first glance, a rowie looks a bit like an unfortunate croissant that you find in the bottom of your bag, crushed by a bag of apples or a stack of books. But it is when you taste a rowie that you learn about its appeal, because it has the richness of a croissant with a bonus of extra heartiness through the addition of lard.

The rowie is a pillar of working-class cuisine and was traditionally eaten for breakfast by workers and fishermen, who could benefit from an extra layer of fat to keep them warm or keep them going. In 1917, the bakeries were briefly forbidden from baking rowies as a result of the introduction of war bread and price controls, much to the dismay of the bakers and their customers. Even the unions protested, stating that the rowie was not bread as defined by the regulations and that it was an important part of the working-class diet. In the *Aberdeen Evening Express*, it was written that the workers' breakfast consisted of porridge and milk, followed by a cup of tea and a buttery rowie.

Every bakery has its own way of making rowies, so it is difficult to establish a recipe. To make rowies you have to push the butter and lard mixture into the dough with your fingertips, just like the Italians do with olive oil while making focaccia. This process ensures that the rowies become soft rather than crisp.

For 14 rowies

2¼ tsp (7 g) dried yeast

1¼ cups lukewarm water

4¾ cups (450 g) plain white flour

2½ tsp (10 g) granulated white sugar

1½ tsp fine sea salt

flour, for dusting

For the filling

1 cup (255 g) butter, at room temperature

½ cup (100 g) lard, at room temperature

Add the yeast to the lukewarm water and stir briefly and gently to activate it. The yeast will start to foam up in clusters, which means it is ready for use.

Mix the flour, sugar, and salt in a large bowl and make a well. Pour the yeast mixture into the well and use a wooden spoon or spatula to mix everything together. Knead for 5 minutes until the mixture forms a smooth dough.

Put the dough back into the bowl, cover, and set aside for 1 hour until it has doubled in quantity.

Meanwhile, for the filling, mix the butter and the lard well and divide the mixture into four portions. This mixture must be spreadable, so leave it at room temperature.

Briefly knead the dough on a floured work surface, then pat it into a rectangle and roll it out into a 18 x 10 inch rectangle that's ½ inch thick. Place the dough lengthwise in front of you.

Spread one of the butter and lard portions over two-thirds of the left-hand side of the dough rectangle. The easiest way to spread the mixture is with your hands, but be careful not to tear the dough; if it does not spread properly, the fat mixture is too cold. The warmth of your hands should help the mixture to spread.

Working from the right-hand side, fold one-third of the dough over onto itself. Then, working from the left-hand side, fold one-third of the dough over the top of the folded dough. Push your fingertips into the folded dough so that the butter and lard mixture mixes with the dough.

Re-roll the dough into a 18 x 10 inch rectangle that's ½ inch thick and repeat the process until you have used up all of the butter and lard mixture.

Roll out the dough once more to a 18 x 10 inch rectangle that's ½ inch thick. Push your fingers into the dough again, but not as deep this time – this gives the traditional face of the rowies. Cut the dough into 14 squares and place them on a baking sheet lined with parchment paper.

Cover the sheet of rowies with a light cotton cloth and wrap it in a large plastic bag (I keep one especially for this purpose). Rest the dough for 1 hour until the rowies have doubled in size. Towards the end of the resting time, preheat the oven to 400°F.

Bake the rowies in the middle of the oven for 20–25 minutes until they are slightly golden brown – the color of honey. Let the rowies cool on a wire rack. They will keep for a few days in an airtight container and can also be frozen.

The "Granite City," Aberdeen, Scotland

Aberdeen buttery rowie (pages 188–189)

Pies and tarts

Britain is a pie country. You'll find pies in the pub, at the bakery, at the butcher, at markets, at fairs, and at home. Although the whole of Europe made meat pies during the Renaissance, it is in Britain that they remain firmly engraved in the identity of the cuisine and culture. A pie can be sweet, savory, or both, as in the meaty mince pies on page 222 that give you a taste of medieval flavors when the boundary between sweet and savory had not yet been determined.

A pie doesn't have to have a pastry bottom and sides, as long as it has a lid made of pastry. Cornish pasties look more like a pastry envelope and are actually hand pies that were taken into the mines. The "Pie & Mash shop" pies were the food of the workers in London, while pork pies formed the lunch of the hunters and are now made famous by a little town that gives its name to Melton Mowbray pork pies.

For hundreds of years, pies – "bake metes" in Middle English – were made exclusively as a means to cook the food inside them, trapping the juices to prevent the meat or fish from drying out but also to prevent it from burning. The crust, originally called a coffin, acted as a baking dish to prepare and serve its contents, which was then divided among dinner guests. It was made of only flour and water, and had to be sturdy and thick to withstand the heat of the temperamental wood-burning ovens and fireplaces. The pastry remnants would not have been eaten by the well-to-do for whom these pies were baked. Instead they would have ended up in alms vessels for the poor, who welcomed a crust with a whiff and taste of whatever had been cooked inside. Often these pie crusts were simply re-used to thicken stews and sauces.

Large pies were often adorned with the feathers and taxidermy head of the game birds that were cooked inside, or with pastry decorations. This meant that guests would know what meat was in each of the pies without having to ask. This custom is also a remnant of medieval times, when it was fashionable to roast a swan, peacock, or crane and sew it back into its feathers for theatrical effect. An eye-catcher like this was called a "subtletie."

As ovens and cooking techniques slowly became more sophisticated, the recipes for the crust became more delicate too, adding fat to the dough and later sugar for sweet pies. The crust was no longer just the decorated baking dish, it was now part of the dish. In the 17th century, it was fashionable to make pies with "cut lids." Templates for different types of these pastry lids, all coordinating with pie recipes within the book, were tucked into Robert May's cookbook *The Accomplisht Cook*, which was published the year of the Restoration in 1660. In a book called *The Queen's Royal Cookery*, published in 1711, we find templates for differently shaped sweet and savory pies and mince pies that form a pattern when placed together. The author specifies shapes for apple, gooseberry, lamb, or mince pie, and the engravings suggest where the pies should be on the table when serving.

Impressive pies like the Yorkshire Christmas pie on page 196 and fruit and mince pies have featured in cookbooks for centuries, but the pies of the working-class people remain solely in the work of diarists like Henry Mayhew, who published an impressive set of interviews with ordinary working people in the middle of the 19th century. On pie sellers, he notes that the "trade in pies is one of the most ancient of the street callings of London." Piemen sold their pies from portable "pie cans," which looked like square tin boxes about 24 inches high where the pies were kept warm by means of a coal fire beneath. The gravy was poured out of an oil can into the pie-crust hole, but consisted only of browned water and salt. The meat pies were made of beef or mutton; the fish pies of eels; the fruit pies of apples, currants, gooseberries, plums, damsons, cherries, raspberries, or rhubarb, according to the season – and occasionally of mincemeat. Even though the selling of pies in the street had been around for centuries, Mayhew remarks that it has now (in the mid-1800s) been destroyed by a new phenomenon, the "pie shops" (see "Pie & Mash shop" beef pies on page 208).

Pie institutions
The first recorded Pie & Mash shop was Henry Blanchard's at Union Street in Southwark, which opened in 1844. It was described as an "Eel Pie House." Eels were one of the few fish that could survive in the heavily polluted River Thames and they were plentiful, making them perfect food for the working classes. Eel pies became convenient food to serve to large crowds and on Eel Pie Island, a small island in the Thames, the Eel Pie Island Hotel served them to Victorian day trippers in the 19th century. The hotel later became rather iconic, hosting concerts with rock legends The Rolling Stones, The Who, David Bowie, Genesis, and Black Sabbath.

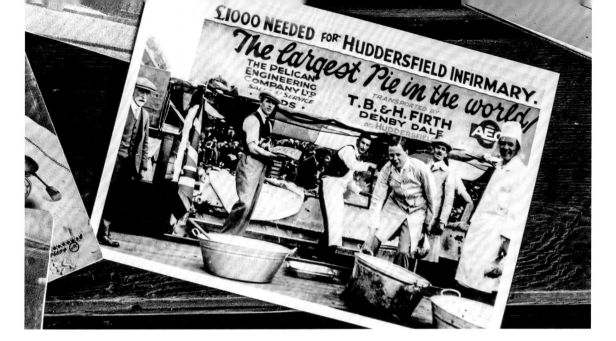

Denby Dale pies

In the Yorkshire town of Denby Dale, they like to bake a big pie.

No one knows just why Denby Dale decided to start baking giant pies. The first one was baked in the White Hart pub in 1788 to celebrate that the "Mad King" George III had come back to his senses. The second was baked in 1815 for the victory in the Battle of Waterloo. A third pie was baked in 1846 to celebrate the repeal of the corn laws that kept the price of grain imports high for 30 years. The law was enforced to keep grain prices high to favor domestic producers, which led many to starvation.

Then, after decades of no pie, the Jubilee Pie was baked in 1887 in honor of Queen Victoria's golden jubilee. However, something went terribly wrong and the pie turned bad due to a combination of careless cooks and a hot summer day. To great embarrassment, the rotten pie was buried in a field near the village. A week later, the women of the village took pie matters into their own hands and baked a new pie to save the village's reputation. This pie was called the Resurrection Pie.

Sometimes an excuse was also sought for something to celebrate. The seventh pie was baked in 1928 to raise money for the local hospital. A large brick oven was also constructed that year to bake the giant Infirmary Pie. Newspapers of the time reported that 40,000 people had shared a piece of this pie.

In 1953, the village wanted to bake a Coronation Pie for Queen Elizabeth II's coronation, but due to war rationing they had to apply to the Ministry of Food for a special allocation of meat and fat. The application was turned down and the pie couldn't be baked, but in 1964 the pie committee decided to bake another pie, this time for the occasion of the birth of four royal children. Any excuse for a pie was good, and for generations they had been waiting in Denby Dale for a new giant pie. It was such an occasion that four members of the pie committee, including the lead baker, were invited to ITV studios near London to film a program about the pie. Tragically, they all died in a car accident on the way home. It was then decided that the pie baking would continue as planned to honor the dead, and the proceeds from this gigantic pie went to building the Denby Dale Pie Hall. The giant pie dish of this pie is now a flowerbed outside its walls.

The Bicentenary Pie was baked in 1988 to commemorate 200 years since the first pie was baked. The BBC came to broadcast the event live and 60,000 people had a piece of the pie. This pie went into *The Guinness Book of Records* as the biggest pie in the world. The last pie was baked in the year 2000 as the Millennium Pie and it was the largest yet, using 5 tons of beef, 2 tons of potatoes, 1 ton of onions, and 200 pints of bitter beer. The pie dish was 40 feet long, 9 feet wide, and 3 feet deep.

In the meantime, it's been decades since the folk of Denby Dale baked a giant pie. I wonder what's keeping them...

Hot water crust pastry

Hot water crust pastry is the most forgiving type of pastry. It doesn't judge you by your experience, and even when you fail, it allows you to start again and make it better – that is, if you keep it warm. When it cools, it doesn't stretch and it will break, and become more demanding.

Hot water crust is sturdier and therefore may be a little less elegant than shortcrust or puff pastry, but as a result it can also handle wetter and heavier fillings without fear of sinking, leakage, or dreaded soggy bottoms. The pastry holds up and sculpts very well and is therefore ideal for hand-raising pies, molding the pastry around a pie dolly or pie block, and for free-standing pies, where the pie mold or tin is lined with pastry and then removed before the last stretch of baking. It should certainly not be kneaded too much – just enough to make sure that everything is blended well. Overworked hot water crust pastry turns into a tougher, chewier crust, but this doesn't mean the result will be inedible, just that it could be better.

Because the fat for the hot water crust is melted, it is much better distributed throughout the dough, which creates a consistent pastry that will color much more evenly while it bakes. Other pastry methods require you to rub the fat into the flour with your fingers, which can lead to inconsistencies in the color of the baked result.

Except for pork pies and Scotch pies, the dough should not be rested before use as it tends to toughen up, dry out, and crumble when cooled. For large pies using a tall game pie mold, you need the pastry to be warm, which means it is pliable so that the pastry can sink into the mold and take its shape, building it up the sides and molding it with your fingers. In contrast, filled pork pies should be rested in the fridge before baking, and for Scotch pies the pastry cases are rested before they are filled and closed. As they are baked without the support of a tin, the pastry has to be dried out to keep its shape while baking. Pastry that has rested also yields a better color when baked. When the pie goes into the oven, the water in the pastry evaporates and the dough becomes crisp. You don't have to grease your tin or mold because the pastry contains enough fat and will never stick.

Of all the different types of pastry, hot water crust is the pastry that is most closely related to the pastry used for the large, impressive pies in the Middle Ages and the Early Modern period. To make your pies look even more impressive, roll out any leftover pastry, let it cool and dry out for half an hour to make it more sturdy, and then cut or stamp out your decoration.

I adore hot water crust pastry because of its versatility and its ability to hold the most challenging fillings and make it look effortless. Even though it's the sturdiest of pastries, I like to compare it to a strong woman who, even though she's had to deal with a lot, on the outside looks incredibly elegant and dignified. A large pie like the ones you find in these pages will impress your dinner guests and make a wonderful table decoration at the same time.

For the hot water crust

3½ cups (415 g) plain white flour

3½ cups (415 g) strong white bread flour (see page 16)

1 egg

½ cup (115 g) butter, at room temperature

1¼ cups water

⅔ cup (150 g) lard

1½ tsp sea salt

flour, for dusting

1 egg yolk + 1 Tbsp milk, for egg wash

Place the flours in a large bowl, mix in the egg and place the soft butter in pieces on top. Bring the water to a boil in a saucepan with the lard and salt, but turn off the heat as soon as it starts to bubble. Set aside until the lard has melted.

Pour the hot mixture over the butter and flour and use a wooden spoon or spatula to mix everything together. Once the dough has cooled down sufficiently that you can touch it with your hands, knead it into a soft dough.

Follow your recipe for further instructions.

Yorkshire Christmas pie

Yorkshire Christmas pies are probably the most impressive pies in the English repertoire that have survived through time. The filling of the pie consists of a remarkable combination: a boned turkey filled with a boned goose, chicken, partridge, and pigeon. The stuffed turkey was then placed into the crust and more meat was put around it as a filler.

In an 18th-century recipe from Hannah Glasse, hare was used to fill the gaps to the left and right of the turkey. In a recipe from Maria Eliza Ketelby Rundell from 1807, she says that the decoration on the top of the pie must be in the shape of a flower, and in her recipe the outer pieces of meat were replaced by a minced meat mixture so that the filling held together when cut.

These pies were often given as Christmas gifts in the 18th century. People in the countryside would even send a pie many miles away, with reports stating that pies that arrived were a health hazard. Their pastry crusts would be made inches thick so they would survive a journey in a horse-drawn carriage, yet they didn't think that the pies should remain cooled.

Engravings of the period show that in 1858 a Yorkshire Christmas pie was served to the Queen at Windsor Castle. The pie was beautifully decorated but also so incredibly large that it had to be carried into the room on the shoulders of four footmen. It would have been a statement piece, just as it was intended to be in earlier centuries.

These types of elaborate pies were the privilege of the very rich, not only because of the pricey contents, but also the precious copper molds that were often used to create them. Only the kitchens of the grandest houses owned one of these game pie molds and they are rarely found today. I stumbled upon one a couple of years ago in an antiques store and it was the price of a small second-hand car. I was very tempted.

The authentic Yorkshire Christmas pie was made by actually stuffing the birds one inside another and then sewing the birds closed, but to get a more refined result it is best to work with fillets and use the surplus meat for another dish or very finely chop it to use instead of the minced (coarsely ground) meat. From the bones you can make broth, which is then reduced to an aspic or jelly that, just like in the pork pies, was subsequently poured through the opening in the crust lid.

For 8–10 people

For the pie

1 lb (450 g) chicken breast

12 oz (350 g) partridge breast

10–11 oz (300 g) pheasant breast

3 oz (80 g) small rooster or
  quail breast

2 saddles of wild hare – about 8 oz
  (250 g), or replace with extra poultry

2½ Tbsp (14 g) ground mace

2½ Tbsp (14 g) ground nutmeg

1 Tbsp + 1 tsp (7 g) ground cloves
  or allspice

2½ Tbsp (14 g) ground black pepper

6 Tbsp–½ cup Madeira or sherry

4 oz smoked bacon, thinly sliced

For the filling

1 lb (450 g) minced (coarsely ground)
  meat (chicken, pork, lamb or off-cuts
  from the poultry used)

2 Tbsp finely chopped flat-leaf parsley

2 tsp finely chopped thyme

pinch of sea salt

For the hot water crust

1 quantity Hot Water Crust Pastry,
  page 194

For a large (2-kg/4.4-lb) game pie mold

Marinate the poultry and the hare a day in advance: mix the meat well with the spices and put it in a resealable plastic bag or a deep bowl. Pour the Madeira or sherry over the mixture, seal or cover, and leave to rest in the fridge for a few hours or overnight.

Preheat your oven to 375°F.

Mix the minced meat with the herbs and salt. Wash the marinade off the poultry and hare and pat dry with paper towels.

Follow the method for the Hot Water Crust Pastry on page 194. Set aside a third of the pastry to make the lid (if possible, keep it warm on a radiator or stove).

Roll out the remaining pastry until ⅜ inch thick. Form an ellipse, place the mold on top, and cut out two triangles on each end about 4 inches wide. Fold the ends into the middle and place the pastry on the base of the pie mold (you don't need to grease it because the pastry contains enough fat). Open out the pastry and make sure there is still some overhanging the edge to attach the lid later. Push the ends together where you cut out the triangles to create a neat seam. If you have cracks or holes, you can repair them with some leftover pastry, provided it is still warm enough.

When the crust is nicely prepared in the mold, take half of the minced meat and spread it over the bottom of the pie crust. Add the fillets of the smallest bird, followed by the second smallest, then put a layer of bacon strips on top. Place the other fillets on top with a layer of bacon in between until all the poultry is added. Lay the hare saddles on both sides, then cover everything with the other half of the minced meat. The filling should now come higher than the edge of the pie mold so that the top of the pie will have a dome shape.

Roll out the pastry for the lid and cut out a hole in the center. Wet the edges of the crust with water or egg yolk and place the dough lid on top. Cut away the excess pastry and crimp the edges well so that the pie is well sealed. Make decorations for the pie with the leftover pastry. Use egg wash to stick the decorations onto the pie, but don't egg wash the entire pie yet.

Place the pie on a baking sheet lined with parchment paper in the lower part of the oven, reduce the temperature to 325°F, and bake the pie for 4 hours. The pie is cooked when the internal temperature reaches 165°F or higher on a thermometer.

Now, be brave – take the pie out of the pie mold using the special hinges, and apply a layer of egg wash. Return the pie to the oven for another 15–30 minutes of baking.

A meat grinder has different applications to create a rough or fine cut of ground meat; ask your butcher to use a coarser one for these pies. In any case the finest grind of meat should never be used for this book.

Sweet lamb pie

The sweet lamb pie from Eliza Smith's *The Compleat Housewife* from 1727 is a good example of the old style of flavoring food using sweet, sour, and savory in harmony. The flavors come through in layers. The pie isn't sweet but the spices used – nutmeg, mace, and cloves – were once considered sweet spices and used as sweeteners. In addition to these spices, dried fruits and candied peel are added to give extra warmth. The original recipe calls for Spanish potato, which is sweet potato, and artichoke hearts. If they're not in season, use a handful of scalded grapes instead.

The pie can be made in a springform tin or a game pie mold, or you can just make a pastry lid and make the pie in a dish. In this case, the pastry crust does still act as the baking dish as the content is like a stew, scooped out and divided among guests. When I was a guest at food historian Ivan Day's house, he made his version of this pie for an extraordinary dinner and cut the pastry lid into wedges so that everyone had a piece of the crust. This is an elegant way to serve the dish and I encourage you to do the same. I like using barberries in combination with currants for some extra tartness.

For 4 people

For the pie

14 oz (400 g) leg of lamb, deboned

1 tsp ground nutmeg

4 cloves, ground

¼ tsp ground mace

⅛ tsp ground black pepper

10–11 oz (300 g) minced lamb neck

1 Tbsp chopped flat-leaf parsley

½ cup (50 g) dried barberries and/or currants

10–11 oz (300 g) sweet potato, peeled, cut into ½-inch dice, and cooked

6 oz (150 g) artichoke hearts, cooked and cut into ½-inch dice

1 Tbsp (10 g) candied citrus peel, finely chopped

For the hot water crust

1 quantity Hot Water Crust Pastry, page 194

For the sauce

juice of 1 lemon

the same amount of white wine

1 tsp granulated white sugar

1 egg yolk

1 tsp butter

For a 7-inch-wide, 2¾-inch-high springform cake tin or a 9-inch (2-kg/4.4-lb) game pie mold

Cut the lamb into ¾-inch chunks and dust with half of the spices. Add the other half of the spices to the minced meat and use your hands to mix the spices with the meat. Mix in the parsley and 2 tablespoons of the barberries or currants, then roll the mixture into meatballs.

Preheat your oven to 400°F and line the base of the springform tin with parchment paper. (If using a game pie mold, follow the instructions for shaping the pastry in the Yorkshire Christmas pie recipe on page 197.)

Follow the method for the Hot Water Crust Pastry on page 194. Set aside a third of the pastry to make the lid (if possible, keep it warm on a radiator or stove). Roll out the remaining pastry until ⅜ inch thick. Place the pastry in the tin, mold it up the sides, and make sure that there is some dough overhanging the edge to attach the pastry lid later. If you have cracks or holes, you can repair them with some leftover pastry.

Put some chunks of meat, meatballs, sweet potato, and artichoke into the pastry crust and sprinkle some barberries or currants and candied peel over the top. Continue making layers of filling until the tin or mold is full. Roll out the pastry for the lid until ⅜ inch thick. Make a hole in the top for the steam to escape. Brush the edge of the crust with the egg wash and place the pastry lid on top. Cut away the excess pastry and crimp the edges together. Decorate the pie as desired with the excess pastry and egg wash.

Bake the pie in the middle of the oven for 30 minutes, then reduce the oven to 325°F and bake for another 1¾ hours.

When the pie is ready, make the sauce. Bring the lemon juice and wine to a boil with the sugar. Beat the egg yolk in a bowl and add the warm sauce gradually while whisking, as you would for a custard. Finish with a little butter and gently reheat. Pour the sauce through the hole in the top of the pie. Serve by cutting around the lid and slicing the pastry into wedges. Scoop out the filling and divide it among your guests.

Derby picnic pie with eggs

In 1900, Frederick Vine published the recipe for a derby pie in one of his books. At first I thought the pie was named after the county of Derby or Derbyshire, but thanks to the introduction to Vine's recipe, I discovered that this pie was so named because it was a popular snack at derby picnic parties. In the past it was popular for people to make a day out of the local derby – a football match between two local teams. There were very extensive picnic options and sometimes people even brought their servants and furniture along to picnic in style and splendor.

Derby picnic parties sometimes turned out very badly, when the pie, which contains cold meat, was kept in unsuitable conditions. The *Manchester Courier and Lancashire General Advertiser* of 16 September 1902 recorded the story "Deadly derby pie." Two older people brought a Derby pie to a party where the pie, which had gone off, made six people sick, one of them fatally. These types of unfortunate events were so common that the culprit was named "salmonella derby." If you keep this pie in the fridge, I can assure you there will be no safety hazard!

Derby pie is still made in a simplified form today, ideal for a picnic or lunch party. You make the pie in advance and on the day it makes a festive table decoration.

This recipe is made with ham hock and minced pork, but 19th-century recipes also suggest veal, chicken, and tongue. Certainly worth a try!

For 8–10 people

For the ham hock

1 onion

1 carrot

1 rib celery

3 leeks

1 ham hock/rear shank

1 Tbsp ground black pepper

1 bay leaf

butter, for frying

For the filling

4 eggs

6 oz (150 g) ham hock

1 lb (430 g) pork shoulder, finely chopped or coarsely minced

8 oz (200 g) pork belly, finely chopped or coarsely minced

¼ cup flat-leaf parsley, minced

¼ tsp ground mace

1 tsp sea salt

1 tsp ground black pepper

10–11 oz (300 g) smoked bacon, thinly sliced

For the hot water crust

1 quantity Hot Water Crust Pastry, page 194

English mustard, for serving

For a 9 x 5-inch loaf tin

Prepare the ham hock a day in advance. Chop the vegetables and briefly fry them in butter in a deep flameproof casserole dish. Add the ham and enough water so that the ham is completely covered, then add the pepper and bay leaf and simmer for 2–3 hours until the meat falls off the bone easily. Remove the ham and let it cool. You can use the cooking liquid as the basis for a soup, such as pea soup. If there is excess ham, you can also add this to your soup.

Now on to the filling. I'm going to tell you how to cook an egg because, let's be honest, we often mess up the simplest things. I start with boiling water, add the eggs, turn down the heat, and cook for 9 minutes for an almost hard-boiled egg with a soft yolk. In this way, the egg can continue to cook during the baking of the pie without becoming too dry. Run the egg under cold water to stop the cooking process and immediately peel it while wet because this is the easiest way to do it. Set the egg aside while you prepare the rest of the filling.

Finely chop the ham hock and measure out 6 oz (150 g) of meat for the filling. Place in a bowl with the chopped or minced meat, parsley, mace, salt, and pepper and knead together. Cover and place in the fridge while you make the pastry.

Preheat your oven to 375°F. Drape the loaf tin with a strip of parchment paper so that the pie can be easily removed later. Greasing is not necessary because the dough itself contains enough fat.

Follow the method for the Hot Water Crust Pastry on page 194. Set aside a third of the pastry to make the lid (if possible, keep it warm on a radiator or stove).

Roll out the remaining pastry until ⅜ inch thick. Fold the pastry inward and place it in the tin. Now fold up the sides and let the excess pastry hang over the edges of the tin.

Line the pastry with the strips of bacon, letting the ends hang over the sides of the tin. Add half of the meat mixture and gently press it into the sides of the tin. Place the eggs on top of the meat and press them into the meat slightly so they stand upright. Add the rest of the meat mixture to fill up the pie. Fold the bacon over the meat, adding more strips so that the entire outside of the filling is covered with bacon.

Roll out the remaining pastry for the lid, brush the edges with the egg wash, and put the lid on top. Trim the excess pastry and crimp the pastry together with your fingers. Decorate with the excess pastry and brush the top with egg wash.

Reduce the oven to 350°F and bake the pie for 1½ hours. The pie is cooked when the internal temperature reaches 185°F on a thermometer. You can remove the pie from the tin 15 minutes before it is ready and brush the sides with egg wash before returning it to the oven to continue baking.

Let the pie cool completely before serving, or keep it well covered in the fridge for up to 3 days. A sharp English mustard is a perfect match and an absolute must!

Derby picnic pie with eggs (pages 202–203)

Pork pies

There is a town in the landlocked Midlands that is famous for its pork pies. A blue commemorative plaque in Melton Mowbray celebrates Edward Adcock as the first baker to have produced the Melton Mowbray pork pie, in 1831. Indeed, advertisements from the mid-19th century show that the Melton Mowbray pork pie was by then considered a local speciality. The Melton Mowbray pork pie is the only pie to have received a protected PGI status from the EU. The PGI statement explains that pork pies became popular in the region after the Enclosure Acts turned traditional sheep farming into controlled cattle husbandry. The surplus cow's milk was turned into another local product, Blue Stilton, and the whey, a by-product of cheese production, went to pig farms to be part of animal feed. With the arrival of fox hunting in the area and pig slaughtering coinciding with the hunting season, pork pies formed the perfect seasonal food for the hunters, or most likely their servants, to carry with them on the hunt.

While pork pies have not changed much in 200 years, quality did vary. There were times in Victorian London when there was a lot of talk in the streets about the dubious content of pork pies. A penny dreadful by James Malcolm Rymer and Thomas Peckett Prest, *The String of Pearls*, is a story written in the 19th century about the dark, tormented barber Sweeney Todd and his henchman, Mrs Lovett, who turned Todd's murdered customers into cheap meat pies.

Most butchers I talked to prefer pork shoulder with an addition of fat from the belly or back, and most use uncured pork. Some use a proportion of gammon (cured ham) or cured bacon to give a pinker color to the filling. The meat for Melton Mowbray pork pies should never be cured, but of course that's up to you. A stiff jelly is made to pour into the cooled pie to fill the cavity between the meat and the crust. This originally served as a preservative, but it is not a must today as not all pie makers use it for their pies. Pork trotters are the best bones to use for jelly and they're something you can buy cheaply at your butcher. The seasoning is simple: fresh sage, salt, pepper, and often nutmeg and mace.

Pork pies are usually eaten cold and are therefore a perfect pie for a picnic or lunch on the go. It is traditional to make this pie with hot water crust pastry, hand-raising it using a wooden pie dolly or pie block, giving it its slightly bow-walled shape when baked. Small pork pies are most popular, but large pork pies are also traditional, with stacked pork pie wedding "cakes" becoming a big hit with my friends at Bray's Cottage, who make pork pies with pork fillings in all its possible guises. So please feel free to experiment after trying this traditional recipe.

Although pork pies are eaten throughout the year, it is the tradition in many regions of England to eat pork pies on Boxing Day, the day after Christmas. At some pie shops or butchers, such as Percy Turner's in Barnsley, the line can be as long or even longer as the line for the latest culinary craze or smartphone in New York.

For 6 pies, each serving 1–2 people

For the jelly (optional)

1 pork trotter

1 onion, chopped

1 carrot, chopped

1 rib celery, chopped

2 bay leaves

1 Tbsp black peppercorns

¼ tsp sea salt

4 cups water

For the filling

(in total 3¾ lb/1680 g of meat)

2 lb (1 kg) pork shoulder, finely chopped or coarsely ground

1½ lb (680 g) pork belly, finely chopped or coarsely ground

¼ cup fresh sage, minced

½ tsp ground mace

2 tsp ground black pepper

1¾ tsp sea salt

For the hot water crust

1 quantity Hot Water Crust Pastry, page 194

Use a 2¾- to 3¼-inch diameter wooden pie dolly or a jam jar or glass

If using the jelly, make it a day in advance. Bringing all the ingredients to a boil in a large flameproof casserole dish. Skim off the impurities with a skimmer. Simmer the mixture for 2 hours over low heat until reduced by half. Strain the broth into a clean bowl and let it cool to form a jelly. The surplus jelly can be frozen and used in soups and sauces.

For the pies, make the filling by mixing the chopped or minced pork with the sage, mace, pepper, and salt. Place in the fridge while you make the pastry.

Follow the method for the Hot Water Crust Pastry on page 194.

Divide the pastry into six pieces, about 6 oz (150 g) each. Shape 4 oz (110 g) of the pastry from each piece into a neat disc and let it cool for 10 minutes so that it is still pliable but not dried out enough to tear. This will ensure that the pastry will release the pie dolly better. Do the same with the remaining pastry, which is for the pie lids.

Preheat your oven to 375°F and line a baking sheet with parchment paper.

Roll the pork filling into balls, using 10 oz (280 g) for each one.

Place a pastry disc on a floured surface, press the bottom of a floured pie dolly or jam jar into the pastry and use your fingers to mold the dough around it, pushing it upwards with your fingers. Remove the mold and place a ball of meat inside the pastry crust. Roll out the lid so that it is a little larger than the pie. Make a small hole in the center. Brush the edge of the crust with the egg wash and place the lid on top. Use your fingers to crimp the edges together. The pie will now look like an inverted top hat. Fold the edge with your thumb and finger to create a rim.

Place the pie on the baking sheet and make the remaining pies. Generously brush the pies with the egg wash. Place in the middle of the oven, lower the temperature to 325°F, and bake the pies for 1 hour and 10–15 minutes. The pies are ready when the crust is golden brown and the internal temperature reaches 185°F on a thermometer.

When the pies have cooled down, add the jelly if you are using it. Heat the jelly slightly until it becomes liquid, then pour it into the hole of the cold pie using a small funnel. Let the jelly set. You can keep these pies in the fridge for 3 days or freeze them. Thaw them in the refrigerator before using.

Pork pies are best eaten cold, with sharp mustard or pickles, maybe accompanied by a beer.

"Pie & Mash shop" beef pies

Pie & Mash shops are traditional eateries for the working class in large cities, especially London, and near industrial areas. They came into being when street vendors of eel stew and pies started to open shops in the middle of the 19th century, the so-called Eel and Pie Houses. Today these Pie & Mash shops are still the places where you can eat a hot dish for less than four pounds, such as hot eels, jellied eels, or a pie with mashed potatoes and liquor – a hot parsley sauce. These eateries are important for nearly all layers of the London community: old people carry piles of pie and mash out in their trolley for a whole week, and taxi and truck drivers park in front to get a quick pie before their next shift. Young mothers with children gather on the benches, students and even men in tailored suits all know how to appreciate a meal in the Pie & Mash shop. Just like the traditional Belgian and Dutch cafe, this is the only place in London where young and old, poor and prosperous meet, and maybe even share a table if it's busy.

Two Pie & Mash shops are protected because of their historic interiors, but shops are closing everywhere because of an increase in rent that affects not only these small businesses, but also the working people who have to move farther and farther outside London in order to be able to afford housing. But it also seems that the middle-class Londoner would rather go to a new hip spot than hold on to an old-fashioned institution.

A pie from a Pie & Mash shop should traditionally consist of two different types of dough: the top of the pie is made from suet pastry, and the bottom from hot water crust or shortcrust pastry, or a combination of one of those pastries mixed with the surplus of the suet pastry from the top. The filling consists of what used to be the cheapest minced (coarsely ground) meat – mutton or lamb. Nowadays it is usually beef for the traditional version, but some shops also have pies with chicken, fruit, and even a vegetarian version.

I can't do a trip to London without visiting a Pie & Mash shop. My favorite one is M. Manze on Tower Bridge Road in London, which was established in 1902. With a large spoon, the ladies of the shop spread mashed potatoes on one side of your plate. The pot with mash is so large that you could hide a small child in it, and it is constantly steaming. The pie is placed next to the mash and the ladies always insist you have liquor, "because it's too dry otherwise, luv." Who am I to say differently? It is pleasantly busy, and although this is not a culinary highlight, I love it and can't resist looking at people from behind my pie and mash with jellied eels on the side and a cup of builder's tea. It's as if time has stood still. Nowhere else can you see the real London like in a Pie & Mash shop.

Serves 6 people

For the shortcrust pastry base

5 cups (600 g) plain white flour

½ tsp sea salt

14 Tbsp (200 g) butter, at room temperature

7 Tbsp (100 g) lard or butter

½ cup + 2 Tbsp water

flour, for dusting

butter, for greasing

For the suet pastry top

2½ cups (300 g) plain white flour

1 tsp baking powder

½ tsp (3 g) sea salt

7 Tbsp (100 g) chilled butter

3 oz (80 g) ready-shredded suet

½ cup ice-cold water

2 egg yolks + 2 Tbsp milk, for egg wash

For the filling

1 onion, chopped

2 lb (850 g) beef chuck steak or hind quarter flank, minced (coarsely ground)

1 Tbsp tomato paste

1¼ cups beef broth

1 Tbsp brown sugar

oil, for frying

sea salt and pepper, to taste

For six 6-inch rectangular pie pans

Make the shortcrust pastry by combining the flour, salt, butter, and lard in a food processor fitted with the blade attachment. Pulse for 8 seconds until the mixture resembles breadcrumbs. Add the water and pulse again until the dough forms a ball in the bowl. Remove from the bowl and knead briefly. Wrap the pastry in plastic wrap and let it rest for 30 minutes in the refrigerator.

Make the suet pastry by rubbing the flour, baking powder, salt, butter, and shredded suet together with your fingers until the mixture resembles breadcrumbs. Add the water and knead until the dough comes together. Wrap the pastry in plastic wrap and let it rest in the refrigerator while you make the filling.

Make the filling by frying the onion in oil until it has caramelized. Add the meat and brown, then add the tomato paste and briefly fry it with the meat. Deglaze with the broth, season with salt and pepper, and add the brown sugar for color. Briefly simmer, stirring, but don't let the moisture evaporate. Let the mixture cool in the pan while still very wet.

Preheat your oven to 350°F and grease the pie pans with butter.

Roll out the shortcrust pastry on a floured work surface until ⅛ inch thick. Roughly cut the pastry into six pieces. Gently lift each piece of pastry over a pie pan and let it sink into the base. Let the excess dough hang over the edges to help attach the pastry lid. Use a piece of excess dough to press the edges into the tins. Brush the pastry bases with the egg wash, then spoon in the filling, using about 4 oz (100 g) of the filling for each pie.

Roll out the suet pastry to the same thickness as the shortcrust pastry, and also cut it into six pieces. Place a piece of pastry on top of each pie and use a sharp knife to cut the excess pastry from the base and top. Squeeze the edges together so that the pies do not open during baking. You can embellish the pies with leftover pastry, but traditionally these pies are left plain.

Brush the top of each pie with the egg wash. Bake in the middle of the oven for 40–50 minutes until the pies are golden brown. You can freeze the pies before baking and then simply bake them from frozen.

Traditionally these pies are served with velvety mashed potato and that is indeed the best combination. Children love this dish.

G. Kelly, Pie & Mash shop, London

"Pie & Mash shop" beef pies (pages 208–209)

Steak & ale pies

This pie is a real pub classic. If you want to eat it like they do in the pub, then serve it with steamed peas, carrots, and thick-cut chips. You can also make these pies with leftover stew – just halve the recipe for the dough if necessary. The variation with Stilton cheese is another example of a classic British pie, and if you want to go Victorian style, add a couple of raw oysters to the stew. This used to be the custom to make the meat stretch further when oysters were poor people's food. Times do change!

For 4 people

For the filling

1 onion, finely chopped

1 carrot, finely chopped

1¾ lb (800 g) beef chuck steak

2–3 Tbsp flour, for dusting the meat

2 Tbsp tomato paste

1 cup Guinness, stout, porter, or bitter dark beer (or use beef stock for an alcohol-free alternative)

1 slice of bread spread with English mustard

oil, for frying

For a steak & Stilton variation

about 3 oz (80–100 g) Stilton cheese

For the shortcrust pastry

5 cups (600 g) plain white flour

½ tsp sea salt

10 Tbsp (150 g) chilled butter, diced

6 oz (150 g) cheddar cheese, grated, or 10 Tbsp (150 g) butter

½ cup + 2 Tbsp water

butter, for greasing

1 egg yolk + 1 Tbsp milk, for egg wash

For six 6-inch pie pans

Make the filling by frying the onion and carrot in oil in a flameproof casserole dish. Roll the meat in the flour, then add it to the vegetables. Briefly brown the meat, then add the tomato paste and stir until well combined. Deglaze the pan with the beer.

Bring to a boil, then add the slice of bread with mustard. Stir until the bread falls apart. Cover and simmer for 1½–2 hours. I do this step in a 325°F oven, because I don't like leaving a casserole full of hot food on the stove top for so long. When the stew is cooked, let it cool.

Make the pastry by combining the flour, salt, butter, and cheese in a food processor fitted with the blade attachment. Pulse for 8 seconds until the mixture resembles breadcrumbs. Add the water and pulse again until the dough forms a ball in the bowl. Remove from the bowl and knead briefly. You can also do this by hand by rubbing the butter into the flour and salt until it is the consistency of breadcrumbs, then add the water. Remove from the bowl and knead to bring the pastry together. Wrap the pastry in plastic wrap and let it rest in the refrigerator for 30 minutes.

Preheat your oven to 350°F and grease the pie pans with butter.

Set aside one-third of the pastry for the lids. Roll out the remainder on a floured work surface until ⅛ inch thick. Roughly cut the pastry into four pieces. Gently lift each piece of pastry over a pie pan and let it sink into the base. Let the excess dough hang over the edge to help attach the pastry lid. Use a piece of dough to press the edges into the tins.

Roll out the pastry for the lids and fill the pies with the cooled stew.

For steak & Stilton pies, crumble the Stilton cheese and add it to the cooled stew before filling the pies.

Place a piece of pastry on top of each pie and use a sharp knife to cut the excess pastry from the base and top. Squeeze the edges together so that the pies do not open during baking. You can decorate the pies with leftover pastry.

Brush the top of each pie with the egg wash. Bake in the middle of the oven for 40–50 minutes until the pies are golden brown. You can also freeze the unbaked pies, and bake them straight from the freezer.

Serve the pub way, with steamed peas and carrots, chips (home fries), or roast potatoes.

Chicken & mushroom pies

This is an example of a savory pie that uses just a top crust. I like these types of pies best with a puff pastry lid, but if you don't want to make puff pastry (even though this is a really quick method), you can make shortcrust instead (see page 212) or use a shop-bought alternative. I won't judge – it's available, so why not use it now and again when you don't have time to make pastry from scratch? You can use chicken breast to make the filling, but a whole organic chicken is cheaper.

Chicken & mushroom pies are a firm favorite with the Brits. They're very uncomplicated but never disappoint when made well. If pies could be hugs, then this would be it.

For 6 people

For the chicken

1 organic chicken

1 onion, chopped

1 carrot, chopped

1 rib celery, chopped

3 Tbsp flat-leaf parsley, chopped

5 black peppercorns

For the quick puff pastry

2 cups (240 g) plain white flour

½ tsp sea salt

1 cup (240 g) chilled butter, diced

½ cup ice-cold water

butter, for greasing

flour, for dusting

1 egg yolk + 1 Tbsp milk, for egg wash

For the sauce

3½ Tbsp (50 g) butter

6 Tbsp plain white flour

1 cup whole milk

3¼ cups chicken stock

pinch of ground nutmeg

sea salt and pepper, to taste

1–1½ lb (500–600 g) cooked chicken (above), cut into small chunks

8 oz (250 g) mushrooms, cut into ¼-inch slices

¼ cup tarragon, finely chopped

For six 6-inch rectangular pie pans

Put the chicken in a large flameproof casserole dish with the vegetables, parsley, and peppercorns and cover with about 6 cups of water. Bring to a boil, then reduce the heat and simmer for 45 minutes–1 hour until the chicken is just cooked. Allow the chicken to cool, then remove it from the stock. Keep the stock separate for the sauce.

Make the pastry following the method on page 137.

For the sauce, make the roux by melting the butter in a pan, adding the flour, and mixing well. Cook, stirring, over low heat until the roux has the scent of biscuits. If you don't do this, your sauce will taste like flour. Add the milk and stir, off the heat. Gently bring back to a boil while stirring so that the roux doesn't burn. Add the stock and stir until the roux is thicker. Season with nutmeg, salt, and pepper.

Add the chicken, mushrooms, and tarragon and simmer for a few minutes. If your sauce becomes too thick, add more stock or milk. Allow the filling to cool before assembling the pies. You can also make the filling a day in advance.

Preheat your oven to 350°F and grease the pie pans with butter.

Roll out the pastry on a floured work surface to a thickness of ⅛ inch. Roughly cut it into four pieces. Spoon the cooled chicken filling into the pie pans. Place a piece of pastry on top of each pie and use a sharp knife to cut off the excess. You can decorate the pies with leftover pastry. At this point you can bake the pies or freeze them to bake another time.

Brush the top of each pie with the egg wash. Bake in the middle of the oven for 40–50 minutes until the pies are golden brown.

You can make these pies with leftover stew or make the filling in advance. It's a good way to make use of leftovers.

Scotch pies

Scotch pies are, as the name implies, a Scottish dish. The pies have an annual "World Championship Scotch Pie Awards" dedicated to them, and they are also the preferred snack at the half-time interval at Scottish football matches. They therefore also go by the name "football pies."

According to the championship judges, minced (coarsely ground) beef flank in combination with minced lamb is favored as a filling, but originally these pies were made with mutton, and some still are to this day. Traditional bakers leave the unbaked hot water crust pastry cases to dry out for two to three days before adding the meat filling and fresh pastry lid. This makes for a crisper pastry that perfectly retains its shape and therefore doesn't sink and get a "belly" when it bakes. However, this is troublesome to do for homemade pies, and I prefer to finish the pies and rest them overnight in the fridge, ready to bake the next day. It is also perfectly possible to bake them the same day.

In contrast to pork pies, which have a decorative crimped rim, the lids of these pies need to be tucked neatly inside the pastry casing to create a smooth finish and get the traditional Scotch pie shape. This leaves a space on top of the pie lid that acts like a basin to pour gravy on, or scoop on some mashed potatoes, baked beans, peas, or another topping or sauce you fancy. When making a pie like this with game meat or even the traditional mutton, it's very striking to finish the top with cranberry or blackberry compote. Although technically they are then game pies and no longer Scotch pies, they are an absolute treat and look very pretty with the colorful jam on top and finished with a fresh green bay leaf or sprig of rosemary.

Scotch pies are traditionally not egg washed and are baked to a rather pale golden color. You are, of course, welcome to egg wash and bake the pie until it has a little more color. Just check that the core temperature of the pie is more than 165°F.

For 6 pies

For the hot water crust
1 quantity Hot Water Crust Pastry,
   page 194
milk, for brushing

For the filling
1⅓ lb (600 g) minced (coarsely ground)
   mutton (for example, from the neck),
   lamb mince, or a combination of
   minced beef flank and lamb mince
   or game mince
1 tsp ground black pepper
¼ tsp ground mace
¼ tsp ground nutmeg
½ tsp salt

**For six 4-inch-high, 1½-inch-wide springform cake tins,
or use a 4-inch diameter wooden pie dolly or a jam jar or glass**

Follow the method for the Hot Water Crust Pastry on page 194. Divide the pastry into six pieces. Set aside one-third of the pastry from each piece for the lid. Shape the pastry for the casings into discs. Roll out the lids to 4½-inch circles and cut a small steam hole in the center of each.

Mold your pie casings in 4-inch springform tins or around a 4-inch pie dolly or jam jar.

Make the filling by flavoring the meat with the spices and salt, and kneading it well so that all the flavors blend together.

Divide the filling among the pie casings, pushing the meat well into the corners so there are no gaps. Moisten the inside of the rims with milk and attach the lids by placing them on top of the meat, then folding up the sides and squeezing them together and up to make a ⅝- to ¾-inch rim. Rest the pies in the fridge for 1 hour (or overnight if you're planning to serve them the next day).

Preheat your oven to 400°F. Bake the pies for 35–40 minutes until they are golden. You can either serve the pies hot, allow them to cool to eat cold, or reheat them another time. These pies can also be frozen, then thawed overnight in the fridge, and baked until the filling is piping hot.

Cornish pasties

Pasties are semi-circular hand pies with a distinctive crimped edge. Today they are often sold in British train stations with a range of fillings, but in the past they were made only with meat, potato, onion, and turnip. They were eaten by fishermen and other workmen, but especially by the miners of Cornwall in the many tin, silver, and copper mines that are still dotted around the rugged landscape of the Cornish peninsula. An 1861 newspaper article from Leeds indicates that the Cornish pasty was already being sold to tourists in the region at the time. By then the pasty was no longer just food for the working people, and Victorian tourists would buy them as the local delicacy.

At the beginning of the 19th century, many Cornish miners emigrated to the American states of California, Montana, Michigan, Wisconsin, and Pennsylvania, and to Mexico and Australia. Known as the best miners in the world with the most progressive tools and the best techniques, they started working in mines that were sometimes even bought up by British investors. They took their culture of pasties with them and, as a result, a pasty culture emerged in those regions. In 1968, Governor George Romney declared 24 May as Pasty Day in the state of Michigan. There you will now find places that sell pasties as Michigan pasties.

In Mexico's state Hidalgo, the pasty is the legacy of the mining past. Here the pasty has Mexican-style fillings such as *mole*, the spicy chile and chocolate sauce, and *tinga*, pulled pork marinated in a sauce of tomatoes, chipotles, and onions. In Real del Monte, Cornish Mexico, *auténtico paste* is decorated with the flag of Cornwall. There is a Museo del Paste and the city holds an international pasty festival every year.

In 2011, Cornish pasties were granted a PGI status by the European Union, which means a pasty can only be called a Cornish pasty if it's made in Cornwall, has the shape of a D, it contains a minimum of 12.5 percent raw beef, turnip, potato, onion, and a light seasoning, and the dough is shortcrust and crimped on one side, never on top. Where the crimped edge should be is debatable, since I have found a postcard from around 1900 showing the pasties crimped on the top and not the side. That goes to show that what is considered authentic or traditional is often not certain.

For 6 pasties

For the shortcrust pastry

5 cups (600 g) plain white flour

½ tsp sea salt

1 cup + 5 Tbsp (300 g) chilled butter, diced

½ cup + 2 Tbsp water

flour, for dusting

2 egg yolks + 2 Tbsp milk, for egg wash

For the filling

1 lb (450 g) onglet, skirt steak, or hanger steak

1 lb (450 g) russet potatoes, peeled

4 oz (120 g) turnip, peeled

2 onions

sea salt and pepper, to taste

Make the pastry by combining the flour, salt, and butter in a food processor fitted with the blade attachment. Pulse for 8 seconds until the mixture resembles breadcrumbs. Add the water and pulse again until the dough forms a ball in the bowl. Remove from the bowl and knead briefly. You can also do this by hand by rubbing the butter into the flour and salt until it is the consistency of breadcrumbs, then adding the water. Remove from the bowl and knead to bring the pastry together. Wrap the pastry in plastic wrap and let it rest in the refrigerator for 30 minutes.

Preheat your oven to 375°F and line a baking sheet with parchment paper.

For the filling, chop the meat, potatoes, and turnip into ½-inch cubes. Finely chop the onions. Combine the meat and vegetables in a large bowl and season with salt and pepper.

Roll out the pastry on a floured work surface. Using a plate as a guide, cut out six 9½-inch circles and brush the edges with the egg wash. Divide the filling among the centers of the circles and fold in half. Use your fingers to crimp the pastry in the traditional way.

Lay the pasties on their side on the baking sheet and brush with the egg wash. Bake for 40–50 minutes until the pasties are golden brown. Serve hot, or reheat the next day.

Mince pies & mincemeat

Mince pies are very medieval in their nature. These rich tarts, filled with dried fruits and spices soaked in alcohol, were a status symbol as only the rich could afford these delicacies. Mince pies are filled with mincemeat – minced meat – and that immediately gives us an insight into the history of this tart. There used to be meat in mince pies, but nowadays only the suet or kidney fat reminds us of the "meaty" history of this pie. Beef was used in the filling, but also veal or ox tongue and mutton. The latter is, in my opinion, the best combination, although lamb also works well in combination with the spices and fruits and for most people it's much easier to obtain than mutton.

The first cookbook in the English language, *The Forme of Cury* from around 1390, contains various recipes for similar tarts, some even with white fish or salmon instead of meat. The Tarte of Fleshe in *The Forme of Cury* is most similar to the mince pie. Gervase Markham used a whole leg of mutton in his mince pies in 1615.

> *Minc't Pie*
> *Take a Legge of Mutton, and cut the best of the flesh from the bone, and parboyl it well then put to it three pound of the best Mutton suet & shred it very small; then spread it abroad, and fashion it with Salt Cloves and Mace: then put in good store of Currants, great Raisins and Prunes clean washed and picked a few Dates sliced, and some Orenge-pils sliced ; then being all well mixt together, put it into a coffin, or divers coffins, and so bake them and when they are served up, open the lids and strow store of Sugar on the top of the meat and upon the lid. And in this sort you may also bake Beef or Veal, onely the Beef would not be parboyld, and the Veal will ask a double quantity of Suet.*
> Gervase Markham, *The English Huswife*, 1615

In the 17th and 18th centuries, mince pies became much smaller and were made in various shapes and then placed together on a serving dish so that all shapes formed a whole, as if they were different parts of a decorative puzzle.

Although mince pies made their appearance on every major festive occasion, they have been connected to Christmas since the 19th century. During the Victorian period, mince pies were made with a base of shortcrust and a top of puff pastry. Only since the 20th century has the meat finally disappeared from the mince pie recipes in cookbooks. Today only one pastry is used at a time, either shortcrust (which has become traditional) or puff pastry (which is rarely seen).

The combination of fruits and spices is often diverse, but raisins, currants, and candied lemon, cedro, and/or orange peel are standard. Some old recipes also contain prunes, dates, figs, or candied ginger. Spices are usually cinnamon, cloves, mace, and nutmeg. There is always grated apple or pear and sometimes also lemon or orange juice – mostly from Seville oranges (these are very acidic and also the basis for English marmalade).

These tarts are made with a finer shortcrust pastry than the other tarts in this book.

For 9 small tarts

For the mincemeat
(makes 2 lb /880 g)

1¼ cup (175 g) currants

1¼ cup (175 g) large dark raisins

6 oz (175 g) stewing apple, in small pieces

⅓ cup (50 g) candied orange peel

2 oz (50 g) prunes, pitted and chopped

4 oz (115 g) shredded suet or ½ cup (115 g) butter, frozen and grated

½ cup (115 g) soft brown sugar

½ tsp ground cinnamon

½ tsp ground mace

½ tsp ground cloves

¼ tsp ground nutmeg

¼ tsp ground ginger

pinch of sea salt

½ lemon or Seville orange, zest and juice

1 cup brandy or rum (or half sherry, half rum), or as needed

For the fine shortcrust pastry

1½ cups (180 g) plain white flour

2 Tbsp (20 g) confectioners' sugar

pinch of sea salt

7 Tbsp (100 g) chilled butter, diced

1 Tbsp cold water

1 egg yolk

butter, for greasing

flour, for dusting

1 egg yolk + 1 Tbsp milk, for egg wash

For the filling

8 oz (200 g) mincemeat (see above)

For a tin with 2½-inch shallow mince pie molds

Put all the ingredients for the mincemeat in a bowl and add brandy or rum to cover the fruit. Stir well, then let it rest overnight. The next day, stir again and then divide among sterilized preserving jars.

To make the pastry, mix the flour, sugar, and salt in a large bowl. Rub the butter into the mixture with your fingers until it is the consistency of fine breadcrumbs. Add the water and egg yolk and knead until the mixture comes together into a smooth dough. Alternatively, use a food processor to make the pastry. Wrap the dough in plastic wrap and let it rest for 30 minutes in the refrigerator.

Preheat your oven to 350°F. Grease the tart molds with butter and cover the base of each with a small circle of parchment paper. Dust with flour.

Briefly knead the pastry until smooth, then pat it into a rectangle and roll it out to a thickness of ⅛ inch. Use a round cutter with a diameter of 2¾–3¼ inches to cut out pastry circles. Gently push the pastry rounds into the tart molds. Prick the base of each tart shell three times with a fork.

Knead the remaining dough back together and roll it out to cut out the lids – you can choose whichever shape you like, but stars are the most traditional.

Divide the 8 ounces of filling among the tarts and press down gently. Place the lids on top and brush with the egg wash.

Bake in the middle of the oven for 20–25 minutes until golden brown.

Serve warm or cold.

Use the extra mincemeat to make Mince Pies with Meat (see page 222) or Cumberland Rum Nicky (see page 229).

You can make the mincemeat in this large quantity and store it in the fridge for up to 6 months in sterilized preserving jars. It's best made a month in advance so that the flavors can mature. You can use it for different recipes in this book, such as the Cumberland rum nicky on page 229 and the Eccles cakes on page 137.

Mince pies with meat

For 9 small tarts

For the fine shortcrust pastry

1½ cups (180 g) plain white flour

2 Tbsp (20 g) confectioners' sugar

pinch of sea salt

7 Tbsp (100 g) chilled butter, diced

1 Tbsp cold water

1 egg yolk

butter, for greasing

flour, for dusting

1 egg yolk + 1 Tbsp milk, for egg wash

For the filling

2 oz (40 g) minced (coarsely ground) or
    finely chopped lamb or meat from the
    leg or shank or neck

1 tsp ground cinnamon

large pinch of black pepper

5–6 oz (160 g) Mincemeat
    (see page 221)

For a tin with 2½-inch shallow mince pie molds

To make the pastry, mix the flour, sugar, and salt in a large bowl. Rub the butter into the mixture with your fingers until it is the consistency of fine breadcrumbs. Add the water and egg yolk and knead until the mixture comes together into a smooth dough. Alternatively, use a food processor to make the pastry. Wrap the dough in plastic wrap and let it rest for 30 minutes in the refrigerator.

For the filling, lightly fry the meat in a frying pan with the cinnamon and pepper, but do not brown it. Mix the meat with the mincemeat and stir well.

Preheat your oven to 350°F. Grease the tart molds with butter and cover the base of each with a small circle of parchment paper. Dust with flour.

Briefly knead the pastry until smooth, then pat it into a rectangle and roll it out to a thickness of ⅛ inch. Use a round cutter with a diameter of 2¾–3¼ inches to cut out pastry circles. Gently push the pastry rounds into the tart molds. Prick the base of each tart shell three times with a fork.

Knead the remaining dough back together and roll it out to cut out the lids – you can choose whichever shape you like, but stars are the most traditional.

Divide the filling among the tarts and press down gently. Place the lids on top and brush with the egg wash.

Bake in the middle of the oven for 20–25 minutes until golden brown.

For a more "meaty" version, you can use half meat and half mincemeat. This recipe gives a more subtle taste.

Banbury apple pie

This is a type of closed pie as we know mostly from America today. These kinds of sweet pies came from England, where they have been on the menu for centuries. Their lids were either decorated with pastry, or the pies were cut into shapes, creating the "cut laid tarts" we find in old cookbooks.

Apple pie was very common in Britain throughout the ages. I like the fact that this recipe is linked to the town of Banbury in Oxfordshire by a recipe I found in a 1928 newspaper. Strangely, it appeared in a very different county than the county in which Banbury is located.

For this pie you need a pie plate, which has a wide rim on which you can rest the bottom pastry and then attach the pastry lid.

For 6–8 people

For the shortcrust pastry

2 cups (250 g) plain white flour

¾ cup (100 g) confectioners' sugar

pinch of sea salt

½ cup (125 g) chilled butter, diced

1 egg

1 Tbsp water

butter, for greasing

flour, for dusting

1 egg yolk + 1 Tbsp milk, for egg wash

For the filling

2¼ lb (1 kg) Cox, Jonagold, or
  other red apples

½ cup (100 g) demerara (coarse raw
  sugar)

1 tsp ground cinnamon

¼ tsp ground ginger

⅓ cup (50 g) currants

2–3 Tbsp (25 g) candied citrus peel

3½ Tbsp (50 g) butter, cubed

For an 8½-inch pie plate

Make the shortcrust pastry by combining the flour, sugar, salt, and butter in a food processor fitted with the blade attachment. Pulse for 8 seconds until the mixture resembles breadcrumbs. Add the egg and water and pulse again until the dough forms a ball in the bowl. Remove from the bowl and knead briefly. Wrap the pastry in plastic wrap and let it rest in the refrigerator for 30 minutes.

Preheat your oven to 375°F.

Cut the apples into slices and then into thirds. Combine with the sugar and spices and mix well. You need 1½ lb (650 g) of chopped apple.

Grease the pie plate with butter and dust with flour. Thinly roll out half of the pastry on a floured work surface and place in the pie plate. Brush the rim of the pastry with the egg wash.

Spoon half of the apple mixture into the pastry. Sprinkle the currants over the top and then add the candied peel. Finish with the remaining apple and the butter cubes.

Thinly roll out the rest of the pastry, lay it over the filling and cut away the excess. Press the rim of the pie well with a fork or crimp with your fingers for a scalloped effect. Make a cross or a hole in the middle of the pie so that the steam can escape. Decorate with the leftover pastry and brush with the egg wash.

Bake the pie in the middle of the oven for 40–45 minutes. Allow to cool for 5 minutes before serving warm.

Serve with ice cream, custard (see page 49), or copious amounts of clotted cream.

Blueberry plate pie

This is the perfect pie if you like lots of lovely fruit and juices. It doesn't have a pastry base, so to serve it you simply cut the pastry top and spoon it out along with the fruit. Fresh or frozen berries both work well in this pie. Be sure to experiment with other berries, such as blackberries and raspberries – anything but strawberries (which hold a lot of water and will create a soupy pie) will be delicious.

For 6–8 people

For the shortcrust pastry

2 cups (250 g) plain white flour

¾ cup (100 g) confectioners' sugar

pinch of sea salt

½ cup (125 g) chilled butter, diced

1 egg

1 Tbsp water

butter, for greasing

flour, for dusting

1 egg yolk + 1 Tbsp milk, for egg wash

For the filling

1½ lb (650 g) blueberries

1½ Tbsp (20 g) demerara (coarse raw sugar)

¼ tsp ground cinnamon

1 Tbsp cornstarch

For an 8½-inch pie plate

Make the shortcrust pastry by combining the flour, sugar, salt, and butter in a food processor fitted with the blade attachment. Pulse for 8 seconds until the mixture resembles breadcrumbs. Add the egg and water and pulse again until the dough forms a ball in the bowl. Remove from the bowl and knead briefly. Wrap the pastry in plastic wrap and let it rest in the refrigerator for 30 minutes.

Preheat your oven to 375°F. Grease the pie plate with butter.

For the filling, mix the blueberries, sugar, cinnamon, and cornstarch together in a bowl, then spoon into the pie plate.

Roll out the pastry until thin, then lay it over the berries and cut away the excess. Crimp the edge of the pie well with a fork or make a nice edge with your fingers. Make a cross or a hole in the middle of the pie so that the steam can escape. Decorate the top with the leftover pastry and brush with the egg wash.

Place the pie on a baking sheet lined with parchment paper to protect your oven from any leaks. Bake the pie in the middle of the oven for 40–45 minutes. Allow it to cool for 5 minutes before serving warm.

Serve with vanilla ice cream, custard (see page 49), or clotted cream.

Cumberland rum nicky

Cumberland rum nicky is a shortcrust pastry filled with dried and candied fruits soaked in rum – you could say it is a giant mince pie. The tart tells the story of the trade in sugar, spirits, spices, and fruits between the Caribbean and Northern England in the 18th century. Unfortunately, it also tells the story of the slave trade on sugar plantations.

For 6–8 people

For the shortcrust pastry
2 cups (250 g) plain white flour
¾ cup (100 g) confectioners' sugar
pinch of sea salt
½ cup (125 g) chilled butter, diced
1 egg
1 Tbsp water
butter, for greasing
flour, for dusting
1 egg yolk + 1 Tbsp milk, for egg wash

For the filling
5 oz (140 g) mincemeat (see page 221)

For an 8½-inch pie plate

Make the shortcrust pastry by combining the flour, sugar, salt, and butter in a food processor fitted with the blade attachment. Pulse for 8 seconds until the mixture resembles breadcrumbs. Add the egg and water and pulse again until the dough forms a ball in the bowl. Remove from the bowl and knead briefly. Wrap the pastry in plastic wrap and let it rest in the refrigerator for 30 minutes.

Preheat your oven to 375°F.

Grease the pie plate with butter and dust with flour. Roll out half of the pastry on a floured work surface until thin and place in the pie plate. Cut away the excess pastry and brush the rim of the pastry with the egg wash. Roll out the remaining pastry.

Spoon the mincemeat into the pastry base. Lay the second piece of pastry on top and cut away the excess. Crimp the edges well or use a pastry stamp, and decorate with the leftover pastry.

Brush the top of the pie with the egg wash and bake in the middle of the oven for 20–25 minutes.

Serve as it is or with custard (see page 49).

Tideswell, Derbyshire, Peak District

Bakewell, Derbyshire, Peak District

Bakewell tart

In Bakewell you'll find a bakery on every street corner, each claiming they bake the one and only original Bakewell pudding that made the little Peak District town famous. Who actually invented the Bakewell pudding? According to the most popular story, the Bakewell pudding originated around 1850 when the maid of the local Rutland Arms pub made a mistake when reading a recipe from her mistress, Anne Grieves, thus creating a new bake that they then baptized as Bakewell pudding. However, recipes for this pudding appear two decades earlier in two manuscript recipe books, and in print in *The Magazine of Domestic Cookery* published in 1836. In *Traditional Fare of England and Wales* from 1948, a recipe says that: "A Mr Stephen Blair gave £5 for this recipe at the hotel at Bakewell about 1835."

But there isn't just Bakewell pudding to be had in Bakewell, there's also Bakewell tart. When researching my first book I was on a mission in Bakewell to uncover the mystery surrounding the Bakewell pudding and Bakewell tart, two very similar bakes, although the pudding has a custard filling and is baked in a puff pastry base, while the Bakewell tart has a more cakelike consistency – often made with frangipane in recent years – and is baked in a shortcrust base. Could the Bakewell tart be a more recent invention based on the pudding? Nineteenth-century cookbooks show recipes for Bakewell tarts, but they are always called Bakewell pudding, which tells us that people were baking two kinds of Bakewell pudding at that time and one of the recipes was simply renamed tart in the early 20th century.

But while the Bakewell pudding was most likely an 18th-century sweetmeat pudding renamed to create a local delicacy to attract the increasing number of Victorian tourists when the railway came to the area, today we find yet another kind of Bakewell in Bakewell, and it was not invented by a kitchen maid. Filming a program with the BBC recently about how the iced "Cherry Bakewell" – the supermarket version of the Bakewell tart – was born, I found out that although five years ago you couldn't find an iced Bakewell tart in Bakewell (at one bakery there was even a sign saying that you shouldn't ask about iced Bakewells because "Bakewell tarts are not iced"), today you can choose between a plain Bakewell and an iced Bakewell. The owner of Bloomers of Bakewell bakery, where the aforementioned sign used to be, told me, rather sadly, that tourists now demand iced Bakewells because they know them from the supermarket shelves and see them as the original Bakewell. You can also make a Bakewell as a traybake (sheet cake). This is known as a "Bakewell slice" when divided up into portions.

The iced "Cherry Bakewell" is a completely different product. Its scallop-rimmed pastry casing and smooth white icing with a lone cherry in the middle did become iconic, even though it had nothing to do with the original. It was developed in the 1970s by Mr Kipling, a major manufacturer of cakes, and today the tart is manufactured on a massive scale throughout Britain. And so the history of this bake changes again. It is only a matter of time before the Bakewell tart – as we know it now – is replaced by the iced version created to meet mass production, with a cherry on top.

The recipe in this book is based on the Bakewell pudding from Mrs Leyell's book, *Pudding*, published in 1927. Although in the book it is called "pudding" rather than "tart," it is what we know today as a Bakewell tart. The only difference with the commercial Bakewell tart is that this recipe uses breadcrumbs and almond meal, which makes for a superior, more dense filling, and not frangipane. So by baking this version, you're keeping the old-style Bakewell tart alive. Due to the dense nature of this tart, it will keep for many days in an airtight container. I think it even improves on the second day.

For 6–8 people

For the pastry

1 quantity of Shortcrust Pastry,
  page 235

For the filling

3 Tbsp (20 g) apricot kernels
  (see page 19)

1 Tbsp rosewater

10 Tbsp (150 g) butter

⅓ cup (75 g) demerara (coarse raw sugar)

1¾ cups (150 g) almond meal

⅔ cup (50 g) fresh white breadcrumbs

2 eggs

pinch of grated nutmeg

3 Tbsp raspberry jam

handful of flaked almonds

flour, for dusting

For an 8-inch round cake tin

Make the Shortcrust Pastry following the instructions on page 235.

Prepare the cake tin (see page 21). Roll out the pastry on a floured work surface to a thickness of ¼ inch. Fold in the sides so that the pastry will fit into the base of the tin, then gently lift it into the tin, letting it sink down into the base. Use a small piece of excess dough to firmly press the edges of the pastry into the tin. Trim the excess pastry with a knife and then pierce the base with a fork. Put the pastry in the fridge to rest for at least 30 minutes or overnight (we don't blind bake this pastry as we want it to blend a little with the filling).

Blanch the apricot kernels in boiling water, then remove the skins. Using a mortar and pestle, bash the apricot kernels with the rosewater to make a paste.

Melt the butter in a saucepan but don't let it bubble. Remove the pan from the heat, add the sugar, almond meal, apricot kernel paste, and breadcrumbs and stir well. Add the eggs and nutmeg and mix well. Let the filling rest for at least 1 hour. Towards the end of the resting time, preheat the oven to 400°F.

Spread the jam over the pastry base and spoon the filling on top. Sprinkle with the flaked almonds and bake for 30–35 minutes until golden brown.

Tamarind tart and custard tarts (recipe page 237)

Tamarind tart

Tamarind was a popular, yet rare, ingredient in the 18th century. It found its way to Britain through the East India Company. Tamarind is a podlike fruit that looks a bit like a smooth peanut shell; inside hides the sticky black flesh that is used in the cuisines of different cultures, especially Indian. Tamarind adds a little sourness and enhances flavor. Combined with the bay leaf and mace, it makes this tart something very special.

Charles Carter has a recipe for a tamarind tart in his 1730 book, *The Complete Practical Cook*. He gives the option of making the cake with plums (which he calls "prunellas") or tamarind. The original recipe was made with puff pastry, but shortcrust works much better.

For 6–8 people

For the shortcrust pastry

2 cups (250 g) plain white flour

¾ cup (100 g) confectioners' sugar

pinch of sea salt

½ cup (125 g) chilled butter, diced

1 egg

1 Tbsp water

butter, for greasing

flour, for dusting

1 egg yolk + 1 Tbsp milk, for egg wash

For the custard filling

2 cups full-cream milk

½ cup + 2 Tbsp cream, with at least 40% fat

¼ cup (50 g) demerara (coarse raw sugar)

1 fresh bay leaf

1 mace blade

6 egg yolks

1 egg

2–3 Tbsp pure tamarind concentrate, unsweetened (or use fresh tamarind pods if you have access to them)

For an 8½-inch tart tin

Make the shortcrust pastry by combining the flour, sugar, salt, and butter in a food processor fitted with the blade attachment. Pulse for 8 seconds until the mixture resembles breadcrumbs. Add the egg and water and pulse again until the dough forms a ball in the bowl. Remove from the bowl and knead briefly. Wrap the pastry in plastic wrap and let it rest in the refrigerator for 30 minutes.

Grease the pie plate with butter and dust with flour. Roll out the pastry on a floured work surface. Gently lift the dough over the tin and let it sink into the base. Use a piece of excess dough to firmly press the edge into the tin. Trim the excess pastry with a knife and then pierce the base with a fork. Freeze the tart shell for 1 hour or refrigerate for a few hours. Preheat your oven to 400°F.

Crumple up a piece of parchment paper, then smooth it out and place it in the tart shell. This will help the paper fit the shape of the tart. Fill the pastry with baking beads or rice and place in the middle of the oven to bake blind for 10 minutes until the edge of the crust is colored. Remove the paper and beads or rice and bake for another 5 minutes to dry it out.

Brush the egg wash over the pastry base to help prevent it from getting soggy and bake for 5 minutes more. Allow the pastry to cool.

For the custard filling, heat the milk and cream with the sugar, bay leaf and mace in a pan. Beat the egg yolks and the whole egg in a separate bowl. Remove the spices and pour a tiny bit of the warm milk and cream mixture into the eggs and beat well; this prepares the eggs for the warm milk mixture. Pour the rest of the milk into the eggs while you whisk continuously.

Drop dots of about ⅛ teaspoon of tamarind onto the pastry base until the base is speckled. Strain the custard into a jug, then pour it over the tamarind.

Reduce the oven temperature to 250°F and bake the tart in the lower part of the oven for 35–40 minutes.

Custard tarts

Custard tarts have been around since the Middle Ages. The earliest recipe can be found in the first English cookbook in the English language, called *The Forme of Cury* and dated around 1390. In the past, custard tarts were made with sturdy pastry to withstand the heat of wood-fired ovens. The pie dough was raised by hand, just like we do with the pork pie. Nowadays, vanilla is added to custard tarts, but this is a rather modern addition. Originally custard tarts used rich spices such as saffron, bay leaf, ginger, mace, cloves, cinnamon, and pepper. Dried fruit such as prunes and dates were also often added to custard tarts, as well as fresh wild strawberries.

You can use a regular cutter to cut out the tart bases, but one with a scalloped edge makes the retro custard tarts that many will remember from their childhood. Today the traditional English custard tart is disappearing from the shops, giving way to richer Portuguese custard tarts, which are made with puff pastry.

For 12–14 small tarts

For the shortcrust pastry

2 cups (250 g) plain white flour

¾ cup (100 g) confectioners' sugar

pinch of sea salt

½ cup (125 g) chilled butter, diced

1 egg

1 Tbsp water

butter, for greasing

flour, for dusting

For the custard filling

1 cup full-cream milk

⅓ cup cream, with at least 40% fat

2 Tbsp (25 g) demerara (coarse raw sugar)

1 fresh bay leaf

1 mace blade

3 egg yolks

1 egg

grated nutmeg

For a tin with 2½-inch tart molds

Grease the tart tins with butter, cover the base of each with a small circle of parchment paper, and then dust with flour.

Make the shortcrust pastry by combining the flour, sugar, salt, and butter in a food processor fitted with the blade attachment. Pulse for 8 seconds until the mixture resembles breadcrumbs. Add the egg and water and pulse again until the dough forms a ball in the bowl. Remove from the bowl and knead briefly. Wrap the pastry in plastic wrap and let it rest in the refrigerator for 30 minutes.

Briefly knead the pastry until smooth, then pat it into a rectangle and roll it out to a thickness of ⅛ inch. Use a round cutter with a diameter of 2¾–3¼ inches to cut out pastry circles. Let the pastry sink into the tart molds by gently pushing it down. Prick the base of each tart shell three times with a fork. Refrigerate the pastry for 30 minutes. Preheat your oven to 350°F.

Crumple up small pieces of parchment paper, then smooth them out and place in the tart shells. This will help the paper fit the shape of the tarts. Fill the pastry with baking beads or rice and place in the middle of the oven to bake blind for 10 minutes until the edges of the crusts are colored. Remove the paper and beads or rice and bake for another 5 minutes to dry them out. Reduce the oven to 250°F.

For the custard filling, heat the milk and cream with the sugar, bay leaf, and mace in a pan. Beat the egg yolks and the whole egg in a large bowl. Remove the spices and pour a tiny bit of the warm milk and cream mixture into the eggs and beat well; this prepares the eggs for the warm milk mixture. Pour the rest of the milk into the eggs while you whisk continuously.

Strain the custard into a jug, then pour it into the cooled tart bases. Sprinkle with grated nutmeg and bake in the lower part of the oven for 35–40 minutes.

Let the tarts cool on a wire rack.

Manchester tart

This tart was once very popular in schools, where it was served for pudding (dessert). In 19th-century recipes the filling was thickened with breadcrumbs, and although this is also very good and more filling, I find this 20th-century version just a little more delicate. The custard is slightly richer than in the custard tarts on the previous pages, and the desiccated coconut and single cherry are essential for a retro look.

For 6–8 people

For the shortcrust pastry
2 cups (250 g) plain white flour
¾ cup (100 g) confectioners' sugar
pinch of sea salt
½ cup (125 g) chilled butter, diced
1 egg
1 Tbsp water
butter, for greasing
flour, for dusting
desiccated coconut, to garnish
glacé cherry, to garnish (optional)

For the custard filling
1 egg
5 egg yolks
¾ cup full-cream milk
¾ cup cream, with at least 40% fat
grated zest of 1 lemon
½ cup (100 g) demerara (coarse raw sugar)
2 Tbsp raspberry jam

For an 8½-inch tart tin

Make the shortcrust pastry by combining the flour, sugar, salt, and butter in a food processor fitted with the blade attachment. Pulse for 8 seconds until the mixture resembles breadcrumbs. Add the egg and water and pulse again until the dough forms a ball in the bowl. Remove from the bowl and knead briefly. Wrap the pastry in plastic wrap and let it rest in the refrigerator for 30 minutes, or make it one day in advance.

Butter and flour the tart tin. Roll out the pastry on a floured work surface until thin. Gently lift the dough over the tin and let it sink into the base. Use a piece of excess dough to firmly press the edge into the tin. Trim the excess pastry with a knife and then pierce the base with a fork. Freeze the tart shell for 1 hour or refrigerate for a few hours.

Preheat your oven to 400°F.

Crumple up a piece of parchment paper, then smooth it out and place it in the tart shell. This will help the paper fit the shape of the tart. Fill the pastry with baking beads or rice and place in the middle of the oven to bake blind for 10 minutes until the edge of the crust is colored. Remove the paper and beads or rice and bake for another 5 minutes to dry it out. Allow the tart base to cool.

Reduce the oven to 350°F.

For the custard filling, beat the egg and egg yolks in a large bowl. In a large pan, heat the milk and cream with the lemon zest and sugar. Bring to a boil and make sure the sugar is completely dissolved. Pour a little of the hot milk mixture into the eggs and beat well; this prepares the eggs for the warm milk mixture. Pour the rest of the milk into the eggs while whisking continuously to make a smooth sauce.

Pour the mixture back into the pan and stir over low heat until the filling becomes heavier on the spoon and starts to thicken. Remove from the heat and set aside to cool slightly while you spread the pastry base with the raspberry jam.

Pour the custard into the tart base over the raspberry jam and bake in the middle of the oven for 20–25 minutes until the filling has set but still wobbles a little when you shake the tart.

Place the tart on a wire rack and sprinkle with the coconut. The lone glacé cherry in the middle is optional and pure retro nostalgia.

Treacle tart

In the fantastic world of Harry Potter, elves often bake treacle tart. In real England it is an old-fashioned school pudding (dessert) and, just like Marmite, you either love it or hate it.

Combining breadcrumbs with a sweet syrup in baked goods dates from before the 19th century, but the treacle tart that we know today came into existence sometime after the invention of the iconic golden syrup in 1883. It's called "treacle tart" and not "golden syrup tart" because "treacle" is the general term for by-products of the sugar-refining process. Pecans are a nice addition to the tart crust, but don't hesitate to replace them with more flour.

For 6–8 people

For the pecan shortcrust pastry

1⅔ cups (200 g) plain white flour

½ cup (50 g) pecans, roasted and ground

¾ cup (100 g) confectioners' sugar

pinch of sea salt

½ cup (125 g) chilled butter, diced

1 egg

1 Tbsp water

butter, for greasing

flour, for dusting

For the filling

1½ cups (450 g) golden syrup, maple syrup, or honey

1 lemon, zest and juice

1 tsp ground cinnamon

¼ tsp ground ginger

1½ cup (120 g) fresh breadcrumbs

3 Tbsp cream, with at least 40% fat

1 egg

For an 8½-inch tart tin

Make the pecan shortcrust pastry by combining the flour, ground pecans, sugar, salt, and butter in a food processor fitted with the blade attachment. Pulse for 8 seconds until the mixture resembles breadcrumbs. Add the egg and water and pulse again until the dough forms a ball in the bowl. Remove from the bowl and knead briefly. Wrap the pastry in plastic wrap and let it rest in the refrigerator for 30 minutes.

Butter and flour the tart tin. Roll out the pastry on a floured work surface until thin. Gently lift it over the tin and let it sink into the base. Use a piece of excess dough to firmly press the edge into the tin. Trim the excess pastry with a knife and then pierce the base with a fork. Freeze the tart shell for 1 hour or refrigerate for a few hours.

Preheat your oven to 400°F.

Crumple up a piece of parchment paper, then smooth it out and place it in the tart shell. This will help the paper fit the shape of the tart. Fill the pastry with baking beads or rice and place in the middle of the oven to bake blind for 10 minutes until the edge of the crust is colored. Remove the paper and beads or rice and bake for another 5 minutes to dry it out.

Make the filling by melting the golden syrup, maple syrup, or honey in a saucepan with the lemon zest, lemon juice, cinnamon, and ginger. Add the breadcrumbs, remove from the heat, and set aside for 10 minutes. Stir in the cream and the egg, then spoon the filling into the tart shell.

Bake the tart for 30 minutes. The crust will become dark, which will give it much more taste.

Treacle tart is lovely served warm with clotted cream and a scoop of vanilla ice cream, or cold with warm custard (see page 49).

Maids of honour

Maids of honour tarts are small cheesecakes that, according to one of the beloved legends, were named after one of the maids of honor of one of the wives of Henry VIII. The king had tasted the tarts and was so besotted with them that he locked up the maid of honor so she could bake these tarts for him.

Recipes for maids of honour do not appear in the time of Henry VIII, but sometimes appear in books in the 18th century. In Richmond near London, where Henry VIII lived, Newens The Original Maids of Honour shop has existed since 1850. Here you can still buy these delicious tarts and the recipe is a closely guarded secret. Recipes in old cookery books vary, with some fillings consisting of custard while others are thickened with cheese, almond flour, and sometimes even mashed potatoes.

This recipe is based on a recipe from the 1792 book *The New Art of Cookery*, by Richard Briggs. The original used sweet curd cheese, which is made with fresh milk to which rennet is added. To make this cheese you need unpasteurized cow's milk, which isn't available (or legal) in many parts of the world. The tarts can also be made with curd cheese produced from sour milk or milk that has been soured by the addition of buttermilk or lemon juice. The result is, however, a more acidic filling. I prefer in this case to substitute the curd cheese for ricotta.

For 18 tarts

For the curd cheese

8 cups (1 half gallon) raw milk

1 tsp rennet

For the filling

½ cup (110 g) butter

6 Tbsp–½ cup cream, with at least 40% fat

½ cup (110 g) granulated white sugar

4 egg yolks

1 egg

grated zest of ½ lemon

2–3 Tbsp (25 g) candied cedro (see page 19), very finely chopped

1 drop of orange blossom water

8 oz (230 g) curd cheese (see above)

For the quick puff pastry

1 cup (240 g) butter, diced

2 cups (240 g) plain white flour

½ tsp sea salt

½ cup ice-cold water

butter, for greasing

For a tin with 2½-inch shallow mince pie molds

To make the curd cheese, start half a day in advance or the day before. Place a clean piece of muslin (cheesecloth) in a colander over a large bowl. Heat the milk in a large saucepan until it reaches 99°F, then remove it from the heat and thoroughly stir in the rennet. Leave to rest for 15–30 minutes until the cheese has set (if nothing happens, then you haven't added enough rennet). Carefully pour the cheese into the cheesecloth. Pour off the whey (you can keep it for baking). Drain the cheese in the cloth above the bowl for 4 hours.

To make the filling, melt the butter, then let it cool and add the cream, sugar, egg yolks, egg, lemon zest, candied cedro, and orange blossom water and mix well. Pass 8 ounces of the curd cheese through a fine sieve into a large bowl, then gradually add the butter mixture and combine well.

Preheat your oven to 350°F and grease the tart tins with butter.

Make the quick puff pastry following the instructions on page 137.

Roll out the dough until ¹⁄₁₆ inch thick (or as thin as possible). Use a 2¾- to 3¼-inch round cutter to cut out the pastry. Use the pastry to line the tart tins and prick each base with a fork three times. Knead the remaining dough back together and continue to cut out rounds. If you're not cooking the pastry bases immediately, put them in the fridge because the pastry must remain cold.

Fill the tarts and bake in the oven for 20–25 minutes until they are golden and the filling is a light golden yellow with a golden-brown blush and the surface has puffed up and cracked. Let the tarts cool, but eat them as soon as possible.

Store extra curd cheese in a clean container in the fridge for up to 2 days. The curd cheese may be substituted with ricotta.

Yorkshire curd tart

Yorkshire curd tart is traditionally eaten at Pentecost. It's an old form of cheesecake that was traditionally made with beestings, or colostrum, the first milk a cow produces after calving. This milk is thicker and yellowish, and is particularly rich in nutrients and fat. In more recent years, the cake has been made with curd cheese, a very light cheese made by hanging curdled milk in muslin and draining it for a few hours. You can also make curd with soured milk or buttermilk, but I've used rennet to avoid an acidic taste.

For 6–8 people

For the curd cheese

8 cups (1 half gallon) raw milk

1 tsp rennet

For the shortcrust pastry

2 cups (250 g) plain white flour

¾ cup (100 g) confectioners' sugar

pinch of sea salt

½ cup (125 g) chilled butter, diced

1 egg

1 Tbsp water

butter, for greasing

flour, for dusting

1 egg yolk + 1 Tbsp milk, for egg wash

For the filling

2 Tbsp (25 g) butter

¼ cup (50 g) demerara (coarse raw sugar)

2 eggs, separated

grated zest of 1 lemon

½ tsp ground nutmeg

8 oz (230 g) curd cheese (see above)

⅓ cup (50 g) currants

For an 8½-inch tart tin

To make the curd cheese, start half a day in advance or the day before. Place a clean piece of muslin (cheesecloth) in a colander over a large bowl. Heat the milk in a large saucepan until it reaches 99°F, then remove it from the heat and thoroughly stir in the rennet. Leave to rest for 15–30 minutes until the cheese has set (if nothing happens, then you haven't added enough rennet). Carefully pour the cheese into the cheesecloth. Pour off the whey (you can keep it for baking). Drain the cheese in the cloth above the bowl for 4 hours.

Make the shortcrust pastry by combining the flour, sugar, salt, and butter in a food processor fitted with the blade attachment. Pulse for 8 seconds until the mixture resembles breadcrumbs. Add the egg and water and pulse again until the dough forms a ball in the bowl. Remove from the bowl and knead briefly. Wrap the pastry in plastic wrap and let it rest in the refrigerator for 30 minutes.

Grease the tart tin with butter and dust it with flour. Roll out the pastry on a floured work surface. Gently lift it over the tin and let it sink into the base. Use a piece of excess dough to firmly press the edges into the tin. Trim the excess pastry with a knife and then pierce the base with a fork. Freeze the tart shell for 1 hour or refrigerate for a few hours.

Preheat your oven to 400°F.

Crumple up a piece of parchment paper, then smooth it out and place it in the tart shell. This will help the paper fit the shape of the tart. Fill the pastry with baking beads or rice and place in the middle of the oven to bake blind for 10 minutes until the edge of the crust is colored. Remove the paper and beads or rice and bake for another 5 minutes to dry it out.

Reduce the oven to 350°F.

For the filling, melt the butter and let it cool, then add the sugar, egg yolks, lemon zest and nutmeg and mix well. Pass 8 ounces of the curd cheese through a fine sieve into a large bowl, then gradually add the butter mixture. Beat the egg whites to stiff peaks in a large bowl, then fold in the butter mixture and the currants.

Spoon the filling into the tart shell and bake for 25–30 minutes. Allow the tart to cool completely before serving.

Store extra curd cheese in a clean container in the fridge for up to 2 days.

Amber tarts

Cookbook writer Mrs Rundell called these "amber pudding" in 1808, but amber tarts are indeed tarts. This used to be made as one large pudding or tart, but it is very nice to make individual ones. In the oldest recipes, the tarts are covered with a pastry lid, but I find they are much nicer without it because you can see the beautiful color of the filling. Amber tarts owe their name to the beautiful golden-yellow color that comes from the butter, egg yolks, and candied orange peel.

For 6 people

For the shortcrust pastry

2 cups (250 g) plain white flour

¾ cup (100 g) confectioners' sugar

pinch of sea salt

½ cup (125 g) chilled butter, diced

1 egg

1 Tbsp water

butter, for greasing

flour, for dusting

1 egg yolk + 1 Tbsp milk, for egg wash

For the filling

½ cup (110 g) butter

¼ cup (30 g) candied orange peel

1 cup (110 g) confectioners' sugar

5 egg yolks

1 egg

grated zest of ½ orange

For 3¼- to 3-½ inch individual tart tins

Make the shortcrust pastry by combining the flour, sugar, salt, and butter in a food processor fitted with the blade attachment. Pulse for 8 seconds until the mixture resembles breadcrumbs. Add the egg and water and pulse again until the dough forms a ball in the bowl. Remove from the bowl and knead briefly. Wrap the pastry in plastic wrap and let it rest in the refrigerator for 30 minutes.

Butter and flour the tart tins. Briefly knead the pastry until smooth, then pat it into a rectangle and roll it out to a thickness of ⅛ inch. Use a round cutter a bit wider than your tart tins to cut out pastry circles. Let the pastry sink into the tart tins by gently pushing it down. Trim the edges with a sharp knife to create a neat rim. Prick the base of each tart shell three times with a fork. Freeze for 1 hour or refrigerate for a few hours.

Preheat your oven to 400°F.

Crumple up six pieces of parchment paper, then smooth them out and place in the tart shells. This will help the paper fit the shape of the tarts. Fill the pastry with baking beads or rice and place in the middle of the oven to bake blind for 10 minutes until the edges of the crusts are colored. Remove the paper and beads or rice and bake for another 5 minutes to dry them out.

Meanwhile, make the filling by melting the butter in a saucepan over low heat without allowing it to simmer. Set aside to cool.

Finely chop the candied peel and mash it to a paste using a mortar and pestle.

Add the confectioners' sugar to the butter and beat until smooth. Add the egg yolks and the whole egg and beat well, then mix in the orange zest and candied orange paste. Let the filling rest and reduce the oven to 350°F.

Stir the filling well, then pour it into the tart shells. Bake the tarts in the middle of the oven for 10–15 minutes until the filling is set and golden.

Apple and blackberry crumble

My British friend Pete Brown, who recently published a book about the uniqueness of British food, says that crumble is typically British because it's warm and comforting, a feeling that the British look to create with their iconic dishes. It's also incredibly easy to prepare and it's quite subdued but silently proud. It is Britain in a nutshell, or, rather, in a ceramic dish.

For 4 people

For the crumble topping

⅔ cup (85 g) whole-wheat flour or whole-grain spelt flour

⅔ cup (60 g) traditional rolled oats or spelt flakes

¼ cup (50 g) demerara (coarse raw sugar)

handful of slivered almonds

pinch of sea salt

5½ Tbsp (80 g) butter, at room temperature

butter, for greasing

flour, for dusting

For the filling

10–11 oz (300 g) red apples (e.g. Cox or Braeburn, or a combination), cubed

2 Tbsp (30 g) butter

2 Tbsp (30 g) granulated white sugar

¼ tsp ground cinnamon

1⅔ cups (200 g) blackberries

For a 4½ x 7–inch ovenproof dish

Preheat your oven to 375°F and grease the dish with butter.

Combine the flour, oats or spelt, sugar, almonds, and salt and rub in the butter. Put the topping in the freezer while you prepare the filling.

Stew the apples for 5 minutes with the butter, sugar, cinnamon and two or three of the blackberries for color. Spoon the filling into the dish, then sprinkle the raw blackberries over the top.

Roughly crumble the topping over the fruit. Bake for 30–40 minutes until the crumble is golden brown and the fruit is bubbling wonderfully.

Serve the crumble with vanilla ice cream or with Greek yogurt, skyr (Icelandic yogurt), or clotted cream. Custard (see page 49) is a classic combination with crumble.

I like to make too much and eat the leftovers for breakfast the next day!

Polperro fishing harbour, Cornwall

ACKNOWLEDGMENTS

First of all I want to thank my husband, Bruno Vergauwen, who is, as always, responsible for the beautiful design and cover of this book. Creating a book all by yourself involves trial and error, and after many late nights and early mornings his help was indispensable. Starting in a clean kitchen ensures that the day starts well right away. Thanks for the many clean-ups and support! Thanks to Mum and Dad for not getting annoyed with me for locking myself away until the book was finished.

This book is extra special for me thanks to Becky Colletti, who was so generous in gifting me the recipe for my wedding fruit cake. The recipe for Aunt Betty's gingerbread came to me because of a chance meeting with Joanne Harold on the Eurostar. In the meantime, it has become one of our favorite recipes, gradually becoming our own family recipe – thank you for that.

Thanks to Christian Reynolds, Jayne Cross, Charlotte Pike, Elinor Hill and Wim Rubbens for sharing their family Christmas cake recipes and to everyone who told me their nostalgic food memories. Your stories brought the bakes to life and flavored them with your words. My thanks also to Sarah Pettegree for her advice about the Pork Pies. Thanks Diane G. and Miss South for our chat about Northern Irish bakes, and Del Sneddon for pointing me towards Aberdeen Rowies.

I also received help from a number of other people so that I didn't always have to bake alone; thanks to food stylist Kathy Kordalis, Stefan de Bruyne, Vanessa Vermandel, and Julie van den Driesschen. Baking is so much more fun when you can share a plate and talk about the flavors and textures together.

In addition, thanks to my *Bake Off* colleague, pastry chef, and chocolatier Herman van Dender, who was always there for me whenever I needed technical advice.

I also collected photos and postcards from old bakeries for this book. For that I also thank those who sent me photos of their still-existing bakeries: Billingtons, who have been making gingerbread since 1817, and Lewis Freeman, sixth-generation baker at Dunn's Bakery in London, not only for the photos, but also for his stories.

Thank you, Greetje, for the beautiful profile photos, and Sarah, for our wedding photo in England. Thank you, Clarence Court, for being wonderfully crazy enough to send me a box of your beautiful eggs. See the result on page 43.

Thank you to Esse and Adek for ensuring that my beloved cooking range was placed on time to work on this book.

Thanks to The Guild of Fine Food and the Farrand Family for their support and for giving me the chance to learn so much about flavors for the past seven years being a judge for the Great Taste Awards and the World Cheese Awards.

Thanks to my publisher, Corinne Roberts, and everyone else at Murdoch Books.

Thank you, Sheila Dillon and Dan Saladino from the BBC Radio 4 Food Programme, for their words of support for my books.

Thanks to Jamie Oliver for his continued support since I started writing in 2011. When he called my blog, which started this whole journey, his favorite blog in the *Sunday Times* in 2013, it gave me a much-needed boost of confidence and motivation.

Thank you, Dr. Annie Gray, for your foreword, for your friendship, your support, and for being the coolest historian on the planet.

Thank you to Ils for welcoming me into your village bakery on nightly visits when I was a teenager. The smells of the bakery and the hustle and bustle of baking have most likely been the trigger for what I do today. I remember I brought you food from the party next door as an excuse, because the bakery was where I really wanted to be. Thanks for all your baking advice over the past 20 years.

Thank you to everyone I have forgotten, but who I really appreciate.

BIBLIOGRAPHY

"A seasonable dish. Banbury pie," *Shipley Times and Express*, 3 November 1928

Acton, Eliza, *Modern Cookery for Private Families*, 1845

Acton, Eliza, *The English Bread Book*, 1857

Armitt, M.L., *The Church of Grasmere, a History*, 1912

"Banbury apple pie," *Shipley Times and Express*, Saturday 3 November 1928

"Bettys of Harrogate tells Whitby cafe to drop Fat Rascal name," BBC, 6 November 2017, www.bbc.com/news/uk-england-york-north-yorkshire-41894004

Borella, S.P. and Harris, H. G., *All about Gateaux and Dessert Cakes, All about Pastries, All about Biscuits,* 1920

Boswell, James, *The Journal of a Tour to the Hebrides with Samuel Johnson*, 1791

Bradbury, Mrs Anna R., *The Dutch Occupation. History of the city of Hudson, New York: with biographical sketches of Henry Hudson and Robert Fulton*, 1909

Bradley, Martha, *The British Housewife ...*, 1756

"Bread," Mapping Variations in English in the UK, The University of Manchester, projects.alc.manchester.ac.uk/ukdialectmaps/lexical-variation/bread/

Brears, Peter, *Traditional Food in Yorkshire*, 2014

Briggs, Richard, *The New Art of Cookery*, 1792

Brown, Pete, *Pie Fidelity: In Defence of British Food*, 2019

Byron, May, *Pot-luck; or, The British Home Cookery Book*, 1914

Carême, Marie-Antoine, *The Royal Parisian Pastrycook and Confectioner*, 1834

Carter, Charles, *The Complete Practical Cook*, 1730

"Chorleywood: The bread that changed Britain," BBC, 7 June 2011, www.bbc.com/news/magazine-13670278

Cleland, Elizabeth, *A New and Easy Method of Cookery*, 1755

Cloake, Felicity, "How to make the perfect custard tart," *The Guardian*, 30 September 2015

Congreve, William, *The way of the World*, 1700

"Cornish pasties," *Leeds Times*, 21 December 1861

Dalgairns, Mrs, *The Practice of Cookery*, 1829, Edinburgh

David, Elizabeth, *English Bread and Yeast Cookery*, 1979

Davidson, Alan, *The Penguin Companion to Food*, 2002

Davies, Caroline, "Wordsworth's village bakers fight over their gingerbread," *The Guardian*, 23 March 2008

"Deadly derby pie," *Manchester Courier and Lancashire General Advertiser*, 16 September 1902

"Eat toasted bread for Energy," *Evening Telegraph*, 1937

Eccles & District History Society, http://edhs.btck.co.uk/HistoryofEccles/EcclesWakes

"Fat Rascals," *Leeds Intelligencer*, 17 November 1860

Fiennes, Celia, *Through England on a Side Saddle in the Time of William and Mary*, 1888

Frazer, Mrs, *The Practice of Cookery, Pastry, and Confectionary*, 1791

Gaskell, Elizabeth, *Sylvia's Lovers*, 1863

"Ginger fairings," *The Cornishman*, 3 December 1908

"Gingerbread Husbands," *Chelmsford Chronicle*, Friday 14 May 1847

Glasse, Hannah, *The Art of Cookery Made Plain and Easy*, 1747

Goldstein, Darra, *The Oxford Companion to Sugar and Sweets*, 2015

"Goosnargh," *Preston Chronicle*, 18 June 1859

Grosley, M., *A Tour of London*, 1772

Hall, T., *The Queen's Royal Cookery*, 1713

Hallam, H.E. and Joan Thirsk, Eds, *The Agrarian history of England and Wales*, Cambridge University Press, 1989

Harris, H. G. and Borella, S.P., *All about Gateaux and Dessert Cakes, All about Pastries, All about Biscuits*, 1920

Heritage, Lizzie, *Cassell's Universal Cookery Book*, 1894

Hieatt, Constance B. and Sharon Butler, *Curye on Inglysch: English Culinary Manuscripts of the Fourteenth Century (Including the Forme of Cury)*, 1985

Home, Gordon, *Yorkshire: Painted and Described*, 1908

Institute of Historical Research, *Letters and Papers, Foreign and Domestic, Henry VIII*, Vol. 13 Part 1, January–July 1538

"Isle of Wight dough nuts," *Portsmouth Evening News*, Thursday 9 May 1878

Jacobs, Henry, "Tottenham Cake," www.haringey.gov.uk, 2010

Jenkins, Geraint H., *The Welsh Language and Its Social Domains, 1801–1911*, 2000

Johnson, Samuel, *A Dictionary of the English Language*, 1755

Joseph, Emmanuel, "2019 sugar harvesting may not be so sweet," https://barbadostoday.bb/2019/02/22/2019-sugar-harvesting-may-not-be-so-sweet/

Kalm, Pehr, *Peter Kalm's Travels in North America: The English Version of 1770*, 1937

Kellett, Adam, "Fat Rascals: bakery trade marks scone wrong," *Dehns*, 8 November 2017, inspiredthinking.dehns.com/post/102ek0h/fat-rascals-bakery-trade-marks-scone-wrong

Kirkland, John, *The Modern Baker, Confectioner and Caterer*, 1907

Kitchiner, William, *The Cook's Oracle*, 1830

Knight, Charles, *The Guide to Trade: The Baker; Including Bread and Fancy Baking: with Numerous Receipts*, 1841, London

Leyell, Mrs C.F., *Pudding*, 1927

Limbird, John, "Chelsea Bun-House," *The Mirror of Literature, Amusement, and Instruction*, Vol. 33: 210–211, 4 May 1839

Markham, Gervase, *Maison Rustique*, 1616 edition

Markham, Gervase, *The English Huswife*, 1615

May, Robert, *The Accomplisht Cook*, 1660

Mayhew, Henry, *London labour and the London poor; a cyclopaedia of the condition and earnings of those that will work, those that cannot work, and those that will not work*, Volumes from 1851 to 1862, reprinted 1968

Mintz, Sidney Wilfred, *Sweetness and Power: The Place of Sugar in Modern History*, 1986

McNeill, Florence Marian, *The Scots Kitchen*, 1929

"Peas and prosperity, Pea in rotation with wheat reduced uncertainty of economic returns in Southwest Montana," American Society of Agronomy (ASA), Crop Science Society of America (CSSA), https://www.sciencedaily.com/releases/2016/06/160601131809.htm

Pegge, Samuel, *The Forme of Cury*, 1390

Pennell, Sara, *The Birth of the English Kitchen 1600–1850*, 2016

Phillips, Sir Richard, *A Morning's Walk from London to Kew*, 1817

Poulson, Joan, *Lakeland Recipes Old and New*, 1978

Poulson, Joan, *Old Yorkshire Recipes*, 1974

Raffald, Elizabeth, *The Experienced English Housekeeper*, 1769

Raine, Rosa, *The Queen's Isle: Chapters on the Isle of Wight*, 1861

Read, George, *The Complete Biscuit and Gingerbread Baker's Assistant*, 1854

"Receipt to make a Sally Lun," *The Monthly* magazine, 1796

"Recipes for the Table," *The Cornish Telegraph*, 10 October 1889

Rundell, Maria Eliza Ketelby, *A New System of Domestic Cookery*, 1807

Skuse, E., *The Confectioners' Hand-book and Practical Guide to the Art of Sugar Boiling*, 1881

Slare, Dr, *A Vindication of Sugars*, 1715

Smith, Eliza, *The Compleat Housewife, or, Accomplish'd Gentlewoman's Companion*, 1727

Smith, Michael and the WI, *A Cook's Tour of Britain*, 1984

Soyer, Alexis, *A Shilling Cookery for The People*, 1845

Soyer, Alexis, *The Modern Housewife, Or Ménagère: Comprising Nearly One Thousand Receipts ...*,1850

Spurr, John, *The Post-Reformation: Religion, Politics and Society in Britain*, 1603–1714

"Stotty Cake," *Daily Mirror*, Friday 9 December 1949

The British Newspaper Archive, www.britishnewspaperarchive.co.uk

"The "Buttery Rowie"," *Aberdeen Evening Express*, 27 August 1917

"The "fat rascals" of Yorkshire," *Yorkshire Evening Post*, 2 August 1912

The Mirror of Literature, Amusement, and Instruction, 6 April 6 1839, 4 May 1839

The Price of Sugar, directed by Bill Haney, featuring Father Christopher Hartley, narrated by Paul Newman, 2007

"The Sim-Nell; Or, The Wiltshire cake," *Wiltshire Independent*, 8 March 1838

"The Widow's Buns At Bow," Spitalfields Life

Traditional Fare of England and Wales, National Federation of Women's Institutes, 1948

Turcan, John , *The practical baker, and confectioner's assistant ...*, 1830, Glasgow

"Viewpoint: The Argentines who speak Welsh," BBC, 16 October 2014, www.bbc.com/news/magazine–29611380

Vine, Frederick T, *Saleable Shop Goods for Counter-Tray and Window*, 1898

Walford, Edward, *Old and New London: Volume 5*, 1878

Wallis, Faith, *Bede: The Reckoning of Time*, Liverpool University Press, 1999

Watkins, C. Malcolm, *North Devon Pottery and Its Export to America in the 17th Century*, The Project Gutenberg EBook, 2011

Wells, Robert, *The Bread and Biscuit Baker's and Sugar-Boiler's Assistant*, 1890

Wells, Robert, *The Modern Flour Confectioner*, 1891

White, Florence, *Good Things in England*, 1932

White, John, *A treatise on the art of baking ...*, 1828, Edinburgh

Whitehead, Jessup, *The Steward's Handbook and Guide to Party Catering*, 1903

"Whitleys Original Wakefield Gingerbread," *Dewsbury Reporter*, Saturday 5 October 1878

Whyte, I. D., "Economy: primary sector: 1 Agriculture to 1770s," in M. Lynch, ed., *The Oxford Companion to Scottish History*, 2001

Wilson, C. Anne, *Traditional Food East and West of the Pennines*, with essays from Peter Brears, Lynette Hunter, Helen Pollard, Jennifer Stead and C. Anne Wilson

"Winster," Discovering Derbyshire and the Peak District, www.derbyshire-peakdistrict.co.uk/winster.htm

Ysewijn, Regula, *Brits Bakboek*, 2019

Ysewijn, Regula, *Pride and Pudding*, 2016

Ysewijn, Regula, *The National Trust Book of Puddings*, 2019

INDEX

USEFUL ADDRESSES

Equipment and crockery
Netherton Foundry for griddles, pie pans, loaf tins, copper, spun-iron, and cast-iron cookware and bakeware: netherton-foundry.co.uk
Barrington Pottery for traditional English pottery like Devon jugs and Pancheons: barringtonpottery.com
Burleigh Pottery for English china: burleigh.co.uk
For Scotch pies, the best sized springform tins I could find are from Jamie Oliver's bakeware. They are 4 x 1½ inches.
For small oblong pies like the "Pie & Mash shop" beef pies, the ideal-sized enamel pie pans can be found at Lakeland, John Lewis, and several other online outlets.

Ingredients
Bob's Red Mill for flours, oats, and other baking ingredients: bobsredmill.com
Dove's Farm for flour and baking powder: dovesfarm.co.uk
King Arthur Flour for baking ingredients and useful conversions at kingarthurflour.com
Organic Scottish oats from Oatmeal of Alford: shop.oatmealofalford.com
Spice Mountain at Borough Market for spices and tamarind concentrate: spicemountain.co.uk

weldon**owen**

Weldon Owen International
1150 Brickyard Cove Road, Richmond, CA 94801
www.weldonowen.com

First published in the Dutch language by Uitgeverij Carrera Culinair
Copyright © Uitgeverij Carrera Culinair, Amsterdam 2019
First published in English by Murdoch Books
Copyright © Murdoch Books, an imprint of Allen & Unwin 2020

This extended version of *Brits Bakboek*, published by Overamstel Uitgevers bv,
The Netherlands, in 2019, has been edited, extended
and translated into English by the author.

ISBN: 978 1 68188 567 4

Library of Congress Cataloging-in-Publication data is available.

10 9 8 7 6 5 4 3
Printed by C & C Offset Printing Co. Ltd., China

MIX
Paper from
responsible sources
FSC® C008047

The paper in this book is FSC® certified.
FSC® promotes environmentally responsible,
socially beneficial and economically viable
management of the world's forests.

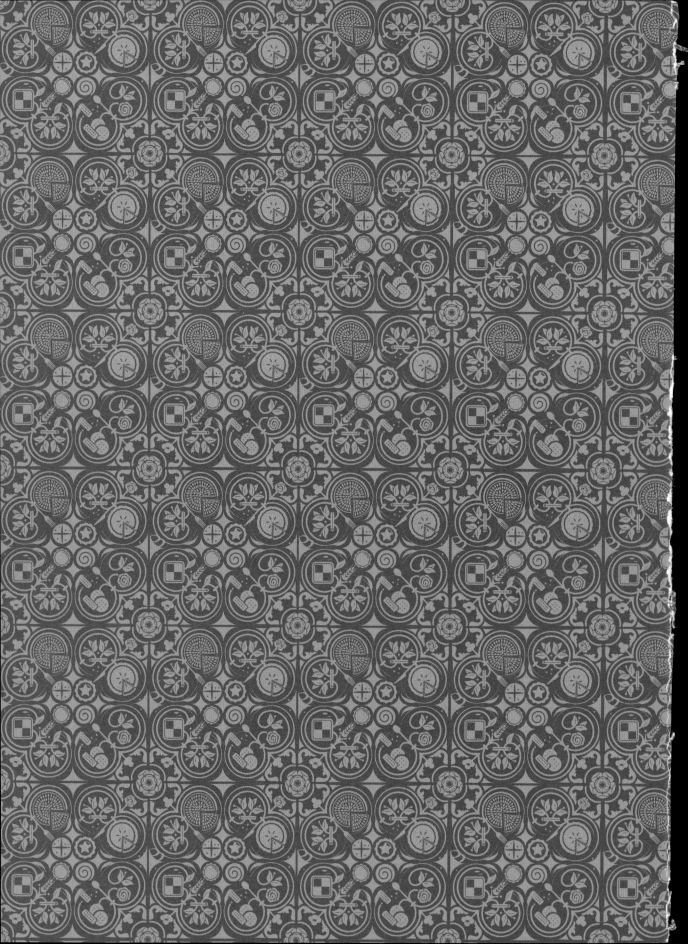